THE AESTHETICS OF BELONGING

THE AESTHETICS

OF BELONGING

Indigenous Urbanism
and City Building
in Oil-Boom Luanda

CLAUDIA GASTROW

The University of North Carolina Press

Chapel Hill

Designed by April Leidig
Set in Calluna by Copperline Book Services, Inc.

Manufactured in the United States of America

Cover art by the author.

Material in chapter 3 previously appeared as "'Vamos construir!':
Revendications foncières et géographie du pouvoir à Luanda,
Angola," *Politique Africaine* 132, no. 4 (2013): 49–72.

Material in chapter 5 previously appeared as "Aesthetic Dissent:
Urban Redevelopment and Political Belonging in Luanda, Angola,"
Antipode 49, no. 2 (2017): 377–96.

Library of Congress Cataloging-in-Publication Data
Names: Gastrow, Claudia, author.
Title: The aesthetics of belonging : Indigenous urbanism and city building
    in oil-boom Luanda / Claudia Gastrow.
Description: Chapel Hill : The University of North Carolina Press, [2024] |
    Includes bibliographical references and index.
Identifiers: LCCN 2024033091 | ISBN 9781469682174 (cloth) | ISBN 9781469682181
    (paperback) | ISBN 9781469682198 (EPUB) | ISBN 9781469682204 (PDF)
Subjects: LCSH: City planning—Angola—Luanda (Luanda) | Slums—Angola—Luanda
    (Luanda)—History—21st century. | City dwellers—Political activity—Angola—
    Luanda (Luanda) | Vernacular architecture—Political aspects—Angola—Luanda
    (Luanda) | Aesthetics—Political aspects. | Indigenous peoples—Material culture—
    Political aspects. | Luanda (Luanda, Angola)—Politics and government—21st century. |
    Angola—History—Civil War, 1975–2002—Influence. | BISAC: SOCIAL SCIENCE /
    Ethnic Studies / African Studies | SOCIAL SCIENCE / Sociology / Urban
Classification: LCC DT1455 .G39 2024 | DDC 305.896/39320673—dc23/eng/20240823
LC record available at https://lccn.loc.gov/2024033091

This book will be made open access within three years of publication
thanks to Path to Open, a program developed in partnership between
JSTOR, the American Council of Learned Societies (ACLS), the University
of Michigan Press, and the University of North Carolina Press to bring
about equitable access and impact for the entire scholarly community,
including authors, researchers, libraries, and university presses around
the world. Learn more at https://about.jstor.org/path-to-open/.

For Chris,
who made this book and
many other things possible.

CONTENTS

ix   List of Illustrations

xi   A Note on Pseudonyms and Terminology

xiii   List of Abbreviations

1   INTRODUCTION
Building Luanda

29   CHAPTER ONE
Making the "New Luanda":
National Reconstruction and
Phantasmagorias of Care

67   CHAPTER TWO
Musseque City:
Indigenous Urbanism in Provisional Spaces

97   CHAPTER THREE
Beyond the Law:
Demolition, Belonging, and the
Moral Economy of Materiality

125   CHAPTER FOUR
The Aesthesis of Class:
Infrastructure and the Politics of Comfort

149   CHAPTER FIVE
Aesthetic Dissent:
Negotiating Worlding from an African Metropolis

171   CONCLUSION
Beyond "Cut-and-Paste" Urbanism

183   Acknowledgments

187   Glossary

189   Notes

197   References

215   Index

ILLUSTRATIONS

MAPS

xviii   Map of Angola

xix   Map of the primary areas and projects discussed in this book

19   The changing boundaries of Luanda province

FIGURES

32   Figure 1.1. "Solving the people's problems"

32   Figure 1.2. "New residential zones across the whole country"

47   Figure 1.3. "The neighborhood of Boavista in Luanda is a zone in constant danger"

47   Figure 1.4. "A new way to solve old problems"

51   Figure 1.5. Luanda Bay

53   Figure 1.6. The new promenade

62   Figure 1.7. Street scene in Cazenga

62   Figure 1.8. "We support the revitalization of our Ilha"

74   Figure 2.1. Musseque squeezed between houses in central Luanda

80   Figure 2.2. Construction in Mundial

81   Figure 2.3. Land occupations in Cacuaco

81   Figure 2.4. Constructing a neighborhood in Cacuaco

93   Figure 2.5. Sign identifying block and sector in Mundial

105   Figure 3.1. Neighborhood "croquis" on the wall of a residents' committee office

119   Figure 3.2. Wooden house built on demolished cement brick foundation

139   Figure 4.1. Kilamba waiting for inhabitants

139   Figure 4.2. Zango 4

159   Figure 5.1. Condominium development near the entrance to Zango

A NOTE ON PSEUDONYMS
AND TERMINOLOGY

When I conducted the bulk of my research between 2008 and 2015, Angola's political context was fraught. The expression of political views, especially open critique of the ruling MPLA, provoked harsh responses. Activists were relentlessly harassed and some even jailed and beaten. I thus initially used pseudonyms to refer to all organizations, locations, and people to prevent those in power from potentially harming my interlocuters. After publishing my first journal article as a graduate student, however, I received complaints from some individuals and organizations I had collaborated with, stating that they felt the use of pseudonyms resulted in their stories and actions going unrecognized. As a result, I have sought to balance the demands of doing no harm with trying to ethically represent the places and people I engaged with during those difficult years. I anonymize individuals by employing pseudonyms but have divulged organization names in those instances in which I have received permission to do so. I have used the real names of locations in some instances so as to provide the reader with a sense of the city's geography as well as to honor the populations who were displaced. Where I have used a pseudonym to name a neighborhood or other location, I draw the reader's attention to this with an endnote.

Angola has a very complex history of racialized identifications. During my time in Luanda, the most commonly used nonderogatory terms to describe racial identifications were *negro* (Black), *mestiço* and *mulato* (for someone of presumed mixed racial background), and *branco* (white). "Mestizo" and "mulatto" have very controversial histories in the Anglophone world and carry with them strongly negative associations, but I do use the Portuguese versions of the words when necessary to recognize local ways race is understood and experienced. I have generally chosen to capitalize Black, not to reify the category above other identifications, but to locate Black Angolans in a broader world of African and African-diasporic geographies, political practices, and identifications that emerged not only, but perhaps most notably, in the wake of the Atlantic slave trade, which is so central to the story of Luanda. In the Atlantic world the reification of Blackness became the grounds for the dehumanization, enslavement, and colonization of Africans. In turn, however, long histories of place-making, struggle, and reconstitution of Black lives both in and beyond

Africa shed light onto not only the remaking of Blackness but the ways in which Black life disrupted imperial and colonial geographies. Describing Black Angolans through capitalization locates them in the transnational worlds of the Atlantic in which Blackness shaped futures and possibilities, and was also key to imagining and enacting other ways of making and inhabiting space. It links the African continent to a broader transnational experience of history, capitalism, and practices of exclusion. In choosing to capitalize "Black," I follow Jordana Matlon (2022, 25), whose scholarship on Coté d'Ivoire recognizes both the potential for the reification and commodification of Blackness as a category, as well as the work it performs as a "hegemonic counternarrative."

ABBREVIATIONS

ANIP   Agência Nacional de Investimento Privado
(National Private Investment Agency)

BCOM/Bricomil   Brigada de Construção e Obras Militares
(Military Works Construction Brigade)

BIR   Brigada de Intervenção de Realojamento
(Rehousing Intervention Brigade)

BNDES   Banco Nacional de Desenvolvimento Económico e Social
(Brazilian National Economic and Social Development Bank)

BPC   Banco de Poupança e Crédito
(Savings and Credit Bank)

CAP   comitê de acção do partido
(party action committee)

CPB   comissão popular de bairro
(people's neighborhood commission)

EDEL   Empresa de Eletricidade de Luanda
(Luanda Electricity Company)

EDURB   Empresa de Desenvolvimento Urbano
(Urban Development Company)

EMPROCI   Empresa Provincial de Conservação de Imóveis
(Provincial Property Conservation Company)

EMPROMAC   Empresa de Materiais de Construção
(Construction Materials Company)

ENAS   Empresa Nacional de Água e Saneamento
(National Water and Sanitation Company)

EPAL   Empresa Pública de Águas de Luanda
(Luanda Public Water Company)

FAPLA   Forças Armadas Populares de Libertação de Angola
(People's Armed Forces for the Liberation of Angola)

FESA   Fundação Eduardo dos Santos
(Eduardo dos Santos Foundation)

FNLA   Frente Nacional de Libertação de Angola
(National Front for the Liberation of Angola)

GARM   Gabinete de Renovação e Reabilitação dos Musseques
(Office for the Renewal and Rehabilitation of the
Musseques)

GOE   Gabinete de Obras Especiais
(Office for Special Works)

GPL   Governo Provincial de Luanda
(Luanda Provincial Government)

GRN   Gabinete de Reconstrução Nacional
(Office for National Reconstruction)

GTRUCS   Gabinete Técnico de Reconversão Urbana de Cazenga,
Sambizanga e Rangel
(Technical Office for the Urban Reconversion of Cazenga,
Sambizanga, and Rangel)

INH   Instituto Nacional de Habitação
(National Housing Institute)

INSTAL/UEE   Empresa Nacional de Instalações Especiais
(National Company for Special Installations)

IPGUL   Instituto de Planeamento e Gestão Urbana de Luanda
(Luanda Urban Planning and Management Institute)

MPLA   Movimento Popular de Libertação de Angola
(Popular Movement for the Liberation of Angola)

PDGML   Plano Director Geral Metropolitano de Luanda
(Luanda Metropolitan General Master Plan)

PGML   Plano Geral Metropolitano de Luanda
(Luanda General Master Plan)

PHS   Programa da Habitação Social
(Program for Social Housing)

PNUH   Programa Nacional de Urbanismo e Habitação
(National Program for Urbanism and Housing)

PRP   Programa para o Realojamento da População
(Programme for the Rehousing of the Population)

SBL   Sociedade de Baía de Luanda
(Luanda Bay Corporation)

SEH   Secretaria de Estado de Habitação
(State Housing Secretariat)

SEUHA   Secretaria de Estado do Urbanismo, Habitação e Águas
(State Secretariat for Urbanism, Housing, and Water)

UNITA   União Nacional para a Independência Total de Angola
(National Union for the Total Independence of Angola)

THE AESTHETICS OF BELONGING

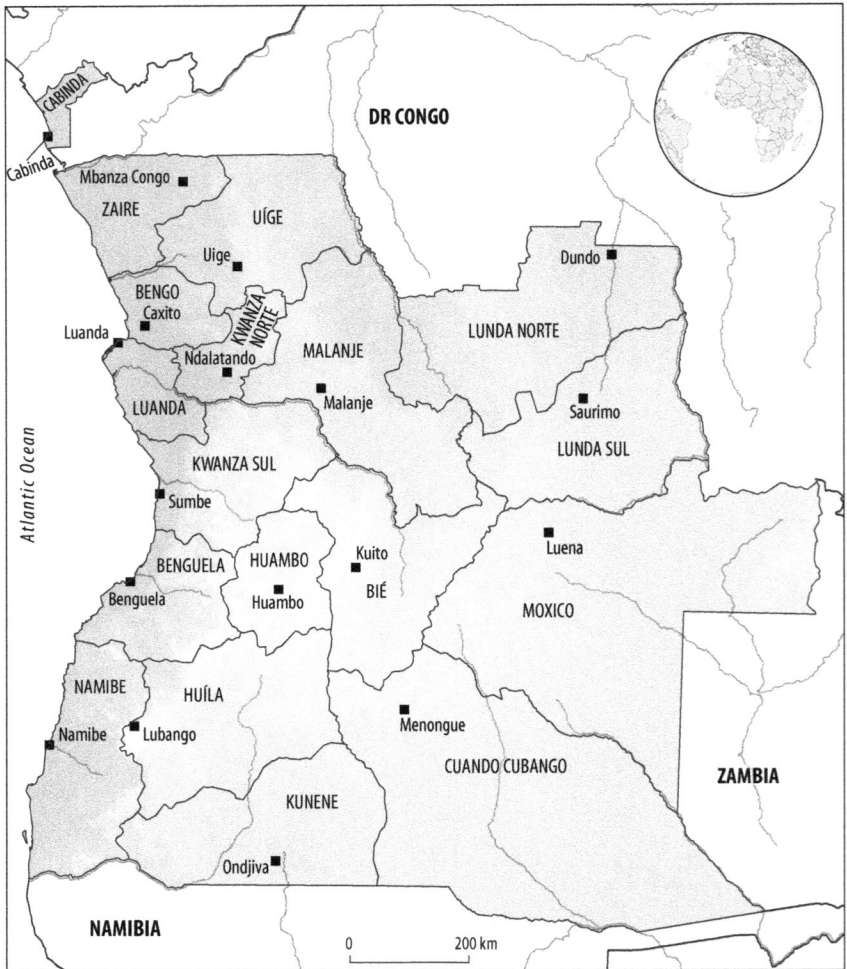

Map of Angola. Created by Aharon deGrassi.

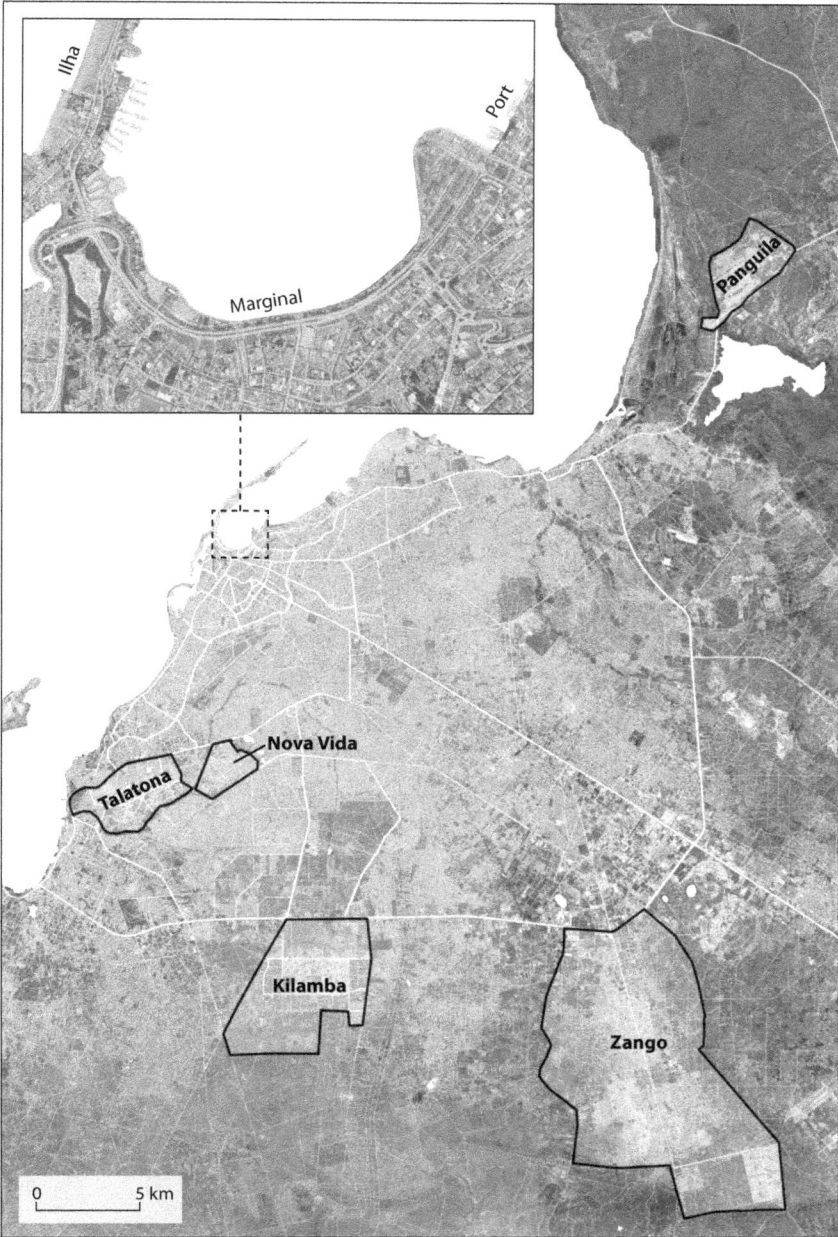

Map of the primary areas and projects discussed in this book.
Created by Aharon deGrassi.

Building Luanda

On 20 July 2009, police, soldiers, and members of Angola's Presidential Guard encircled the neighborhoods of Iraque and Bagdad.[1] It was 3:00 a.m. The areas' dirt roads were relatively quiet during this unusual hour of deep slumber in a city of late-night celebrators and early risers. Moving between concrete-block homes, police forced startled sleepers out of their houses, harassing and beating those who resisted. Over the next six days, residents watched their homes crack and collapse in front of them as demolition teams flattened the neighborhood. Piles of concrete blocks, twisted iron rods, and broken planks remained of what had been homes. One local paper described the scene as "a cavalry of iron . . . tearing everything down" (Mateus 2009). Police later set fire to the temporary accommodation that the despondent former inhabitants had assembled from the rubble, making sure that people would not be able to rebuild (Amnesty International 2009). By the time the operation was over, approximately 3,000 houses, home to 15,000 people, had been destroyed. A luxury residential complex commissioned by the Camama Consortium, a private investment group, was earmarked for building on top of the ruins.

Housing demolitions had become increasingly common in Luanda since the end of the civil war in 2002, as an oil-fueled postconflict building boom consumed the city. While the growing numbers of elites, middle-class Angolans, and wealthy foreign migrants benefiting from oil were usually apathetic about demolitions, the scale of this one drew public attention—enough, at least, to provoke a response from the provincial government. Despite a court's having declared many of the residents' tenure claims valid in 2007, after a previous attempted demolition (SOS Habitat 2012, 95–96), when questioned, a representative of the Luanda Provincial Government (GPL) explained that it would not be providing compensation to those affected, as residents had knowingly built in a state land reserve ("GPL descarta culpa" 2009). The representative appeared unconcerned that the land reserves (*reservas fundiárias*) had only been formally delimited in 2007, long after many of the areas that developers were targeting had been established. His explanation for the lack of compensation, however, rested on not only legal but also aesthetic concerns. In an interview with Rádio Ecclésia, the mouthpiece of the Catholic Church in Angola, when asked about the provincial government's refusal to provide compensation, the GPL representative explained that it was not houses that had been destroyed but "cabanas de chapa" (corrugated iron shacks). His statement indexed how urban and political belonging are fundamentally shaped by entrenched aesthetic orientations rooted in urban materialities that distinguish and classify who and what can be included as part of the city, and therefore as part of the broader political community. In his eyes, the materials of the "cabanas" rendered them incapable of being considered real houses. His classification of the cabanas as aesthetically beyond the category of "house" recast the horror of the loss of home as an excusable act undertaken in the name of improving the city. This appeal to the aesthetic surfaced repeatedly during my time in Luanda as the question of who and what belonged in the city, and who and what was considered to embody a desirable form of urbanism, was rooted in aesthetic assessments of materials, design, and infrastructures.

This book explores how aesthetics came to mediate understandings of political belonging in Angola's capital, Luanda, during the country's remarkable postconflict oil boom (c. 2002–14). It is a story of the remaking of Luanda and the dreams, tensions, and negotiations that emerged from this remaking, as oil aesthetics turned out not to quell political debate but to catalyze it. By tracking how arguments about urbanism, materials, architecture, and design shaped the possibilities of urban inclusion and exclusion in this period, this book shows how construction spectacle was undone by an aesthetic politics that emerged from Luanda's *musseques*. Although musseques could simply be described as "informal areas," in Luanda, they are better understood as an Indigenous urbanism, productive of a sense of urban belonging, community, and political rights via deep histories of formation, construction, and design, which the notion of "informality" fails to capture. While new projects drew people in with promises of state care in the form of aesthetic comfort, the materials and building practices of Luanda's musseques provide a political critique of the violent actions and historical erasures that urban redevelopment involved. The primary research for the book was conducted over a period of eighteen months in 2011 and 2012, followed by approximately eight months of follow-up research between 2013 and 2018. The text, however, covers the period following the end of Angola's twenty-seven-year civil war in 2002 until about 2014, when the international price of oil began to crash. During this time, Angola's state, dominated by the ruling Popular Movement for the Liberation of Angola (MPLA), embarked on an ambitious, multibillion-dollar program of "national reconstruction." Arguing for the need to restore a country shattered by more than three decades of war,[2] the state invested heavily in infrastructure and housing as a means to stabilize the economy and build political legitimacy. Projects included the rehabilitation of the national transport system, the extension of water and electricity grids, and the construction of vast state-subsidized housing projects across the country. State money also funded the building of a new international airport, sports stadiums, and leisure areas.

Nowhere was the building boom more evident than in Luanda. As oil profits soared, a surge in private investment paralleled state efforts. Developers poured money into luxury high-rises, gated communities, business parks, and conference centers to meet the consumer demands of local elites, international companies, and a growing middle class. These actions were matched by the efforts of Luanda's poor, who rapidly expanded the city's informal areas. Construction materials such as cement, stone, iron, and wood flooded the ports. Freshly built concrete-block houses stretched out for kilometers as new migrants and people seeking a respite from crowded neighborhoods quickly transformed the urban edge. Like their wealthier counterparts, many speculated on real estate opportunities, occupying land to build additional homes, or erecting new rooms to rent in existing plots. Land and housing quickly became the most lucrative negotiations in the city as concrete-block self-built homes, high-rises, corrugated-iron houses, and suburban developments competed for space, catering to the needs and tastes of the diverse and growing population that was hoping to cash in on the excesses of the oil bonanza.

Luanda's remaking emerged at a key moment in the reconfiguration of urban planning in Africa. While the MPLA-state's visions for the city appeared fantastical to many observers, they were part of a larger turn across Africa to "new city" building and megainfrastructure investments. In Kenya, Ghana, Nigeria, the Democratic Republic of the Congo, Equatorial Guinea, Sudan, Mauritania, Rwanda, and Senegal among others, urban megadevelopments that sought to radically reshape the governance, aesthetics, and everyday experience of cities were being designed by international real estate and engineering consulting companies. Investors presented these projects as solutions to what they portrayed as the seemingly intractable problems of African cities. While some of these projects, such as Ciudad de la Paz in Equatorial Guinea, imagined the construction of entire new cities, others focused on the construction of privatized urban districts such as Appollonia in Accra, new urban precincts, housing developments, or even the redevelopment of existing urban areas. What united these discrepant projects was their embodiment of a "utopian urban fantasy"

(Mendelsohn 2018, 456) that drew on globally circulating ideas about what constituted a "world-class city" in order to perform and implement a postcolonial urbanism that appeared freed from the legacies of inequality, poor governance, and uncontrolled growth that government and residents believed marred African cities (Datta 2016). They constituted an attempt at urban "worlding," a search to redefine the existing global urban imaginations of cities and Africa. The political economies of their planning and realization also shared characteristics. Built from scratch, often on land that had been violently cleared of existing inhabitants, new city projects have been controversial in scholarly discussions of contemporary African urbanism. Researchers have described them as an "escapist urbanism" (Moser and Côté-Roy 2021, 2) driven by elite aspirations and have accused them of diverting funds away from the poor, promoting segregated urbanism, accelerating environmental destruction, ignoring the underlying political and economic conditions that have contributed to urban problems, and funneling policy attention away from improving the conditions of existing cities (Watson 2014; van Noorloos and Kloosterboer 2017; Murray 2015; Mendelsohn 2018). Despite developers' claims that these cities symbolize a new direction in African urbanism, studies have suggested that they reproduce colonial urban planning practices and logics of racialized violence, even when initiated by new partners from the Global South (Moser 2015; Sawyer 2019; Choplin and Frank 2010; Kimari and Ernstson 2020). Broader participatory planning and consultation processes are virtually nonexistent, resulting in limited local input as regards the design and implementation of projects. Such projects have also tended to entrench existing class divisions into new urbanscapes. Across the continent, local anxieties about what these investments mean for sovereignty and financial stability are reflected in repeated rumors that key national assets or major tracts of land have been mortgaged to lenders.[3] Local opposition to new city developments and large infrastructure projects therefore reflects anxieties about the possibilities for equality and sovereignty in the face of rampant speculation, elite capture of economies, and urban financialization in an age of neoliberalism.

In Luanda, the massive investment in housing and infrastructure generated conflicts over the conditions under which people could claim urban belonging. These struggles were most visceral in the conflicts over urban land that accelerated from the early 2000s onward. A new land law and recently legislated state land reserves, which earmarked areas for urbanization initiatives, took little heed of existing constructions. Overnight, signs appeared in the midst of completed homes informing residents that it was illegal to build there. The result was the state's adoption of mass demolitions as a tool of city building.

People watched as their neighborhoods were flattened for new real estate ventures. Nevertheless, as the GPL representative's statements suggested, not merely a legal regime but also an aesthetic one enabled these actions. It was the existence of alternative aesthetic orientations, however, that enabled a questioning of them.

New city developments have been marked by the ways utopian aesthetic visualizations of new projects have acted as a form of "political propaganda" for their implementation (Datta 2016, 21). In much the same way as Ayona Datta (2016, 18) has argued regarding the logic of masterplans, the state thereby legitimizes its "mega-urbanization dreams . . . to its citizens as if [this] were the only rational solution to urban crisis, and in doing so it mobilizes mass dreams and future aspirations." Given the power of these utopian aesthetics, many planners and bureaucrats assumed that musseque residents viewed their homes in the same way as official discourses framed them: as illegal and "provisional." In contrast to the pronouncements of developers, however, Luanda provides clear insight into the fact that "informal settlements" are carefully built, designed, and honed according to shared aesthetic criteria. Residents of neighborhoods like Iraque and Bagdad made precise decisions regarding the design and material constituents of their homes, building an urban aesthetic world that was in dialogue with, but not determined by, official norms shaped by histories of enslavement and settler colonialism. While they desired the aesthetic comforts that new city projects promised, musseque residents were proud of the homes they had built. Those I spoke to explained how they had carefully added on to their houses, chosen certain kinds of materials for construction, and decided what kinds of flora (fruit trees or medicinal plants) should be grown in their yards. These decisions established bonds between residents, the city, and the state. But now these bonds, rooted in the bricks, roads, and planning practices of the musseques, were unraveling. Conflicts over the built environment increasingly mediated relationships between the state and Luanda's inhabitants, becoming central to the conceptualization and reconfiguration of political belonging.

As new city projects have spread across the Global South over the last two decades, Luanda's experience provides insight into the kinds of struggles and political contestations that emerge from their political aesthetics. The utopian visuals of the building of new cities appealed to many Angolans, who yearned for the comforts of working infrastructure, indoor plumbing, and public spaces that projects promised. Despite developers' dreams of building a tabula rasa urbanism, however, these projects could not escape the tensions over race, class, and belonging from which they emerged. Their entanglement in these histories became visible in Luandans' engagements with design, infrastructures, and building materials, showing the need to understand the micro-lives of materiality and aesthetics as central to the politics of master planning and city making. Discussions with Luanda's residents revealed the existence of strongly held beliefs about the built environment that mediated notions of political inclusion and permeated practices of governmentality. It also emphasized that people held multiple, sometimes conflicting aesthetic judgments in tension. The same individual might argue that musseques were an eyesore that required intervention while simultaneously affirming that musseque homes were valuable assets and proudly commenting on the materials they had used to construct their house. Aesthetic judgment, rooted in orientations to materials, embodied experiences, and design, therefore opened up space for negotiation and critique as Luandans explored the ramifications of urban development. The battles that emerged during the remaking of Luanda are representative of broader contestations unfolding globally regarding the political implications of urban redevelopment: What constitutes the imaginary of the desirable city, who is entitled to inhabit this space of desirability, and under what conditions? As such, this book is about urbanism, architecture, city planning, Indigeneity, and how aesthetics provided and continues to provide a means through which to understand how the limits of political belonging are remade and imagined in everyday life.

Oil and the Aesthetics of Belonging

Oil lay at the center of Angola's postconflict transformation. The MPLA-state had, after all, been made through oil. The commodity became the primary source of state revenue in 1973, two years before Angola's independence from Portugal (Hodges 2004). While other state institutions struggled for most of the postindependence period, the national oil company, Sonangol, and oil extraction activities, were given special attention to ensure the smooth flow of revenues (Soares de Oliveira 2015). Oil profits enabled the MPLA-state to withstand the pressures of the prolonged civil war by funding the purchase of weapons and food. While the fickle nature of international commodity prices regularly put the Angolan economy on edge, in 2011, when I began my long-term fieldwork, the country was experiencing one of the most lucrative oil booms of its postindependence history. In 2002, when the civil war ended, the international oil price stood at US$24 a barrel. By 2005 it had climbed to $52.48, peaking at $111.82 in 2011 (EIA 2024). The country shifted from a wartime economy of debt to being awash in petrodollars.[4] Its gross domestic product grew from $15.285 billion in 2002 to $145.712 billion in 2014.[5] The MPLA-state drew on this mushrooming oil wealth to enact "one of the world's most capital-intensive and spectacular reconstruction processes of recent decades" (Soares de Oliveira 2015, 3).

As foreign exchange poured into Angola, it induced intense shifts in the temporal and material experiences of everyday life. Angolans described these changes in terms of the emergence of a "culture of immediatism," in which the desire for fast money and the symbolic power of consumerism began to pervade everyday interactions and desires (Schubert 2017). Oil money allowed a growing number of Angolans to not only aspire to but actually achieve a better life. Lucrative employment opportunities enabled an ascendant middle class to access unprecedented educational, real estate, and travel opportunities (Auerbach 2020). Class mobility and new consumer desires paralleled each other. In a country with little of its own industrial production and growing consumer demand, imports of everything from basic goods to luxury consumables surged. Luanda rapidly became classified as the most expensive city in the world for expatriates (Tutton 2011). Housing and food prices skyrocketed. One-bedroom apartments in Luanda's city center were being rented out for up to $12,000 a month (Zenki Real Estate 2013, 16). A four-bedroom house cost $30,000 a month (Zenki Real Estate 2013, 16). In one headline-grabbing incident, a customer lodged a court case against an Angolan supermarket, Casa dos Frescos, after it attempted to charge him $105 for an imported melon ("Preços elevados sem justificação" 2011). Accounts of Angolans spending their oil dollars in Cape Town, Lisbon, and Dubai filled daily discussions, and the country's elites soon became infamous for their high-profile investments in significant sectors of the Portuguese economy, leading to the publication of a book with the sensationalist title *Os donos angolanos de Portugal* (The Angolan owners of Portugal) (Louçã, Costa, and Teixeira Lopes 2014). The street economy flourished. Informal money changers, known as *kinguilas*, sat brazenly in front of banks, shaking wads of kwanzas at passersby, offering them a prime exchange rate for the dollars that they knew jangled in many a pocket. On the weekends, packed nightclubs pumped to a mixture of kuduro, kizomba, and the latest Brazilian hits. Even in poorer neighborhoods, the oil boom shaped rhythms, materialities, and prices. A plate of peanut chicken and cassava porridge easily cost five dollars. People poured into the city seeking a better life. From approximately 3.3 million in 2002, the city's population reached 6.4 million people by 2014, a quarter of the country's inhabitants (Cain 2013; INE 2016). Oil wealth created an atmosphere of capricious spending as Angolans (and foreigners), regardless of social class, hustled to access the money that spilled over from elite patronage networks.

While the impact of oil money was felt in almost every aspect of life, nowhere was the quotidian experience of it more evident than in the remarkable metamorphosis of Luanda's built environment. Angola's capital became the center of an oil-enabled postconflict display of state presence and power. The kinds of aesthetic politics it kindled, however, contradict existing writings about oil spectacle. Many writers have commented that oil produces what Andrew Apter (2005) has described as a "seeing-is-believing" ontology, in which observers mistake oil-fueled consumption and construction spectacles for signs of systemic economic transformation (Coronil 1997; Watts 1992). These arguments have implied that oil aesthetics transforms citizens into spectators of, rather than participants in, the state, as state institutions' mobilizations of massive financial flows to transform the material world take on a dreamlike quality that stages the state as a spectacle to be marveled at, rather than engaged with. Show projects provide the illusion of state capacity and national wealth even when the structural underpinnings of the country continue in colonial patterns of raw export and the import of secondary goods (Coronil 1997). Instead of demanding political and economic transformation, citizens become spellbound by the possibilities of oil. Oil spectacle has thus historically been understood to entrance, dim, and nullify critical capacity, much like the commodity phantasmagorias that Walter Benjamin (2002 [1935]) critiqued in early twentieth-century Paris. Work in urban studies has made similar points about megaproject and infrastructural aesthetics' ability to quell dissent. Not only do developers and governments mobilize aesthetic criteria to stigmatize the poor and remake the city in the interests of the middle class and elite (Chatterjee 2004; Murray 2015), but normative aesthetic notions of the desirable "world-class city" are, scholars argue, often internalized by urban populations, leading them to accept violent interventions in their neighborhoods as necessary to produce the promised future city (de Boeck 2011; Ghertner 2015; Harms 2012).

In oil-boom Luanda, however, the state's centering of aesthetic spectacle did not always quell dissent; instead, it positioned the aesthetic as an ambivalent site of politics. While residents often embraced the promises that inhered in visual representations of a future Luanda, aesthetic judgments were also informed by local histories of construction and existing understandings of Angolan politics, which framed elite aesthetics as sites of corruption and exclusion. New projects became the objects of desire but also political critique. By "aesthetics," I refer to both the material aspects of buildings and infrastructure such as design, form, appearance, and architectural features, as well as analytical understanding of the term as defined by almost unconscious judgments based on sensuous engagement with the world. Luanda's residents rooted their urban politics in both meanings. Inhabitants of the city with whom I interacted spoke passionately about the materiality of their homes, criticized (and praised) the architecture of new constructions, and dwelt extensively on their embodied experiences of infrastructure. Their impressions of these material conditions, as well as desires and expectations about what the city was and how it should be, produced the grounds for the contestation of oil spectacle. Their political sensibilities and ensuing arguments about belonging were catalyzed by and expressed through their aesthetic engagements with the city.

As an experience grounded in the senses, aesthetic experience and its accompanying evaluations of good, bad, beautiful, and repulsive tend to present themselves as "natural" and therefore universal. Given this, aesthetic claims are often "a particularly insidious (because deeply embedded) way of naturalizing power relations" (Mazzarella 2006, 104). In contrast, scholars have shown aesthetic orientations to be highly variable, determined by the sociohistorical conditions of their formation (Benjamin 1968; Bourdieu 1984; Elias 2000). It is precisely in the tensions between the pretension to universality and the fact of the sociohistorical constitution of aesthetic orientations, then, that the question of aesthetic judgment provides a window into contestations over categories, conventions, practices, and imaginaries. Even the most hegemonic aesthetic discourses cannot obliterate the necessarily subjective character of aesthetic experience, which thereby always provides a possible source of critique of prevailing power relations. Jacques Rancière (2010) identifies these moments of what he calls "dissensus," that is, dissent from a shared aesthetic consensus, as the epitome of politics. For him, aesthetic perception is limited by what he refers to as the "distribution of the sensible," a phrase that describes how the production of a hegemonic "common sense" regarding who and what can be perceived, classified, and identified as a legitimate participant in a community circumscribes possibilities for participation inasmuch as it determines "what is visible and what not . . . what can be heard and what cannot" (Rancière 2010, 36). Certain kinds of people, objects, and topics do not appear as legitimate participatory subjects or as legitimately included in the polity, while others, who are recognizable within norms determined by the "distribution of the sensible," do. Politics, for Rancière (2010, 38), emerges at the agonistic moment when people and objects who are excluded from the existing community of sense "make visible the fact that they belong to a shared world that others do not see." Rather than hegemonic, aesthetic judgment is inherently unstable.

Oil spectacle dazzled, but it also produced multiple crises. These included mass forced displacements, the delegitimization of musseque architecture, and the erection of buildings deemed "foreign" by many of Luanda's residents. The ambivalences that surfaced as Luandans negotiated their relations to emerging projects brought into focus the existence of various registers of the aesthetics of belonging, the aesthetic criteria through which urban inclusion (and with that political belonging) was produced. These registers provided a means for appeals for inclusion in, as well as radical dissent from, developers' oil-fueled urban "utopias." As state institutions and private developers mobilized aesthetic criteria to exclude certain places and people from the emerging city, thereby justifying violent actions against them, alternative aesthetic logics concerning what a house was, what a city was, what these should look like, and who belonged in them surged into everyday awareness. Contesting normative aesthetic logics is political because it involves not simply a call for inclusion in existing parameters but also the actual transformation of those parameters (Gordon 2018). In order to experience inclusion, one's aesthetic worlds must be valued on their own terms. Aesthetic dissent is therefore defined as a contestation not simply to expand the existing boundaries of aesthetic recognition but also to fundamentally reshape the conditions and possibilities of inclusion and recognition so as to reconfigure the very understanding of the categories, objects, and people in question. Through the shifting and often ambivalent appeals to aesthetic belonging and utterances of dissent, Luandans negotiated their relationships to the city, state, and each other, in the process battling for the recognition of multiple registers of aesthetic belonging.

Indigenous Urbanism and Luanda's Musseques

Musseques constitute an Indigenous urbanism. They are also a form of Black urbanism, for, as Hugo ka Canham (2023, 24) notes, in Africa, divorcing Blackness from Indigeneity "is to bifurcate identities of relation that are inseparable." Indigeneity has at times been a controversial analytic in African studies. Some anthropologists have argued that it simply recasts patronizing notions of essentialist "primitive" identities into contemporary terminology (Kuper 2003). The mobilization of appeals to Indigeneity in the form of autochthony claims, often with violent results, has created unease about it as a scholarly category (Nyamnjoh 2007; Geschiere and Nyamnjoh 2000). In the wake of a long scholarship that has documented the colonial invention of ethnic identities, there is an anxiety among scholars that any notion of Indigeneity in Africa almost always collapses into exclusionary and artificially constructed categories

(Mamdani 1996; Mbembe 2002; Nyamnjoh 2007). Furthermore, African state representatives have historically been hostile to Indigenous peoples' legal activism, arguing that (with the exception of diasporic and settler populations from other continents) the notion of indigeneity as a political identity is nonsensical inasmuch as "all Africans are indigenous and should have equal access to resources" (Pelican 2009, 53; see also Hodgson 2009; Nyamnjoh 2007).

The conceptualization of Indigeneity found in contemporary Indigenous studies, however, moves beyond both essentialist claims and arguments about Indigeneity as a colonial construct (Dorries 2022; Coulthard 2014; Gordon 2013; Tallie 2019). Specifically, scholars approach Indigeneity not as a pure ontological condition but as a historically emergent category produced through relations to other people, beings, places, and objects (Canham 2023). As Heather Dorries (2022, 2) argues, Indigeneity should be understood as not primarily an identity but rather as a "political relation" that not only recognizes historical connections to land and place but also acknowledges people's relational positioning to power, more specifically, in the context of North America and southern Africa, settler colonialism. In her intervention into literature on Indigenous urbanism, Dorries (2022, 5) therefore argues that Indigenous urbanism constitutes an "analytic" that enables scholars to understand how Indigenous people mutually remake Indigeneity and urbanism through the use, production, and contestation of urban space. Although Dorries does not see Indigenous urbanism as referring to architectural formations, I nevertheless draw on her and Canham's (2023) theorizations of Indigeneity as emergent from practice and historically transforming relationalities to understand Indigeneity as constituted through urban construction, suggesting that, in the case of Luanda, urban Indigeneity emerges in concert with spatial and architectural practice. There are suggestions of this possibility in the work of other scholars. Rahul Mehrotra (2008, 206), although focusing on emergent spatial productions that challenge the formal city, refers to India's "Kinetic City," the provisional, informal areas of the country's large urban areas, as "an indigenous urbanism that has its particular 'local' logic." In the context of Madagascar, Tasha Rijke-Epstein (2023) has followed the historical transformation of Comorian migrants into Indigenous urban dwellers through city building. The description of musseques as Indigenous, then, refers to a relational identity of personhood and built form that emerges through construction, but also in the shadow of the often-violent enforcement of normative urbanisms.

While scholars have recognized the existence of urban spaces that predate colonial encounters and encroachment, as well as their ongoing influence on contemporary urban practices (Monteith 2019; Anderson and Rathbone 2000;

Coquery-Vidrovitch 2009), the possibility of an African Indigeneity being born from colonial urbanism has not been as actively addressed. Colonial-era ethnographers struggled to locate a language to describe the unique urban practices, associations, and forms of life that were emerging in the settler-colonial towns of Africa (Mitchell 1956; Wilson 1941–42). In a context of colonial oppression, not only were African sites of residence purposely deprived of infrastructure, resources, and rights, but colonial officials also conceived the city as a space that stood in opposition to imagined "traditional" African practices and identities. As in the North American context, settler colonialism in Africa was premised on not only a *terra nullius* but also an *urbs nullius*, in which cities were imagined as white spaces devoid of any Indigenous influence on their formation and the Indigenous were represented as alien to the urban (Coulthard 2014). While studies of popular culture and politics have long contested these depictions (Callaci 2017; Gluckman 1960), material formations have not generally enjoyed the same recognition. This discursive elimination of Black African material practices from imaginations of urbanism makes it difficult to move analyses of areas such as musseques beyond those of lack or abjection.

Today the distinction between the material conditions of former settler areas of dwelling and African residential areas is often captured in terms of degrees of formality or informality. However, as Menna Agha and Léopold Lambert (2020) have argued, the term "informality" "does not tell us what it is describing; it only tells us what it is not." The material and aesthetic complexities of large swathes of African urbanism disappear in such descriptions. In Angola, the term "cidade" was originally used to refer to Luanda's planned colonial core but subsequently was deployed in everyday language to describe areas of formality and historically contingent desirable urbanism (Roque 2011). In contrast to "cidade," nowadays the words "musseque" or "bairro" are used to refer to areas that deviate from normative imaginations of urbanism in some way. In this sense, the terms "musseque" and "cidade" sometimes act as a relational latent grammar through which different material forms and spaces can be described, compared, and comprehended in a world of shifting aesthetic norms. However, musseques are not simply the negation of the cidade, they are historically emergent Indigenous material formations.

In Luanda, although the term "musseque" encompasses a diverse array of historical settlement types, locations, and degrees of incorporation into the formal logics of the city, all of them, with the exception of musseques partially constituted by colonial-era social housing, are products of historical practices of self-building (Development Workshop 2005). Simply describing them as "informal" erases not only the histories that have constituted them but also the material politics that emerges from them (see chapters 2 and 3). While the diacritics of musseques might change over time in the sense that the materials from which houses are made have varied historically, a number of authors have highlighted certain recurring features that define the musseque beyond simply positioning it as a negation of the cidade, specifically architecture, infrastructure, class, and race (Monteiro 1973; Moorman 2008; Mendes 1988). The musseque is a product of African place-making, but it is also apprehended through racialized aesthetic judgments of urban materiality. Ramiro Monteiro (1973, 30) captured this aesthetic understanding in his study of musseques in the late colonial period when he wrote, "The factor which typifies most obviously the musseque is the nature of housing: 'huts' or provisionally constructed homes. But there are other indicators to take into account for the characterization of these clusters, such as lack of sanitation, communication infrastructure, and the professional, economic, and cultural ties existing between its inhabitants." Marissa Moorman (2008, 33), who studied colonial descriptions of musseques, concurs when she argues that "when planners retrospectively applied the term 'musseque' to conglomerations of huts occupied by African free and enslaved workers, they plied a definition of musseque that encompassed notions of labor and race, not simply location." What these descriptions point to is a need to understand musseques on their own terms rather than define them only through a relation of lack to the cidade. There is no doubt that, as Sandra Roque (2011) has shown, many musseque residents describe their areas as "backward" and "underdeveloped." However, people also proudly invest in homes and neighborhoods, an economy of informal professional housebuilders, or *pedreiros*, advise on construction and design, and by all accounts these practices seem to have decades-long, if not centuries-long, continuity (see chapter 2). Cidade and musseque, rather than opposites, are better understood as different ways of belonging to the city that coexist and infiltrate each other in a generative relationship. They constitute intertwined but different modes of urban belonging rooted in shared material and symbolic practices that have their roots in African experiences of enslavement, colonialism, and struggle. Recognizing areas such as the musseque as Indigenous moves them away from being defined through negation, while simultaneously bringing into focus the ways Africans have produced meaningful political community through their spatial and material practices. Luanda is a promising location from which to think through the possibilities of an African Indigenous urbanism inasmuch as its history deeply complicates any framing of African cities within a conceptual terrain of urbs nullius. Luanda's history demands the recognition of Black Indigeneity while simultaneously disturbing any simplistic racialization of urban form.

The fundamental social and material distinction in early Luanda between "enslavers and the enslaved" was marked by those who lived in formal houses versus those who lived in yards and barracoons (referred to as *quintais*) (Tomás 2022, 42). The city's most prominent early property holders and bureaucrats included many Africans who were central in the management of the Atlantic slave trade. António Tomás (2022, 42) argues that the prominent role of Indigenous Angolans in the slave trade "constitutes the original sin of the city" and results in an ambiguous relationship to colonial-era urban heritage inasmuch as it indexes local elite complicity in processes of enslavement. This material and spatial distinction between the free and the enslaved transformed into the division between cidade and musseque with the surge of settler presence in the early twentieth century and the growing racialization of urban life (see chapter 2). During this time, urban planning began to model itself on the same practices of racialized colonial planning that characterized twentieth-century colonialism across Africa. This history of complicity points to the fact that the cidade is as much an African production as the musseques. In fact, in the 1960s, Fernando Batalha, a Portuguese colonial architect, identified *sobrados*, houses inhabited by elite Luanda society at the time of the slave trade, as being a form of indigenous architecture, a unique mixture of "Portuguese technique and local materials" (Tomás 2022, 43). Recognizing Indigeneity to be an emergent political relation means that the cidade might be indigenous but not Indigenous, inasmuch as its "formality" carries with it histories of enslavement, extraction, and settler-colonial logics of displacement. If we recognize that settler colonialism is rooted in structural patterns of dispossession, extraction, and violence, then the logics of formality and historical legacies of enslavement that run through cidade (and similar urban formations in the rest of Africa) are premised on the disavowal of the legitimacy of alternative material formations of the urban. The cidade might be partially constructed by people Indigenous to Angola, but it does not stand in a political relationship of questioning to settler colonialism and extractive practices of racial capital. In contrast, as I will show, the histories of musseque formation have been fugitive in nature, glossed as "informal" because they constitute, as Agha and Lambert (2020) suggest, sites that fall outside of centralizing "state epistemologies." They are an Indigenous urbanism, not simply because they were largely built by Angolans but because they emerged as sites that revealed ways of making the city entangled with, but not captured by, the colonial logics of the cidade. They "share the same space" with the cidade but "understand and use it differently" (Mehrotra 2008, 205). They remake urban identity and urban politics through their material forms.

National Reconstruction and the Politics of Concrete

It was the Angolan state that introduced a material politics into the postconflict arena by centering construction as *the* sign of national rebirth. Angola's independence on 11 November 1975 was marred by the country's immediate entry into a civil war, which had unofficially begun months before the Portuguese rapidly departed. Driven by complex fractures that emerged not so much from deep ideological differences as from elite fallouts over power-sharing, the conflict was quickly captured by Cold War logics. The Luanda-based MPLA turned to the Soviet Union and Cuba for support against its enemies, the National Front for the Liberation of Angola (FNLA) and the National Union for the Total Independence of Angola (UNITA), the latter supported by the United States and apartheid South Africa. While the FNLA, the oldest of the three movements, was quickly crushed, UNITA was gradually able to build its strength in the interior and east of Angola. What followed was a decades-long war driven by international interests, as well as domestic tensions expressed through discourses of rurality, race, urbanity, African identity, and ethnic belonging,[6] all funded by Angola's bountiful oil and diamonds. When the international political conditions that had enabled it collapsed at the end of the Cold War, the conflict quickly lurched into a ruthless resource-driven fight. The final decade of war in the 1990s was the most brutal. During this period, the MPLA became increasingly convinced that military victory, rather than negotiation, was the only means to end the conflict. Both warring parties became increasingly destructive (Roque 2021).

When the war finally came to an end in 2002, following the killing of UNITA's longtime leader, Jonas Savimbi, the victorious MPLA, which had "won the peace" after twenty-seven years of combat, was forced to assess the damage. Angola was shattered. The war had cost the country an estimated $200 billion (deGrassi 2015, 13). Fighting had destroyed entire towns and most of the national road and railway network. Landmines made farming impossible in much of the interior. In all, 4.1 million people were internally displaced, with hundreds of thousands more having fled the country entirely (Human Rights Watch 2003). Angola was deeply indebted, owing large amounts to lenders who had funded the government's wartime purchases of food and weapons. The government's estimates put inflation at 113.9 percent for 2002 (GURN

2002). Education and health services had collapsed (Sikiti da Silva 2009; Shoko 2002). In 2002, the infant mortality rate was 192 per 1,000 births, and life expectancy stood at forty-seven years.[7]

State efforts soon focused on what was referred to as "national reconstruction" (*reconstrução nacional*). The term had its origins in the immediate postindependence period, when it was invoked to describe the construction of a new socialist order. Now it was recycled as a catch-all term to describe not a unitary policy but a variety of sweeping public investments in infrastructure and housing. Although national reconstruction would come under severe criticism from many sides, it is important to note that there was a strategic logic to the approach. Shortly following the end of the war, the government drew up a number of policy documents that recognized the urgent need to address the serious social problems confronting Angola, ranging from national reconciliation and HIV-AIDS to the improvement of health and education.[8] Collectively, these documents argued that social problems could only be resolved once the economy was stabilized, which, they contended, could only be done by extensive investment in infrastructure. Infrastructural investment was presented as the key to rebuilding the postconflict economy, which, in turn, would enable the realization of the government's broader social goals.

When the war ended, the Angolan government was deeply indebted, still servicing the oil-backed loans it had taken on during the conflict in the face of an extremely low international oil price. In need of significant resources to initiate the investments required by national reconstruction, the Angolan government first approached Western allies and the Bretton Woods institutions requesting the organization of a donors' roundtable such as had been held in 1995. At that time, European states, the United Nations, and the United States had pledged $1 billion to assist postconflict reconstruction (*Africa Confidential* 2002). More than a decade later, however, these same countries were reluctant to disburse funds to Angola, arguing that it was in greater need of good governance than financial support (*Africa Confidential* 2002). Citing concerns about corruption, they demanded that International Monetary Fund (IMF) reforms such as a staff-monitoring program and cutbacks on public expenditure be introduced before they would release money. The Angolan government balked at these demands, arguing that austerity measures were inappropriate for a country seeking to recover from a decades-long war. Conditionalities would not only delay the commencement of reconstruction but would also significantly reduce Angolan autonomy over the country's spending, and with that, the political and economic power that flowed from reconstruction (Corkin 2011; Malaquis 2012). Amid rising oil profits, Angola reevaluated its reconstruction strategy. It turned to its long-standing practice of mobilizing oil-backed loans but this time with new partners, most notably China.[9] Between 2000 and 2015, China is estimated to have advanced Angola about $21 billion through resource-backed lending (Brautigam and Hwang 2016). While some of the loans were direct financial payments, others were extended in the form of technical expertise, construction materials, and labor. Soon, new lenders, eager to profit from the oil boom, began to engage in similar agreements, with previous demands for conditionalities evaporating. Brazil's National Economic and Social Development Bank (BNDES) granted a credit line of $1.5 billion in 2009, Spain pledged $600 million in construction aid, and Canada's Export Development Bank signed an agreement with the Angolan state Savings and Credit Bank (BPC) to fund infrastructure projects (Corkin 2012).

While the money from oil-backed loans was for broader reconstruction efforts, it was soon mobilized by the Presidency to bolster its power. This was made possible through the creation of special offices that managed a significant number of high-profile national reconstruction projects. Although the funds from oil-backed lending were meant to be managed by the Ministry of Finance, a sizeable amount was ultimately siphoned to two offices, the Office for National Reconstruction (GRN) and the Office for Special Works (GOE). The GOE was created in 1998 to enable the Presidency to manage the construction of a new political administration center in central Luanda. While the political administration center was never completed, the office became an avenue for the Presidency to insert itself into urban planning and construction projects in the province (Gastrow 2020a). The GRN was created in 2004 and answered directly to the Presidency. Voicing concerns that existing state institutions lacked the capacity to manage the large financial flows connected to reconstruction, the president created this office to supposedly facilitate efficient project management. Headed by the chief of the Presidency's military cabinet (Casa Militar), Manuel Helder Vieira Dias Júnior "Kopelipa," it was in charge of a number of the projects funded through largely private Chinese oil-backed loans, including, but not limited to, the construction of the "new centralities" and the international airport in Bom Jesus. In 2010, amid rumors that the president had grown concerned with the power amassed by Kopelipa, as well as significant delays in the execution of key projects, the GRN was dissolved. Its projects were passed on to the GOE and Sonip (the real estate arm of the state oil company, Sonangol). The GOE was now described as an office to support "the President of the Republic in the conception and implementation of the program for the Political Administration Center and other works determined by the Head of Executive Power."[10]

In Luanda, this presidential interference was visible not only in the GOE's and GRN's involvement in various projects but also through the Presidency's coordination of several new schemes linked to reconstruction. This included activities that fell under the auspices of the Luanda Special Economic Zone (Zona Económica Especial), the Technical Office for the Urban Reconversion of Cazenga, Sambizanga, and Rangel (GTRUCS), and the Program for the Rehousing of the Population (PRP) (see Gastrow 2020a). Political influence also ran through private developments. The Kinaxixe Complex, a mixed-use commercial and residential development built on the site where Kinaxixe Market, a public municipal market, had stood, was developed with $1 billion from the Cochan Group. This was a conglomerate headed by General Leopoldino "Dino" do Nascimento, then the head of the president's communication service. The GEMA Group, whose shareholders had strong family connections to the Presidency, ministers, and the Angolan national bank, held significant interests in the Torres do Carmo development, the V-Gardens condominium, and the Commandante Gika complex (Dias 2021; Marques de Morais 2009).[11]

In a political structure in which there were no locally elected representatives, little opposition mounted to the Presidency's overreach into the city's administrative structures. In fact, administratively speaking, there was no city of Luanda. Until 2012, there existed only a province of Luanda, which was considered synonymous with the city. Luanda as a city is more a product of history, identity, and popular culture than a set of officially sanctioned administrative divisions. In Angola's highly centralized political system there was (and still is) no independent local government.[12] Luanda did not have a mayor or a city council. The president appointed the provincial governor, who appointed the municipal administrators, who appointed the commune administrators, who then managed the province/city's neighborhoods. In the wake of the redrawing of provincial and municipal borders in 2012, there emerged the municipality of Luanda, whose administrator had also been appointed through these processes. In these kinds of circumstances, there was little appetite for official administrative criticism of central government policies.

While the financial logics of national reconstruction centralized resources into the MPLA, symbolic politics were also a powerful tool of regime legitimation. The focus on infrastructure and housing framed the destruction of war as "a technical, material issue" rather than a broader emotional and political experience (Schubert 2017, 30). The discourses and performances framing national reconstruction therefore centered the MPLA-state as the institution that had the technical competence to heal the broken nation. State advertisements used images of construction and freshly built housing developments to

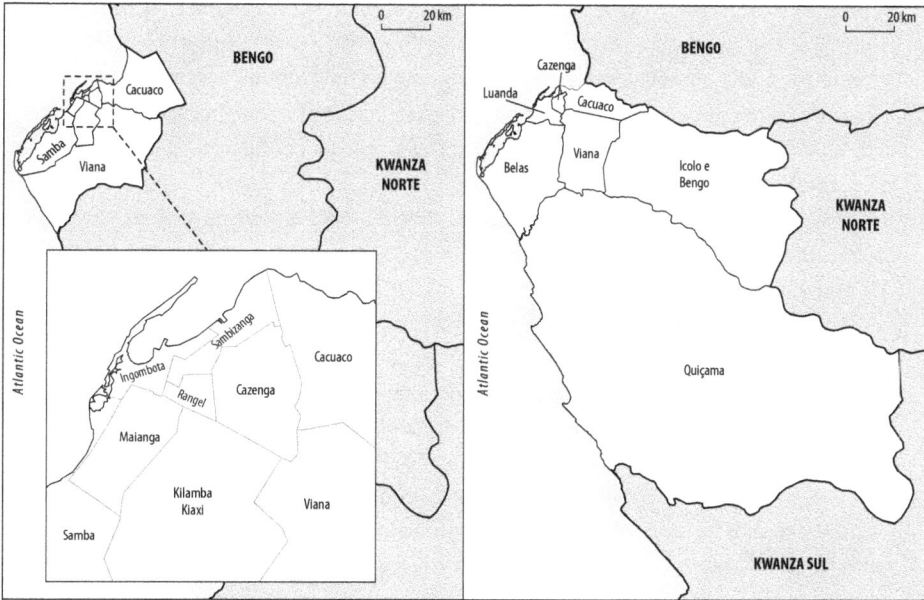

The changing boundaries of Luanda province. Created by Aharon deGrassi. The map on the left shows the boundaries of the province when I began my fieldwork in March 2011. On the right, the map shows the boundaries in September 2011. As can be seen, for the first time since independence, a municipality was given the name Luanda, as opposed to the province simply being conflated with the city. A significant portion of rural land in the form of the Quiçama region was also incorporated into Luanda Province. Further alterations were made to municipal divisions in 2016–17. However, these two maps provide an overview of the areas covered by the province during the time discussed in this book.

broadcast the state's care and capacity to Angolans. The Angola Press Agency (Agência Angola Press) had a permanent section on its website titled "National Reconstruction," which reported not only on key projects but also, in minute detail, on how many meters of road had been built in small provincial towns that day. The MPLA also made liberal use of state investments in its own public communication and propaganda, continuing to confound the division between state and party. The state newspaper, the *Journal de Angola*, the only print news medium available across the entire national territory, regularly featured front-page photographs of President José Eduardo dos Santos inaugurating recently completed constructions or showed images of high-profile projects. In this way, the media and the MPLA strategically aligned dos Santos with the celebration of national rebirth through construction, especially notable in their description of dos Santos as the "Architect of Peace." The moniker had its origins in the late war period, when the MPLA sought to redefine dos Santos as a figure of peace in opposition to Savimbi as a symbol of war. Now the term personalized peace and its maintenance in the body of dos Santos as an individual, rather than portraying them as a collective achievement (Lázaro 2010).

The political use of national reconstruction became singularly apparent when it moved to its "second phase" in 2007–8, which focused on housing delivery, not just basic infrastructure (Croese 2011). In 2008, the government launched the National Housing Development program, promising to construct 1 million houses by 2015 (Cain 2017a). Later that year, during the run-up to Angola's first postconflict national election, President dos Santos shortened the timespan of the plan, announcing the state's intention to build 1 million houses by 2012. This promise was officially made national policy with the adoption of the National Program for Urbanism and Housing (PNUH) in 2009, which came to be known as the "1 million houses" initiative.[13] While the state would coordinate the program, the plan saw the realization of the 1 million houses goal as only achievable through spreading responsibility for construction. Only 115,000 residences were meant to be provided through the public sector. Private-sector actors, cooperatives, and "directed auto-construction" initiatives would build the rest (Cain 2017b). The program retroactively incorporated existing state-subsidized housing initiatives. These included the 2001 emergency housing program, which had catalyzed the creation of rehousing areas in Luanda, and the Nova Vida Project, a state-subsidized housing development aimed at civil servants, which had broken ground in 2004. The PNUH also envisioned the building of multiple new satellite cities across Angola, referred to as "new centralities," aimed at an emerging middle class. The first phase of the flagship new centrality, Kilamba, which opened in 2011 with 20,002 units, alone cost an estimated $3.5 billion to construct, an indication of the massive financial investments undertaken by the state during this period (Buire 2017, 19). These housing initiatives became decisive tools of the MPLA-state's propaganda efforts and attempted legitimation over the next four years. They featured prominently in party election advertisements and state media as signs of not just technical capacity and provision but care. After all, a state able to deliver houses was arguably concerned not exclusively about the economy but also about its citizens' comfort.

The entrenchment of party presence and power in the city through financial and political networks made the built environment a touchstone for critiques of the MPLA and the country's economic status quo. New gated communities and luxury towers were the objects of both desire and anger. While they were sites of aspiration, they also inflicted harm. Public buildings were sold and demolished to make way for private construction (Silva 2011). Gated condominiums that advertised private infrastructures and amenities such as pools, expansive lawns, and clubhouses strained the city's run-down colonial-era infrastructure. These infrastructural demands ate away at public spaces in cases such as that of the new Sonangol building, in which an alleyway was closed to house the building's generators. In a context in which "there is no hard-and-fast distinction between legitimate and illegitimate wealth" (Barber 1982, 436), many Angolans believed the luxury real estate developments to be the material manifestation of illicit profits, a means of money laundering and distributing wealth among friends and family. International organizations such as the US Agency for International Development raised similar concerns (USAID 2010). These views were reinforced by the reality that much of the new real estate was not only beyond the financial means of most Angolans but also stood empty. Multistory apartment blocks in the city center were dark at night, and in some condominiums only a few lights flickered to indicate their sparse occupation. Rumors abounded that leading business figures used their political standing to force oil companies to rent out their buildings or risk losing valuable contracts. Voicing these suspicions and criticisms, however, was risky. Political centralization and intolerance grew steadily alongside Luanda's skyscrapers as a victorious MPLA framed a commitment to it and its projects, as "*in and of itself* a sign of commitment to 'national' unity and reconciliation" (Messiant 2008, 120). Those who differed in their views were portrayed as bellicose, threatening to reignite the civil war, thereby continuing the wartime tendency to frame "any support for its opponents as an act of treason rather than an act of political opposition" (Pearce 2015, 78). Contesting national reconstruction and urban redevelopment therefore meant implicitly contesting the president and the MPLA, whose control over contracts, finances, and companies—both public and private—congealed in the new constructions and roads that transformed the capital.

Fieldwork and Methods

I first went to Angola in September 2008, arriving just a few days before its first postconflict election. My Portuguese was only just conversational at the time and, despite my earnest reading during my first year of graduate school, to describe myself as woefully ignorant of the nuances of the country's political moment would be charitable. Over the next decade, various residents of Luanda—Angolans, Portuguese, Canadian, Germans, Congolese, Lebanese, and South Africans—would be kind enough to put up with my questions and observations. While I had undertaken short visits to the city, the long-term fieldwork began in March 2011, just two weeks after the first antigovernment protests in Luanda since 1977 had taken place. The coming to light of public disillusionment with MPLA rule in what had long been considered the heart of its support would challenge not just me but many researchers to begin to think more complexly about dissent, complicity, and everyday politics in a country where analysis of its fate had long focused on elite actors.

I had initially planned my research to be based on a classic neighborhood study, in which I would deeply engage with the residents of one or two areas of Luanda in order to develop an intricate understanding of their views and experiences of national reconstruction. After a few weeks, however, I realized the inadequacy of my approach for understanding not only Luanda's residents' lives but also the political stakes of the city's transformations. As I crossed the city in minibus taxis, the 4×4s of nongovernmental organizations (NGOs), and friends' luxury vehicles, I was exposed to a cross-section of urban life that appeared radically divided, but whose elements were inextricably bound by the rhythms of the oil boom. Rapidly expanding concrete-block musseques drew from the same influx of petrodollars as the areas where restaurants served foie gras and champagne. Every evening, I returned from engagements with these starkly different kinds of urbanism to the shelter of my apartment in a 1950s colonial-era midrise from where I could watch the enormous Kinaxixe Shopping complex beginning to carve out its place in the ruins of late-colonial Luanda. I later moved to Chicala I, a self-built neighborhood branching off from the Ilha, which was continuously threatened with a "requalification" that never arrived. My research began to demand an approach to and conceptualization of the city that could take into account the radical diversity of experiences and geographies that I was engaging with.

As Filip de Boeck and Marie-Françoise Plissart (2004, 257–58) highlight in their landmark study of Kinshasa, a city is best understood by engaging its fragments rather than attempting to capture it as a cohesive whole. The significant mobility of populations, the large geographies to be covered, the obvious explosion of any appeal to "a unitary cultural and symbolic system" (Ferguson 1999, 226), and the multisited nature of urban lives means that limiting oneself to a single urban location is often not only impossible but can undermine the integrity of the research. The first change to my original research plan was that I was forced to let go of any notion that I could confine my investigations to a limited number of sites. Although I concentrated my efforts in certain areas, the people I was interacting with—demolition victims, musseque residents, planners, and government officials—were spread out in space, linked by the shared and yet varied imaginations of the current and future city. Rather than presume the preexistence of a defined locality, which I would then explicate, I allowed the people and objects I interacted with to produce the city as "an emergent object of study" (Marcus 1995, 102). I therefore shifted my focus to trying to track specific projects, institutions, and actors and their reach across the city rather than define my investigation by location per se.

My research began in Cazenga, at the time the most densely populated of Luanda's nine municipalities,[14] and the object of a large (yet-to-be-realized) state-driven urban development project. Work there provided significant insight into long-standing political allegiances and grievances bound up with land and housing. It was a site of multiple interventions from state institutions and nongovernmental organizations, meaning that conversations about service provision and urban development were often raised in a variety of official forums. In Cazenga, I conducted interviews about histories of construction in the municipality and prevailing understandings of urban redevelopment. I participated in and observed multiple community and NGO meetings on topics connected to urban redevelopment. I was interested in how people living in such a politically key neighborhood, when faced with removals, interpreted postconflict reconstruction. My entry into the area was facilitated by Development Workshop, a leading Angolan NGO focusing on questions of urban poverty. Given the fiercely controlled nature of Angolan neighborhoods and high levels of suspicion aimed at researchers, I doubt I would have been able to do the research without Development Workshop's assistance. Nevertheless, entering with the organization meant that for a long time, regardless of my explanations to the contrary, residents believed that I worked for the United Nations, an NGO, or a Chinese construction company. As I spent time returning to specific neighborhoods, residents grew accustomed to my presence and included me slightly more in their everyday discussions. Still, it was difficult to shake my perceived status as an NGO employee, especially given my race, comparative wealth, and accented Portuguese. I believe many of the discussions that emerged from my time in Cazenga reflect this.

My interactions with Angolans quickly forced me to negotiate the complex regional histories that I embodied as a researcher. While my gender, age, class status, and race shaped my relationships, it was my nationality that primarily mediated the meaning of the other vectors of identity. During the initial few weeks of my research in Cazenga, I was approached by a resident asking me if I had contacts in Johannesburg. His relative was active in the diamond trade in Angola's northeastern Lunda provinces, and he claimed he could source diamonds for me. The encounter was overdetermined by the historical South African presence in processes of resource extraction in southern Africa. These kinds of incidents accumulated as I settled into my research. In one telling moment, a friend of mine introduced me to a table of people saying, "This is Claudia, she's South African. Don't worry though," she continued with a laugh, "she's not a *mercenário*." The reference to mercenaries spoke to my country's extraordinarily violent (and in South Africa largely unacknowledged) role in Angola's postindependence history. The apartheid government had actively supported UNITA, supplying not only funds and weapons but also medical and other kinds of social support. Thus, South Africa played a significant role in enabling and driving the many years of war that Angola endured.

Francis Nyamnjoh (2012, 71) writes about how, unlike their Black counterparts who are often marginalized or not taken seriously as researchers because of their perceived proximity to the societies they study, white African anthropologists' race leads to their escaping the category of "native anthropologist." The result is that they are able to present themselves to those they research as well as the professional community "as if they were not part of the society." My nationality, however, meant that Angolans did not allow me to place myself outside of our mutually shared histories and geographies. Selina Makana (2018, 365), a Kenyan scholar who also conducted research in Angola in the 2010s, notes that while being a Black African woman at times enabled her to build relationships of trust based on racial and pan-African solidarity, at other times the intersection of her race and gender resulted in incredulity that she was a researcher. As someone holding an African nationality, but of white settler origin, I found that the "uneasy interactions" Makana describes took on different forms. While my status as a researcher was typically not questioned (unless I was thought to be working for an international organization), my presence was overdetermined by a strained conviviality based on the shared experience of both apartheid subimperialism and anticolonial struggle that bound South Africa and Angola together. While the apartheid government had supported UNITA, the MPLA had aided the African National Congress (ANC),[15] allowing it to run military training camps in the country. Many South African exiles lived in Angola. South Africans, even white South Africans, were therefore not an alien feature of Luanda's historical landscape (Keniston 2022). Being a white South African, my history was viewed as deeply intertwined with the postindependence history of Angola, making me both a foreigner and an ambivalent insider to the processes of struggle, war, violence, and collaboration that had intimately linked and shaped both countries. Friends and colleagues reminded me of their country's contribution to the destruction of apartheid and South Africa's long presences in Angola.

These interlinkages, experiences, and knowledge of processes of settler colonialism and apartheid in South Africa and Angola shaped the kinds of issues that people raised during my research, as well as the questions I asked. It was difficult not to see parallels, for instance, between apartheid-era forced removals and contemporary demolitions in Angola, when, after roughly four months of work in Cazenga, I shifted my focus to the question of demolitions and victims of demolition who had not received compensation. To do this I became a part of the SOS Habitat team, an organization formed by demolition victims in 2002 to advocate for housing and land rights. For about nine months, I spent most of my days at SOS Habitat's office in Benfica and then Camama, joining in banter, discussing policies, interviewing and engaging with victims of urban land grabs and demolitions, and visiting people spread out across Luanda. Much of what I understand about Angola comes from daily banter with Bernardo, Nuno and Walter, who commented on local politics, explained the histories of different neighborhoods, and made it clear to me that despite many scholars' pronouncements, the MPLA was not hegemonic in its reach or appeal.

My investigations during this period encompassed a huge geographical area, as SOS Habitat's activities spanned the city, from residents of Benfica in the extreme south to people living in the northern areas of Cacuaco, where new land occupations were transforming this formerly agrarian region. While my presence was still routinely associated with either international organizations or journalists, the long period I spent working with SOS Habitat meant that I was at least partially viewed as a permanent presence on the landscape, and my position as a researcher was more clearly understood. It was my time with SOS Habitat that opened up Luanda as a geography of financial, material, and emotional destruction. There was no area of the city whose population was not affected by demolition. The "new Luanda" was being erected on the ruins of lives, creating a traumatized landscape of violence and expulsion. With at least 200,000 people forcibly removed by 2012, and thousands of others unaccounted for, demolition was a central experience of oil-boom Luanda. The antagonisms demolition catalyzed were central in shedding light on the constituents of belonging in the transforming city.

My work with SOS Habitat furthermore confirmed what I had begun to understand in Cazenga, that the process of musseque establishment had long historical roots and astounding durability. During my archival research in my final four months in Luanda, the ongoing, often violent interactions between musseque and cidade emerged out of the documents I read. My reading covered eight years of SOS Habitat's records concerning the communities it had worked with. Thereafter, I worked extensively in CEDOC (Centro de Documentação), Development Workshop's library, which comprised an extraordinary collection of books, gray matter, and newspapers on urban policy stretching back to the 1980s. Finally, I read through thirty-six years of Angola's state newspaper, the *Jornal de Angola*, to create a record of government urban policies since independence. My goal was to gain some sense of Luanda's urban history as well as popular attitudes toward the musseques over the years. This archival work was accompanied by extensive research into the maze of legislation governing land, housing, and redevelopment in Luanda so that I could build a framework of the linkages between various institutions, policies, and urban spaces. These research activities were supplemented by interviews with state representatives, architects, and planners involved in projects across Luanda, as well as civil society members, youth activists, NGO employees, human rights activists, and almost anyone else I thought could help me to better understand the city and its remaking. I kept a photographic record of Luanda to capture the aesthetic and material experience of this rapidly changing urban environment. Buttressing these activities was the bread and butter of ethnography: the everyday discussions across lunch, in taxis, at birthday parties, waiting in queues, and multiple other moments and encounters that so often illuminate more than any voice-recorded interview ever will.

The above sites, people, and research practices began to create a representation of the city that revealed the multiple political-economic scales and processes that produced the everyday actions and experiences I encountered. However, I soon realized that a central actor had been excluded from my initial research: the city itself. My discussions clarified to me that the city could not be thought of as a passive object. Luanda—its government buildings, pipes, air conditioners, luminescent high-rises, and generators—was an active participant shaping political worlds. While my interactions with Luandans provided the interpretations, information, and viewpoints that make up the heart of this book, all of us were pushed and moved by the city. From traffic jams that determined daily work rhythms, to everyday hassles of dealing with water cuts and timing transcription of fieldnotes for when electricity was available, the city fundamentally shaped my writing and research. The city was a central actor in my life, from the first time I set foot in Luanda in 2008, through my fieldwork in 2011 and 2012 and subsequent regular visits between 2013 and 2019. How urban materials, infrastructures, and sensations shaped politics and relations came to stand at the center of my research as I gradually witnessed my own practices and judgments shift to manage changing conditions and new information. Musseques became neighborhoods, and I learned how to manage water shortages and power outages. Through the relations that these material conditions forged in my own life, I began to better understand how materials, infrastructures, buildings, and other objects produced various orientations toward and understandings of political belonging through their entanglement with Luanda's residents' lives, actions, and imaginations.

Organization of the Book

The pages that follow explore how oil boom construction, architecture, demolition, materials, and infrastructure reconfigured, and sometimes reinforced, urban residents' understandings of the constituents and limits of political belonging. They trace the political ambiguity of aesthetic registers and show how state and private investors' actions transformed the aesthetic into a space of contestation in an authoritarian environment where obvious forms of criticism were not always possible. To explore these contestations, the book guides the reader through Luanda's experience of the civil war, into the postconflict period where it tracks the state's attempts to produce a new aesthetic consensus, along with the everyday forms of dissent that emerged in the face of this. I show how political belonging was steeped in the aesthetics of the built environment and how interventions into the city then sparked broader political discussions. Chapter 1 introduces the reader to the state's politicization of aesthetics in the postconflict period. It does this by providing a detailed account of Luanda's perceived decline during the civil war, which afforded the MPLA-state the opportunity to present its violent remaking of the city in the oil boom moment as an assertion of care. State institutions sought to transform their image from one of negligence to one of provision by promising to build a "world-class city" that would bring people into a condition of aesthetic comfort that until then had been denied to them. In these discourses, violence was represented as necessary to bring about the promised future city. Chapter 2 enters the world of Luanda's musseques to show how they anchored competing imaginations of urban belonging. As musseque residents built their concrete-block homes, they produced an Indigenous urbanism and a political consciousness of urban autochthony that rejected state projects' implicit claims that their presence was illegitimate. An aesthetic challenge to oil spectacle therefore emerged from the very locations that planners sought to eradicate. Chapter 3 investigates how aesthetic and material considerations permeated relations between urban residents and state institutions. It argues that despite appeals to legal norms, the state and Luanda's residents implicitly drew on a moral economy of materiality to determine questions of property, ownership, and belonging. The demolitions that destroyed thousands of homes in the city betrayed not only human and political rights but also the moral economy of materiality that had long governed the everyday norms through which land tenure and property ownership were assessed. Chapter 4 returns to the politics of comfort by examining the question of rehousing during national reconstruction. The chapter shows how Luanda's informal infrastructures provided the basis for material and aesthetic class distinctions between residents and traces how these distinctions were designed into the national housing policy. Rather than bringing about a new sense of inclusion, rehousing often simply reproduced existing class distinctions through the aesthetic experience of infrastructure. Finally, chapter 5 explores how urban aesthetics became the basis for dissent against not just the project of national reconstruction but also the MPLA regime. Focusing on ordinary residents' interactions with architectural design and aspirational urban plans, it shows how these projects stimulated suspicion and anger toward the regime, allowing political contestation to emerge through the register of aesthetic judgment. The book concludes with a reflection on Angola after the oil boom and an exploration of the possibilities for the democratization of urban aesthetics.

CHAPTER ONE

Making the "New Luanda"

National Reconstruction and Phantasmagorias of Care

"A resolver os problemas do povo" ("Solving the people's problems") read the government-sponsored billboard erected along the Rua da Samba, one of Luanda's main traffic arteries that linked the city center to the wealthy neighborhood of Talatona in the south. The image depicted the Cacuaco Centrality (Centralidade de Cacuaco), one of five state-subsidized satellite cities, referred to as "new centralities," constructed across Luanda Province beginning in 2008. The new centralities were the primary representation of the "second phase" of national reconstruction, which included a turn to housing provision rather than simply big infrastructure (Soares de Oliveira 2015). The use of the slogan "Solving the people's problems" was not accidental. The phrase was a direct reference to Angola's first president, Agostinho Neto, who had famously remarked that "the most important thing is to solve the people's problems" ("O mais importante é resolver os problemas do povo"). The billboard was one of a series sponsored by the Angolan government displaying a project in process or completed during the period of national reconstruction. They included images of hospitals, dams, and housing. Every sign bore the slogan "Building a prosperous and united Angola," accompanied by the name of the project and the province it was located in, as well as a phrase linking the image to ideas of progress and development. The billboards suggested that the nation was being reconstituted through the countrywide provision of infrastructure and housing, thereby fulfilling the long-delayed promises of independence to "solve the people's problems." Just how precisely these projects were "solving the people's problems" and exactly which problems were being solved, however, lay at the center of political disputes during Angola's oil boom.

Literature on Angola's oil boom has concentrated on the politics of the large-scale investments in infrastructure and housing that characterized what became known as "national reconstruction" (see, among others, Soares de Oliveira 2015; Tomás 2022; Croese 2017; Buire 2014; Cardoso 2016; and Croese and

Pitcher 2019). In general, scholars have criticized the state's focus on top-down planning and infrastructure delivery (see Vines et al. 2005). The common view is that megaproject investments eclipsed the urgent need for broader post-conflict political reforms, ignored social needs, failed to diversify the economy, and allowed the MPLA to avoid grappling with postconflict reconciliation, as well as enabling it to use provision to strengthen its control over the state apparatus, financial flows, and popular support. Ricardo Soares de Oliveira (2015), for instance, argues that infrastructure and housing projects became a means of extending the MPLA-state's presence into areas of the country from which the ruling party had long been absent, linking its image to that of provision and thereby further entrenching its hegemonic control. Jon Schubert (2017) also sees construction processes as key to the production of political hegemony. He notes that the destruction of Luanda's existing cityscape, which accompanied major postconflict private and public urban investments, resulted in the purging of mnemonic references to other political pasts and futures, thereby materially imposing the MPLA's imagination of the postconflict state on the country. As Justin Pearce (2015, 110) notes, in a context where the MPLA and the state were "conceptually indistinct," national reconstruction discursively elided the MPLA's culpability in wartime destruction, framing its intervention as one of "undoing the damage caused by UNITA during the war." Investments in housing and infrastructure thereby tied material improvements in people's lives to the MPLA (Buire 2014). As such, national reconstruction positioned the MPLA as the party of provision, peace, and healing enacted through a technopolitics of megaproject implementation.

The means through which the MPLA attempted to construct hegemony using the built environment were, however, more complex—and therefore more unstable—than existing accounts of Angola's oil boom have accounted for. Oil booms have regularly been characterized by the experience of temporalities of rapid change, as leaders use oil rents to launch projects and enable consumerist possibilities that provide a phantasmagoria of "instantaneous modernization" (Coronil 1997, 10), through the replication of feigned signs of material progress in the form of large infrastructure, lifestyle projects, and the latest in consumer goods. As was the case in Angola, these practices of state spectacle are typically analyzed as discombobulating dreams, sparkles that blind an undefined public into recognizing the state as the producer of wealth, modernity, and progress. Oil spectacle is therefore treated as a phenomenon that transforms citizens and others into passive spectators of the state. In the context of similar mobilizations of development rhetoric in contemporary building of new cities, Ayona Datta (2016, 15) has noted that "'development' as both a logic and solution to the crisis of urbanization becomes a tool for asserting the material and symbolic power of the state over its citizens."

Rather, however, than anaesthetizing citizens, spectacle arguably engages with their aspirations. Choices of investments signal understandings of local histories, needs, and imaginations. The billboards that lined the Rua da Samba, which included images of hospitals, dams, and housing represented not some ill-defined notion of progress or modernity but a politics of provision and care that spoke to Angolans' widespread desires for a responsive state.

During the war, the MPLA had won rural populations to its side through its ability to provide consumer goods such as salt and soap in areas ravaged by violence and cut off from trade routes (Pearce 2015). In doing this, it fulfilled long-standing historical expectations of the material forms through which state presence and concern were enacted. In the oil-boom moment, the MPLA-state would scale these perceived acts of material care into a larger systemic program, one backed by fabulous oil wealth. The megaprojects and infrastructures of national reconstruction constituted a visible peace dividend that not only promised a better future and signaled state reach throughout a previously fractured national territory but also attempted to build a particular imagination of the state as a caring state.

This chapter traces how histories of material decay, shortages, and infrastructural breakdown provided fertile ground for the appeal of oil spectacle. This was achieved by repackaging violence as care. Luanda's remaking was rooted in the expulsion of hundreds of thousands of urban residents from their homes. For those affected, peace was experienced as displacement. People spoke fearfully about the early morning arrivals of police and military in their neighborhoods, which marked the initiation of citywide demolitions. Nevertheless, the state institutions represented these evictions as acts of care. Daniel Mains (2019, 2) has argued that the visual performances of construction that often accompany building booms "obscure the process of construction." In Luanda, advertisements, media reports, and the everyday experience of new buildings and infrastructure obscured the violence and neglect that facilitated national reconstruction. By obscuring these processes, spectacle not only promised modernity but also remade the wartime state into a "caring subject" through aesthetic performances (McKay 2017, 10). In claiming to solve the people's problems, the MPLA-state sought to redefine itself from a wartime state to a caring state. Rather than dazzling spectators, this ultimately deeply engaged citizens in the world of political aesthetics.

Figure 1.1. "Solving the people's problems," December 2014. Used by permission of Maka Angola.

Figure 1.2. "New residential zones across the whole country," December 2014. Used by permission of Maka Angola.

The Suffering City: Luanda, 1975–2002

The appeal of care can only be understood in the shadow of Luanda's postindependence history, and especially the country's protracted civil war. Other than in the months leading up to independence and the days following the country's first election in 1992, almost no fighting occurred in Luanda itself, turning the city into a relative haven for Angolans. Nevertheless, the reverberations of war were strongly felt in the capital, which struggled to cope with the demands emerging from the rapid demographic growth and state inefficiencies produced by colonialism, independence, and war. In the accounts of many Luandans, the wounds of war shaped the city's geographies and materialities. Time and again, before explaining anything else, interviewees would begin with an explanation of the city, what they viewed as the essential background to contemporary Luanda. In short, they explained that Luanda had initially been designed for 500,000 people. However, with the arrival of the war, the city was demographically overwhelmed by people fleeing fighting, a process that intersected with the collapse of much state capacity in the postindependence moment. By the time the war ended, Luanda was a desperate city, characterized by dilapidated buildings, drastic shortages of basic services, and kilometers of informal settlements. The in-house magazine produced by the Luanda Urban Planning and Management Institute (IPGUL), for instance, in an article about the redevelopment of Luanda, argued that

> the war disrupted the social systems of Angola's cities, in which populations, at the time of rural exodus, turned to the provincial capitals, especially Luanda. Much of this population, without the necessary knowledge, took over public and private spaces. In this way, the city suffered an occupation of areas previously destined for gardens, building sites, parks and public rights, and public utilities such as urinals and other city facilities. These places were transformed into precarious residences lacking basic sanitation, leading migrants to live in crowded conditions in the capital city. These residents were not concerned with "living in the city" but with surviving in it. (Rita 2010)

The above description was swiftly followed with the explanation that President dos Santos's "1 million houses" initiative would address these historical challenges. An employee of IPGUL explained to me that the war had resulted in the emergence of *bairros desordenados* (disorganized neighborhoods). Because the government did not provide support for people, he continued, they built with whatever they could find in any place they could find. The housing that resulted had no link to Angolan "culture," he claimed. Rather, it was an architecture of "necessity" (Carlos, interview, IPGUL, Maianga, Luanda, 7 June 2011). State institutions were not the only ones offering such accounts; so did those who contested them. Activists often repeated the same narrative of suffering to explain why the state was responsible for the irregular occupation of land and informal construction in the city. Bernado and Nuno, members of the land and housing rights organization SOS Habitat, explained in their first encounter with me that

> the war . . . lasted many years and created many problems. . . . During the war, there were areas that were safe and areas that were not. Those that were safe received many people. The people came, then, from various places. They came to Luanda, to the big centers and city where there was security. When these people arrived in the city, there wasn't a capacity, a technical capacity to receive them. So, these people built, they erected constructions in their own way. Even if they were poor, they built in their own way in these cities. One of them was Luanda. As you know, today Luanda is one of the most populous cities and it was precisely during the war period that the population of the city increased. (Bernardo and Nuno, interview, Maianga, 5 May 2011)

If in the case of the humanitarian organizations studied by Miriam Ticktin (2011, 14), the "universal suffering body" is the "political device to create conditions of care," then in the context of Luanda, it was the built environment of the city that acted as evidence for the necessity of state intervention, seemingly demanding the technical prowess of master planning and infrastructure initiatives to heal it. It seemed almost impossible to argue that the city should continue to be characterized by water shortages, roads should not be widened, or new housing not constructed for the neediest. To understand how this material urgency could be mobilized, however, it helps to better understand the postindependence history of the city. For the claims regarding material degradation, breakdown, and need emanated not only from the state but also from the general population, as the urban experience of war became one powerfully mediated by the perceived ruination and unraveling of the built environment.

1975–C. 1990: DECLINE AS DISCOMFORT

Luanda's inhabitants experienced the immediate challenges of independence as viscerally material. At the heart of these experiences stood the difficulties of reconstituting viable state institutions. In the run-up to independence, about 300,000 settlers fled Angola, including 90 percent of white public servants and many skilled technicians. With much of the technocratic expertise of the country now living abroad, the MPLA inherited a state "with few functioning institutions that could be adapted to new political circumstances" (Birmingham 2016, 86). Rather than simply taking over the skeleton of the colonial state, the MPLA often found itself forced to reinvent the country's political and administrative institutions from scratch. The evacuation of state capacity was notable when it came to urban real estate, governance, and planning. Settlers had little time to organize their departure, resulting in the haphazard abandonment of most of Luanda's formal housing stock. Gradually, Angolans began to occupy the abandoned housing. Some bought the homes from departing settlers (Sr. Walter, interview, Cazenga, 26 September 2011), while others were given the keys to homes by their former employers and asked to care for the properties until their return (Mais Velho João, interview, Cazenga, 2 September 2011). Many, however, just broke into and occupied abandoned homes, claiming them as their own.[1] People's Neighborhood Commissions (CPBs) also played a role in distributing housing, calling on owners to appear in person at their offices to claim their properties or risk having them distributed to others (Gastrow 2021).

Through the *Jornal de Angola*, representatives of the Angolan state made it clear that they disapproved of what the newspaper referred to as the "anarchic occupation" of the city's real estate. The government therefore quickly began creating laws, offices, and institutions to bring processes of occupation under control. To this end, immediately following independence, the government established the Rehousing Intervention Brigade (BIR). It tasked this organization with registering abandoned housing, collecting residence keys, and distributing housing in a controlled manner. The politically sensitive war context, however, meant that people who invaded houses were generally left in place, rather than evicted (former Angolan civil servant, interview, Alvalade, Luanda, 9 February 2012). The BIR's activities were a step toward a general policy of expropriation and nationalization that came into effect in 1976. Under the auspices of Law 3/76 and Law 43/76, the MPLA nationalized much of the existing housing stock.[2] Law 3/76, according to what it described as a "political economy of resistance," enabled the expropriation and nationalization of companies, goods, and properties that had been abandoned or belonged to a persona non grata.[3] Law 43/76, also known as the "Confiscation Law" (Lei de Confisco), stated that any property whose owner had been absent from the country for more than forty-five days could automatically be confiscated in the name of the state, with no right to compensation.[4] Announcements of the law played over the radio to warn people of its imminent implementation (Dona Lili, interview, Kinaxixe, 20 March 2012). Through these laws, the state granted itself official ownership over most of the abandoned housing in the city, as well as the legal mandate to expel occupants and reward those who qualified with housing. The BIR was dissolved in 1976, and management of the housing stock was transferred to the National Housing Institute (INH), which replaced the colonial Housing Board (Junta da Habitação).[5] The state now owned much of the formal housing stock, for which it introduced legislation determining rents in 1978 and 1979.[6] Luandans describe the rental prices as symbolic rather than market driven. In fact, the low rents meant that even when the government raised them in the 1990s, official state rents in Angola remained some of the lowest in the world (Dar al-Handasah 1996a, 1.5).

While laws existed, nationalization in Angola was a chaotic process. When properties were nationalized, the relevant administrative decree sometimes did not identify the exact building, only stating that several buildings on a certain road in the city had been expropriated. Some buildings, although occupied, were never officially expropriated and remain in legal limbo to this day. Others were nationalized in the name of a variety of ministries and special offices, making it at times difficult to determine who was in charge of real estate in Luanda. In addition, it was almost impossible to evict people for infractions, and despite official attempts to dissuade residents, people quickly realized that the best way to lay claim to a property was to occupy it (Gastrow 2021). With demand high and control over the housing stock tenuous, corruption quickly emerged in the distribution process. Caretakers of buildings were said to collect money from people after informing them of the existence of empty apartments, while members of the INH were accused of *amiguismo* (nepotism or cronyism) in their distribution practices ("Distribuidas chaves de 100 novas residências no acto central do Dia do Construtor" 1979). People also tried to bribe those linked to housing distribution, approaching them at parties or even coming to their homes at night to ask for special consideration (former Angolan civil servant, interview, Alvalade, 9 February 2012). By the 1980s, random occupations and clashes over housing had dwindled, but housing in the coveted infrastructurally connected and officially planned city center had become scarce. As a result, people began "denouncing" one another, reporting (and often lying) to authorities that residents living in a desired property had been absent for forty-five days, or that they were occupying a house that the complainant considered too large given the size of the family (Kianda, interview, Maculusso, 16 November 2014). People hoped to acquire the house if those they had denounced were evicted. This messy practice of denunciation was exacerbated by corruption and political connections, with people paying officials to access housing or drawing on political connections to have others evicted. To remain in a property, one had to be endlessly vigilant. To talk of "nationalization" in Angola, then, is to speak of a relatively disorganized and uncontrolled process rather than the formation of a judiciously state-managed housing stock.

State incapacity revealed itself in the material properties of the built environment and with that the everyday embodied experiences of dwelling in the city. The flight of skilled technicians and divestment of assets in the buildup to independence contributed to the crash of the city's late colonial construction boom and eviscerated maintenance and property management competencies (Greger 1990). Newspaper interviews with construction workers revealed a dire shortage of basic building and finishing materials, with locks, tiles, and door handles identified as scarce ("Nacionalizar a construção civil" 1975). After a few years, the cumulative effects of flailing institutions and shortages of parts and human resources became apparent. In 1979, the *Jornal de Angola* reported on a ten-story building on Avenida Comandante Valodia in the neighborhood of Marçal that was in the process of disintegration. Home to 120 people, the highrise's electricity, water, and sanitation systems had collapsed. Residents were forced to fetch water from a tap eighty meters from the apartment block and carry it up the stairs, as the elevator has long ceased functioning. The smells emanating from the stopped-up pipes were so repugnant that inhabitants tore out the toilets and wash basins and cemented shut the sanitation system. With no working elevators, many people grew tired of transporting their rubbish down multiple flights of stairs and began to simply throw it out of their windows ("Cento e vinte famílias habitam sem condições de alojamento" 1979). In the SUNIVOR/FAGOR building in Coqueiros, the ceilings of some apartments had collapsed because of water infiltrations (Eduardo 1983). In the Prédio Oliva in downtown Luanda, water was literally coming out of the some of the walls, forcing residents to evacuate the lower-level apartments. The residents approached the National Water and Sanitation Company (ENAS) for assistance. The company's employees arrived and shut down the water supply to all of the taps and showers in the building. Unfortunately, they did not return to fix and replace the damaged taps and plumbing, or to restore the water (Eduardo 1982).

The MPLA-state attempted to address the pressing maintenance questions by creating a series of state companies dedicated to caring for Luanda's buildings. These included the National Company for Special Installations (INSTAL/UEE), which, among other things, was tasked with fixing elevators, and the Provincial Property Conservation Company (EMPROCI), which was in charge of general maintenance. Unfortunately, these companies were subject to the same shortages of materials and human resources that haunted Luanda's buildings, with representatives from both of them claiming they were unable to fulfill their duties because parts had to be imported and they were not always familiar with the technologies they were called to fix (Ramiro 1980; Perdiz 1985). This slow unmaking of the materiality of colonial modernity caused many people to begin to describe the city as undergoing a process of *mussequização* (mussequeization). For residents of the city center, postindependence state incapacity was experienced through the everyday discomforts produced by the seeming collapse of technical expertise and infrastructure—the drying up of showers, the darkness of rooms at night, the smells that wafted on the breeze from decaying sanitation systems, and the heavy bags residents had to carry up many flights of stairs because of a broken elevator.

It was not only the formally planned city, however, whose materiality and embodied experience was shaped by the struggles of the new state to build institutions and implement policies. In the face of significant shortages of construction materials, the musseques emerged as sites of material illegality. As it became increasingly difficult to access abandoned housing in the city center and the new state constructions were too few to meet demand, people turned to self-building (*autoconstrução*) as a way to house themselves. Provincial and municipal authorities threatened to demolish these constructions, describing houses built without approval as *construções clandestinas* (clandestine constructions). They warned that these homes contradicted planning norms and failed to meet basic health and safety requirements ("Construção clandestina: Chegou a hora de resolver a problema" 1977; "Comissariado de Luanda: Comunicação sobre a construção clandestina" 1977). Several initiatives were announced to combat informal construction. These included the attempted introduction of land registration in the musseques in the 1980s, the unsuccessful creation of a program of *autoconstrução dirigida* (site-and-service) to try and direct the city's growth, and the creation of an Office for the Renewal and Rehabilitation of the Musseques (GARM), which launched its first "slum-upgrading" pilot project in the municipality of Sambizanga in Luanda.[7] These initiatives collapsed in the face of high demand, a shortage of trained technicians, and the inability of state bureaucracies to manage and implement the policies.

The animosity directed toward self-built houses, however, was not just about their disruption of planning orders; it was also a direct criticism of the political economy that their materials signaled. The production of construction materials had plunged since independence (Greger 1990, 133). With the introduction of a centralized economy, the provision of these materials was technically reduced to the public sector, where they had to be officially requisitioned from and supplied by state companies such as the Construction Materials Company (EMPROMAC) (Dar al-Handasah 1996a, 4.34). Like many other state companies, EMPROMAC faced considerable difficulties in delivering its goods and services, with companies that relied on it for parts, such as EMPROCI, complaining that they were unable to obtain their requested materials from EMPROMAC and were therefore unable to fulfill their mandates (Perdiz 1985). Reports complained that zinc sheets, brick, cement, and sand were difficult to access at "official prices" (Eduardo 1984). Items such as paint, locks, and taps were almost never available except through personal connections (Dar al-Handasah 1996b, 4.34). In the face of significant shortages, Luandans turned to what Angolans referred to as *candonga*—illicit informal economic activities— to access goods. Given the growing shortages, worthwhile profits could be reaped from the illegal sale of construction supplies. Factory workers were sometimes paid in kind and would then sell the materials on the parallel market at inflated prices. Goods siphoned off from ports, the airport, and state shops (known as *lojas do povo* or "people's stores") found their way into the expanding informal economy (dos Santos 1990a, 169). Many people bought materials, especially cement, from Cuban *cooperantes* who had pilfered them from state construction works (Samuel, interview, Cazenga, 31 August 2011).[8] One contributor to the state newspaper had been informed by the State Housing Secretariat that it was not its responsibility to construct new housing. The contributor angrily wrote, "Faced with the incapacity of [officials] to provide a response to the housing crisis, in the case of Luanda, we see an unbridled movement toward autoconstruction at the cost of innumerous sacrifices; from the water to the cement, the majority of autoconstructors acquire everything through candonga" (Ramiro 1986). The musseques represented candonga in material form. The proliferation of illegally built houses using materials not available in stores pointed to the limits of state control. The very materials of the musseque home were evidence of the state's incapacity to deliver on the promises of order and uplift—in other words, care—that it had promised to the Angolan people upon independence.

THE 1990S: DEVELOPMENT AND DESTRUCTION

The circumstances of Luanda's inhabitants and buildings worsened in the 1990s, despite the initial glimmers of hope that characterized the first few years of the decade. In 1991, the MPLA and UNITA signed the Bicesse Peace Accord, opening the way for Angola's first multiparty elections in September 1992. Of equal significance, the MPLA abandoned Marxist-Leninism as its defining political principle. The shift in economic and political policies led to a renewed interest in Luanda as a site of profit. While there had been an informal market in land and real estate throughout the socialist period, investors could not officially speculate. The formal opening up of the urban land market resulted in a boom in private and public projects. Soares da Costa, one of Portugal's largest construction groups, announced that, in conjunction with Angola's Grupo Atlântico, it planned to build a twenty-five-story building for luxury housing and offices on Luanda's famous Marginal promenade (dos Santos 1990b). The *Jornal de Angola* ran a number of articles detailing new state and private real estate developments, the return of construction companies to Angola, the restoration of the city's defunct elevators, the redevelopment of the Ilha, and the rehabilitation of the national road network.[9] Peace promised to heal the suffering city.

The MPLA-state, facing an election for the first time in its history, sought to deliver on some of the material promises of independence. In late 1990, it launched the Emergency Housing Program, an initiative to restore existing properties as well as build new housing across the country.[10] The MPLA government also introduced legislation that began a process of real estate privatization by allowing people living in state-owned housing to purchase their residences.[11] To facilitate the sales process, a National Commission for the Sale of State Housing (Comissão Nacional de Venda de Património Habitacional de Estado) was established under the auspices of the SEH and represented locally by provincial commissions. Those who could prove they had regularly paid their rent (receipts were needed) and had steady employment (if a loan was required) or cash at hand, could purchase their homes. The sale value of the properties was determined by the existing rent, as well as the location, quality, age, and condition of the building. Given that the rental prices had been set in 1979 and that the kwanza had markedly devalued since then, people were sometimes able to purchase prime property for as little as $100 (Dar al-Handasah 1996a). A 1996 study by the consulting firm Dar al-Handasah observed that the sales price of properties was not related to their market value, noting that a house that would have been worth $600,000 on the open market was sold by the state for $13.05 (Dar al-Handasah 1996a). By June 1997, the state newspaper claimed that 80,000 houses, worth $2.5 million, had been sold. If this is true, then on average, each house was sold for $31.25 (Santana 1997). Houses were, to all intents and purposes, being given away. Many Luandans viewed the privatization of the housing stock as an MPLA strategy to solidify its urban base in the run-up to the election, as well as to ensure that should

UNITA win its members could not automatically take control of urban real estate.

Dreams of rebuilding the nation were, however, cut short. In the wake of the 1992 election, war broke out once again. The 1990s would be the most brutal decade of the country's war. Scorched-earth policies and forced recruitment devastated rural areas. Although Cold War interests no longer fueled the conflict, the MPLA's access to oil and UNITA's control over the northeastern diamond fields financed the ongoing violence. Fleeing the fighting, thousands of *deslocados* (internally displaced people) headed for the relative safety of Luanda, overwhelming the city's infrastructure and exacerbating the existing housing shortage. Properties were swiftly subdivided, added on to, and remodeled as arrivals sought to locate themselves in the few areas with infrastructure. Existing residents were forced to accommodate relatives and growing families. People occupied incomplete constructions from the colonial era and transformed roofs, balconies, and parks into residences. The musseques exploded as the housing shortage pushed people to the urban edge to construct.

The promised peacetime construction boom disappeared overnight, and housing became ever more central to urban survival. In the face of skyrocketing inflation, which reached 1,236 percent in 1993 (Aguilar 2001, 3), housing became an important source of foreign exchange. To gain access to valuable US dollars, people moved in with friends or family and rented out their apartments in the city center to foreigners. With the money earned, a family could feed itself, pay school fees, purchase a car, and build a house somewhere else in the city, thereby contributing to the growth of informal areas. Construction, though, was not easy. Rapid inflation drove up the cost of materials. As one report by the UN Development Programme observed, "The Angolan population is busy building expensive *musseques*" (UNDP 1999, 63). The desperation to access housing, exacerbated by the lack of clarity regarding the ownership and management of properties in the city, led to rising levels of corruption and conflict, and increased scheming. Accounts emerged of employees selling the same apartments to multiple buyers (Carima 1994), of physical altercations to claim prime properties ("Fui espancado por 20 homens" 1993), and of schemes to evict people from state housing by accusing them of having illegally sold off the property (Baptista 1993). In one of the most shocking accounts, a letter to the state newspaper described how someone had begun to build a restaurant in the writer's backyard, but the victim had been unable to convince the police to evict the culprit (Lopes 1994).

The growing public concern with the state of the city was paralleled by similar pronouncements from state institutions, with each post-1992 provincial governor initiating a new policy for urban rejuvenation. In 1993, then-governor Oscar de Carvalho launched Vamos Salvar Luanda (Let's Save Luanda), an initiative aimed at combating the "degradation of the city" ("Vamos salvar Luanda" 1993). The program attempted to harness broad public involvement in urban renewal with discussions focused on, among other things, the rejuvenation of neighborhood residents' committees, a restructuring of the provincial government, and tackling the city's housing and water problems ("Luanda cuide-se" 1993; "Luanda continua em debate" 1993). The initiative collapsed after tensions between the central and provincial governments flared, as the project would have shifted control of key potential income opportunities to the province (Gastrow 2020a). A few months after Carvalho requested that all state property in Luanda be transferred to the control of the province rather than split between various ministries and institutions, he was relieved of his position and replaced with Justinho Fernandes, a close friend of President dos Santos.

Under Fernandes, Luanda witnessed the rise of state-subsidized speculative urban investment as a development strategy. In 1995, Angola's first public-private urbanization initiative, the Luanda Sul Project, was launched. This was a partnership between Brazilian companies Prado Valladores and Odebrecht, and the Urban Development Company (EDURB), created by the GPL. Imagined as "self-financed," the project involved the central government's transferring state land to the private control of EDURB. Odebrecht and Prado Valladores would plan and install infrastructure and be remunerated through the sale of plots to private developers. These sales would fund the development of low-cost housing as part of the broader project. Although the project foresaw the construction of high-, middle-, and low-income housing, it only made good on its promises in the construction of Talatona, an area now famous for its gated communities aimed at the wealthy. The first company to purchase a set of plots in Luanda Sul was Sonangol, the state oil company, which signed a contract with EDURB for enough land to build 400 houses. Justinho Fernandes encouraged other companies to follow Sonangol's lead.

The construction of Luanda Sul not only heralded a new era in serious urban investments but also raised the specter of housing demolitions. Although rumors of pending demolitions of musseque areas circulated throughout the postindependence era, the general consensus was that, given war conditions, it was politically inexpedient to undertake them (former employee of Empresa de Obras Especiais, Afonso, Maianga, 30 November 2015).[12] However, the act of demolition suddenly began to be presented as necessary, with the state newspaper quoting GPL representatives describing how they would remove "anarchic constructions" (*construções anárquicos*) in the earmarked areas ("GPL concede terreno à Sonangol" 1994). By 1997, when the new governor Ánibal Rocha launched the Luanda, Nossa Casa Comum (Luanda, Our Common Home) initiative, the program openly threatened to demolish housing. A regular page in the *Jornal de Angola* dedicated to the Nossa Casa initiative published articles criticizing informal construction and advocating what one piece described as "disciplinary action" ("Desestimular a ocupação illegal de terrenos" 1999). What such action involved was clear. Warnings printed in the newspaper advised readers that "anarchic constructions" would be demolished. In late 1999, EDURB began to demolish houses within the perimeter of Luanda Sul, leading to protests and sit-ins in front of municipal buildings ("GPL atira cidadãos a rua" 1999; "GPL continua a desalojar" 1999). Despite the protests, the demolitions would become a central part of urban remaking over the next decade and a half, as a system of speculation and rehousing set in that was marketed to Luandans as an act of provision and care.

BOAVISTA: INTRODUCING VIOLENCE AS CARE

In April 2001 unusually heavy seasonal rains left 1,000 homeless and 11 dead in Luanda. With the city in shock, President dos Santos called an emergency meeting of the GOE and the Ministry of Public Works. They framed the tragedy as a product of poor urban planning ("PR convoca reunião de emergência" 2001). The president then created a working group to reassess urban planning as well as a number of major laws, including the Land Law and the Territorial Organization Law. In the meantime, however, the president announced that provisional steps would need to be taken to "eliminate the current anarchy that reigns in the domain of urban planning and management" ("PR aponta soluções para acudir sinistrados" 2001). About a week later the Permanent Commission of the Council of Ministers (Comissão Permanente do Conselho dos Ministros) approved an "emergency program" to provide $10 million in assistance to flood victims across the country and called for a study to analyze the underlying problems that had led to the tragedy, namely, poor urban conditions ("CM aprova programa de apoio aos sinistrados" 2001). The *Jornal de Angola* reported that "these proceedings envisage the adoption of concrete measures in the realm of public sanitation, infrastructures for storm water drainage, the treatment of urban solid wastes, the prevention of anarchic construction in areas of risk, the rehabilitation of roads, and the combating of erosion." In sum, urban planning would be the panacea for the city's woes.

One neighborhood quickly became the focus of government intervention: Boavista, a largely informal area perched precariously on the cliffs between the elite neighborhood of Miramar and Luanda's port. Eight of the eleven deaths had occurred there. Shortly after the president's convening of representatives, the minister of planning declared that residents of the neighborhood were to be rehoused ("Garantido apoio às vítimas das chuvas" 2001). On 28 April 2001, the *Jornal de Angola* reported that as part of the emergency program, 6,000 families would be removed from Boavista to the municipality of Viana, where they would receive assistance in building new houses as part of a program of *autoconstrução dirigida* (directed self-building / site-and-service) (de Melo 2001).[13] The announcement catalyzed resistance to the decision, with Boavista's inhabitants resurrecting their long-defunct residents' committee (Amnesty International 2003). In a letter to the GPL, the committee expressed concern that homes not at risk from landslides were nevertheless being registered for demolition. When, on 30 June 2001, police and demolition crews arrived, Boavista's residents built barricades and burned tires to keep them out (Amnesty International 2003). While these actions worked temporarily, the police returned the next day with a larger contingent that included the Rapid Intervention Police, the canine unit, and helicopters. They began to physically remove people from their homes, clashing with residents who chanted "House for a house, not a house for a tent" (Pearce 2005, 16). Police responded by firing into the air, killing two people and injuring at least five others. Havoc broke out as residents attacked the Sambizanga municipal administration building, with thirteen people subsequently being arrested (Amnesty International 2003).

The violence of the intervention and the dumping of the population in a tented camp, referred to as Zango, more than 40 kilometers from the city center, were described by the state newspaper as a benevolent undertaking. Articles insisted that the protests were the work of local criminals and that no one was being moved involuntarily ("Zona da Boavista regista tumultos" 2001). The government's actions were portrayed as an act of care, with the editor of the *Jornal de Angola* arguing, "In requesting the intervention of the police in order to proceed with the eviction of Boavista's residents, the Luanda Provincial Government not only made use of a legal instrument but principally fulfilled one of the tasks of the state: the protection of its citizens" ("Proteger os cidadãos" 2001). This portrayal of the use of force as not only legitimate but an act of magnanimity marked a new trend in framings of state-citizen relations. If previously there had been a struggle between state representatives and ordinary citizens regarding culpability for Luanda's dilapidation and the housing crisis, state institutions now presented themselves as recognizing their duty to provide for the population through the provision of urban services. The supposed imperative to enforce "order" as a means to provide services became a justification for brutal interventions. Violence was repackaged as care.

This shift in rhetoric was evident in the mobilization of the Zango project as proof of care rather than neglect. While independent journalists were chased away from the zone, the governor invited the diplomatic corps and NGOs to tour Zango and Boavista so as to view the assumedly better living conditions that would be offered to the residents ("Rocha leva embaixadores à Boavista e Zango" 2001). The provincial government even arranged for Se Bem, a wildly popular musician, to hold a concert in Zango for Boavista's former residents ("Se Bem canta em Viana" 2001). Most telling, however, was a government-sponsored media campaign that actively represented displacement and rehousing as acts of care. The campaign was made up of a series of full-page advertisements published in the state newspaper during October 2001. The advertisements used images of Boavista and housing construction in Zango, along with explanations of the benefits of rehousing, to insist on the altruistic nature of the removal. One of these advertisements included an image of Boavista after a landslide with concrete-brick homes crumbling off the side of the cliff (Figure 1.3). In the top right-hand corner was an explanation, "Landslides killed many people here." In much larger bold writing below the image was a text stating, "The neighborhood of Boavista is a zone in constant danger." This was followed by a long paragraph explaining the necessity of removal: "To protect the residents, the government decided to rehouse this population. More than 3,000 families are already living in Zango and Terra Nova II in Viana. With the support of the government, they are building a different life. Houses that are safer, with potable water, basic sanitation, a more tranquil life. With the help of residents, the government found a new way to solve old problems."

A second advertisement (Figure 1.4) focused on life in Zango and Terra Nova II. In stark contrast to the seemingly haphazard construction portrayed in the first advertisement, this one showed men at work, building in officially sanctioned ways indicated through the depiction of hard hats, straight lines, and careful measurement. The advertisement boldly stated, "A new way to solve old problems," again riffing on Agostinho Neto's statement that the primary purpose of the government was to "solve the people's problems." Instead of warning of death, the small text in the right-hand corner spoke of emergent possibilities: "In Zango and Terra Nova II many families are building a better future." Finally, the main text explained how the images of construction could be linked to state care: "Safe houses, more peaceful families, a different life. This is the current situation of more than 3,000 families that [have] already moved to Zango and Terra Nova II in Viana. A great challenge that the government set itself to protect the lives of many people and build a better life. With the help of the community itself, the government found a way to solve old problems" (Figure 1.4). In this explanation, "the community" worked hand-in-hand with government to enable it to fulfill its mandate—to provide and protect. Violent and unpopular demolitions were erased through a repackaging of the process of removal and rehousing as an act of care. On the ground, however, government promises of care rang hollow. The area had no infrastructure for basic services and few employment opportunities. In Zango, each family was assigned a tent, which many were too scared to leave for long periods of time, even to work, as the police patrolling the area ripped down empty tents, depriving their occupants of their right to a new house (Pearce 2005, 20). Ready-built homes were not provided. Instead, the forcibly removed were obliged to build their new homes themselves.

While by the 2010s, Zango was a sought-after site for many (see Croese 2013), inhabitants' accounts of the zone's early years spoke of devastation and disconnection. A daily roll call was made of who was present and amenable to providing labor. Those absent due to work demands elsewhere were told they could be forfeiting their right to a new house (Pearce 2005, 20). Under extreme economic pressure some gave up the possibility of a house in Zango to return to the city center where their work was located; others rented the tents out to even more desperate individuals. One women explained to me that at the time, the area was so isolated and empty that she could have lain down in the middle of the road that led to the encampment for the whole day and not be hit by a car (Helga and Jorge, interview, Zango, 13 May 2012).

The destruction of Boavista and the subsequent rehousing of its residents institutionalized the nexus of demolition and rehousing that would stand at the center of strategies of urban redevelopment under national reconstruction. Despite resistance to the removals and much public criticism, the minister of social affairs, Albino Malungo, announced the government's intention to implement similar "rehousing" projects across the country ("Projectos de realojamento serão estendidos a todo o país" 2001). The Presidency pushed for houses in Zango to be constructed at a faster pace, with private companies being invited to collaborate on a plan to accelerate construction to twenty houses a day (Croese 2013, 97–98). By early November 2001, under a new Emergency Housing Plan, 7,500 additional houses were commissioned to be built in Zango, Terra Nova II, Bitá, and Sapú. Those to be removed were not in Boavista but around the Cidade Alta—the site of the presidential palace and where many

Figure 1.3. (*Left*) "The neighborhood of Boavista in Luanda is a zone in constant danger." Government of National Unity and Reconciliation advertisement. *Jornal de Angola*, 9 October 2001, 23.

Figure 1.4. (*Right*) "A new way to solve old problems." Government of National Unity advertisement. *Jornal de Angola*, 16 October 2001, 16.

party elites lived—which fell within the area of projects being managed by the GOE ("Governo constrói 7,500 casas em Luanda" 2001). Zango subsequently became the largest rehousing zone in the country under the auspices of post-conflict reconstruction.

Demolition and rehousing were the flipside of an emerging large-scale process of urban redevelopment that was tightly tied to presidential and ruling party interests that predated the end of the civil war (Cardoso 2015; Gastrow 2020a). When the president called for the speeding up of the construction of Zango and the elaboration of an urbanization plan for the area by the Ministries of Public Works and Urbanism, it was the Eduardo dos Santos Foundation (FESA), a philanthropic organization of which the president was the symbolic head, that was approached to act as a liaison between the Presidency and private companies during the contracting process. FESA would supervise the plan until the project could be handed over to the Ministry for Social Assistance and Reintegration (Ministro de Assistência e Reinserção Social) (Croese 2013, 98). FESA contracted Dar-al-Handasah, a company whose Angolan branch president, Ramzi Klink, also headed FESA's finance committee, to create the Zango masterplan (Croese 2013).[14] Dar-al-Handasah was the financial consultant for a luxury housing development to be built on the ruins of Boavista (Pearce 2001). Sonils, a subsidiary of Sonangol, was also involved in the real estate development, which was to include 583 upscale apartments, a swimming pool, private electricity and water provision, and pristine ocean views ("No Place for the Poor" 2001). Claims that the removals were merely spurred by the need to provide care for the population by removing them from "risky zones" or to provide them with better living conditions seemed suspicious. The public was given a glimpse into the nexus of presidential power, oil money, violence, and high-end real estate development that would typify the oil boom. After April 2002, as Angolans began to grapple with what it meant to live in a country at peace, state and private institutions continued to characterize evictions and demolition as acts of care, the restoration of urban "order" represented as a means of bringing people into the rights of citizenship.

National Reconstruction: Promising Comfort

"Future City: Why Luanda Is the New Dubai" read the cover of the Winter 2008 edition of *Universo*, the magazine of Sonangol, Angola's state oil company. The cover's image showed a cluster of brightly lit high-rises surrounded by lush lawns, and a Gucci advertisement. Puzzlingly, in the background, there was a mountain range, suggesting, despite the text, that these buildings were not in Luanda at all. But in some ways, it did not matter. What mattered was the world of modernity and international status that image and text suggested lay in the city's future. This image was one of many such visuals that graced magazines, billboards, and television advertisements during Angola's oil boom. In addition to the cover's portrayal of promised luxury, the issue included depictions of new projects such as an international conference center, luxury hotels and retail spaces, and the city's promenade, which it christened "Miami on the Marginal." *Universo*'s editor promised to provide readers with "a glimpse of the new Luanda—the modern, international city that it will inevitably become."

The cover captured the ambience of Luanda's oil-fueled reconstruction, which was experienced through the apparently endless flow of wealth into the city via public works, private investment, and consumer goods. The obvious repetition of a "world-class city" aesthetic in the postconflict representation of Angola's capital characterized discussions and images of the real estate and public works boom it was experiencing. Investors from Brazil, South Africa, Spain, Portugal, and China devoured Angola's oil profits. The Angolan state employed planners from Singapore and Lebanon to advise it on developments, government officials made trips to Curitiba, and new projects were inspired by Barcelona, Cape Town, and Rio de Janeiro. Kate Cowcher (2014, 142) describes this period as distinguished by "the making of a new national fairy tale in Angola" pervaded by a "rentier aesthetic," which produced a startling visual realm of modernity through prestige projects while eliding the sticky political questions of violence and exploitation associated with oil.

The *Universo* cover, along with many other state media aesthetics, often drew on circulating ideas of a generic "world-class city" to project normative notions of urbanism onto Luanda's redevelopment. The details of these aesthetics, however, did not simply promise some vague idea of modernity to capture the popular imagination. Instead, they revealed the ways that appeals to the promised comforts of technology could be politically mobilized. On the *Universo* cover, the three brightly lit towers implied the existence of technocratic expertise that could not only design and build such structures but also provide the electric power to keep them running. The green landscaping suggested the easy provision of water. Modernity was appealing not simply because it promised membership in a global community through the alignment of Luanda's aesthetics with imagined international benchmarks but also because it promised to bring Luandans into a world of aesthetic comfort through the mobilization of technocratic means. It would enable the city's residents to leave behind the harms of the war, by providing what Angolans referred to as *condições*, the comforts of infrastructure provision. It is little surprise, for instance, that when the MPLA-state officially opened the flagship satellite city of Kilamba in late 2011, the glossy special magazine published to celebrate the opening (and distributed free with the state-owned *Jornal de Angola* that day) emphasized the physical and social infrastructures of the project more than the actual housing. These included images of electricity substations, a water treatment plant, rainwater drainage canals, and a sewerage treatment plant. All of these infrastructures—typically hidden from sight—needed to be made visible to perform state legitimacy through the promise of comfort. Schools brought students to visit Kilamba's show apartment so that they could engage with the taps, the indoor plumbing, and the gleaming tiles. Infrastructure and domestic comforts merged into a sense of national pride.

Luanda's remaking through the imagination of a "world-class city" was legitimated by the promise to introduce not only order but also a new urban sensorium. If the experience of the "suffering city" had been shaped by material breakdown embodied in the aesthetic discomforts of infrastructural failure and the rise of informal construction premised on the illicit purchase of materials, then the moment of the oil boom promised to relieve Angolans of these burdens. D. Asher Ghertner (2015), in the context of Mumbai, has shown how appeals to a desirable urban sensorium have become integral to the enactment of "world-class city" imaginations. In the absence of statistical and technocratic means to manage urban growth, the aesthetic has become a means of justifying often violent interventions and the management of urban populations (see also Doherty 2019; and Ndjio 2005). The aesthetics of a generic "world city," as regards both the style of housing and the sensuous experience of urbanism, have become a means for excluding populations seen to be infringing on the realization of generally middle-class and elite urban desires. Official discourses explaining the need to redevelop not just the musseques but also Luanda as a whole, leaned on similar justifications, arguing that interventions promised to create a sensorium of comfort facilitated by new infrastructures and housing.

TECHNOLOGIES OF COMFORT

Appeals to sensorial comfort were integral to justifications for radical interventions into not just informal areas but also the formal part of the city—the cidade. This was marked in discussions regarding the remaking of the city's iconic promenade, the Marginal. "The Future Is Arriving in Our Bay," read the cover of the promotional pamphlet handed to me at the information kiosk that stood at the end of Luanda's promenade. It was September 2008, during my first visit to Luanda. Within just a few hours of arriving in the city, a friend had whisked me down to the kiosk at the end of the promenade so that I could see what was being advertised as a major initiative in the postconflict redevelopment of Luanda—the restoration of its iconic promenade. Five years since the original floating of the idea, and following serious disputes over its implementation, dredging had been initiated for the project, which was meant to reestablish Luanda's bay as one of the most beautiful in the world. Those in favor of the Luanda Bay Project (Projecto de Baía de Luanda), as it was officially known, saw it as a platform for advertising Luanda's new "world-class" status to domestic and international audiences. For those opposed to the development, it was a dangerous capitulation to what they described as the ongoing *dubaização* (Dubaization) of the city, a process in which existing buildings and sites rich in memory and cultural significance were being replaced by nondescript architectural designs that stripped the city of its history.[15]

Figure 1.5. Luanda Bay, 2012.

Luanda's bay had long been the focus of imaginations and plans for the city (Croese 2017) and its decline during the postindependence period had periodically been discussed in the state newspaper as a source of concern as increasing pollution made it impossible to safely swim in it. However, when Portuguese businessman José Carlos Moreira Récio and his Angolan partner António Mosquito, an entrepreneur with close links to the MPLA, proposed a new plan for its redevelopment in 2003, tensions among the city's elites soared. The project, promoted by the Luanda Waterfront Corporation, a business based in the Cayman Islands but whose public face was Tecnocarro, the company run by Récio and Mosquito, was proposing a public-private partnership to transform the bay. In return for investing about $600 million in the cleaning and dredging of the bay, Tecnocarro requested permission to build two artificial islands, which it planned to develop for luxury real estate (Guardiola 2003). When some of the urban elite caught wind of the project near the end of 2003, they wrote a letter to President dos Santos denouncing the lack of public consultation over an intervention of such magnitude and arguing for the historical significance of the bay and the city's downtown. With 185 signatories, including high-ranking members of the MPLA such as former prime minister Lopo do Nascimento, the letter claimed that the project constituted "a dangerous attack against Luandans' traditions and identity and could lead to the destruction of the city's soul and its *ex libris*, its bay, considered one of the most beautiful in the world" (Mukuna 2003). The initial plan was canned, but the drive to redevelop the bay was not over.

After engaging in a public relations campaign advertising the investment and jobs that the project would bring to the city, the Luanda Waterfront Corporation presented a modified plan to the public. It would continue, it claimed, to carry the financial responsibility for the project and in return requested parcels of reclaimed land along the bay for private redevelopment. This plan was eventually passed, with the licensing and designs finalized in 2006 and 2007, respectively. Work on the dredging of the bay began in mid-2008, just as the country readied itself for its first national election in sixteen years in October 2008. Over the next four years, the project unfurled in front of the city, visible and yet, like so many other key projects, inaccessible to the public. Behind the corrugated iron barriers that blocked the development off from the city, a new promenade was forming. What it would ultimately look like, who would benefit, and how it was being funded remained obscure to most urban residents.

The Luanda Bay Corporation (SBL), the company set up in 2005 to facilitate the financing of the project, explicitly promoted the redevelopment of the promenade as the symbol of an emerging "world-class" Luanda. Some of this reiterated what is now a much criticized yet common claim among developers, that the rollout of "internationally recognized" schemes would attract investment. The promotional material promised that the "international and national projection of Angola's capital will promote and attract investment in diverse sectors generating economic growth for our country."[16] The promenade's development was therefore entangled in broader planning ideologies underpinning Luanda's redevelopment that sought to position the city as "a future regional and global hub that is 'open for business'" (Croese 2017, 202). The project tried to advertise its international worth by emphasizing that the design for the bay had been developed by studying many of the best promenades in the world, including the Copacabana, Barcelona, and Cape Town's Waterfront. Much was made of the fact that the palm trees for the project had been shipped from Miami in refrigerated containers, which required that they be watered every three hours. In a homage to the trees' celebrity cachet, they were paraded through the city with a police escort on their arrival.

What was most interesting about the publicity surrounding the Luanda Bay Project was not the assurance of economic fortunes to come but the appeal to the improved urban sensorium that the development promised. The promotional pamphlet I was handed, for instance, spent two full pages explaining in significant detail exactly how the bay would be cleaned, the sewerage

Figure 1.6. The new promenade (Marginal) on the day of its official opening in 2012, which coincided with then president José Eduardo dos Santos's birthday.

system fixed and upgraded, public lighting installed, and traffic flow eased. This included how many lanes would be constructed in the new highway that would run parallel to the promenade, that water would be treated in accordance with World Health Organization guidelines, and that an additional 500 kilovolt-amperes of electricity would be produced by a system of generators to be installed along the walkway. It especially highlighted the project's role in improving the environmental health of the bay, whose pollution it reminded the reader was the cause of "the appearance of dead fish and bad smells." The SBL sought to build legitimacy through concrete promises of infrastructure and the imagined sensorium of health and comfort that would emerge from this, rather than with empty appeals to spectacle.

This appeal to the sensuous benefits of infrastructure was used as a counter to claims that the project was destroying the city. In August 2011, I gathered with dozens of others on the back veranda of the "Swedish Building" perched near the top of Marien Ngouabi Avenue in the neighborhood of Alvalade, where many high-ranking party officials and expatriates lived.[17] In this space, the

Viking Club, an expatriate association, organized regular meetups and, when possible, invited speakers to present on topics they thought would be of interest to the club's members. This week, they had invited someone from the SBL. It was *cacimbo*, the cool dry period of the year that stretches from about May to September, and those who had not dressed for the cold evening were huddled in their seats. People clutched their drinks and chattered excitedly in a mixture of languages as they waited for what was a relatively rare opportunity—a presentation open to the public about a significant urban construction project (Presentation on the Baía de Luanda, Viking Club, Luanda, 25 August 2011).

Clad in a well-tailored suit and tie and speaking perfect English, typically the default medium of conversation at the Viking Club, the representative began his presentation. It consisted of PowerPoint slides followed by a video clip about the project, advertising its goals. Then the audience was invited to ask questions. Hands shot up. One of the first questions was whether the project would break open the reclaimed land linking the Ilha (a tiny peninsula that shot off the edge of the bay) to the mainland in order to allow the ocean's current to properly circulate through the bay. The representative responded that this was not possible, first, because Chicala, where the land bridge was, belonged to another project, and, second, because the water in Chicala was too polluted. The SBL did not want the pollution from Chicala to undermine the effort it had put into cleaning the Marginal area. Despite his attempts to smooth over concerns, the crowd remained suspicious of the plan. The suspicion simmered until one expatriate raised an issue that I had heard discussed many times, namely, whether or not the SBL was concerned about ruining Luanda's heritage, with the additional concern that the project involved the construction of skyscrapers along reclaimed land that would block the view of the bay, and access to it, for much of the city. An Angolan woman raised her voice in agreement, reminding everyone that there had been various plans prior to this one, all of which had generated unhappiness. The speaker nodded his head. He had clearly been prepared for such a question. As far as he was concerned, he explained, "the past" was the sewerage that until recently had clogged the bay's sands, its putrid odor wafting into the nostrils of those walking along the promenade. When he first came to Luanda, he continued, it was impossible to run on the Marginal because the smell was so bad. But now it was different. The Marginal, was, in his words, about to become a "real" public space.

When I later visited the Luanda Bay Project's offices, I asked Manuel, who had given the presentation, what he thought the primary success of the project was. He again emphasized the cleaning of the bay, which had been heavily polluted. He gave me a video to watch, in which the company laid out the decisions it had made about each species of tree that was planted, highlighting the planning expertise and research that had contributed to what was described as the "arborization" of the bay, with the intention to provide shade, re-create a "natural" environment, and control pollution. He went into extreme detail to explain the technologies and experts they had consulted to clean up and maintain the sewers that fed into the bay. An Italian company had sent a robot equipped with a global positioning system through the sewers to ensure that the project had an accurate map to guide planning of where filters should be installed and interventions made. For those people who felt that the project was "meddling" with the city's heritage and identity, he repeated the gist of what he had said in the presentation: "We can't stay stuck in the past." For Manuel, the past was a foul-smelling bay and a lack of public space in the city. His assistant, sitting at a desk surrounded by images of brightly lit skyscrapers, chimed in: "People are scared of change, but we are not destroying anything. On the contrary, we are building an environment that is more beautiful and much cleaner than what exists at the moment and than what existed in the past" (Observation at Projecto de Baía, Luanda, 14 September 2011).

As Manuel's comments suggest, the aesthetics of national reconstruction that advertisements, videos, and planning documents presented found popular support by appealing to a broader sensorium of sound, touch, and smell, which established the parameters of what "good urbanism" meant in Luanda. This appeal to a future infrastructural sensorium of light and freshness involved the repackaging of the existing city as a place of dirt and aesthetic ruin, rather than a space of history, heritage, and national identity. While new city plans in Africa may be "fantastical" inasmuch as they constitute a "wholesale rejection" (Murray 2015, 97) of the existing realities of informal urbanism, weak regulation, and high levels of poverty that constitute the everyday of the majority of Africa's urban residents, they nevertheless reverberate with local desires. Members of a rising middle class invested substantially in their bodily and domestic aesthetic comfort (Auerbach 2020), and there was support for a state that would make similar investments. Through mobilizing an aesthetic imagination of comfort and cleanliness embodied in fresh and pleasant odors, the issues of destruction, resistance, and suffering had been papered over. It was the sensorial promises of comfort, the aesthesis of infrastructure, enabled by oil and reconstruction, that the state mobilized in an attempt to extend what it had begun with Boavista: to represent violence as care.

The Discipline of Care: Requalifying Cazenga

I was sitting at a desk in the architecture department of Agostinho Neto University. Rather than answer my carefully crafted questions, the architect I was interviewing suggested that I look through his PowerPoint presentations while he worked; if I had any questions stemming from the slides, I could pose them. I was despondently clicking through images, trying to think about what I should be analyzing or asking as he diligently sat near me in case of any queries. The slide that eventually caught my eye was focused on policies of urbanization in Angola. It showed a red box with the words "Irregular occupants (without rights)," which then morphed into a green box whose text read, "Regularized citizens (with rights, duties, and obligations)." The slide suggested that the transformation of the built environment involved a transformation of state-citizen relations. It represented state intervention as a means of expanding substantive citizenship by bringing people into a clear legal status.

The architect's slide was not an outlier in official discourses about Luanda's redevelopment. In explaining the need to regularize land tenure and launch redevelopment projects in the musseques, a representative of IPGUL explained in its inhouse magazine that "the process of the regularization of irregular occupants is an operation to rescue citizenship and enable the recuperation of consideration and respect for public administrative authorities" (José 2011, 9). This statement was accompanied by images showing the reordering of the supposed chaos of the musseque into gridded logics. This emergence into citizenship was visually represented not only by the order of gridded urbanism but by an environment of aesthetic comfort. Many of the architect's slide presentations that addressed various requalification plans showed self-built musseque housing, usually surrounded by trash and poor infrastructure. These images were generally immediately followed by a slide that presented an imagined redevelopment of the houses and streets depicted in the previous images. While the original pictures were bereft of people, the "requalified" versions showed children playing, clean rivers flowing under picturesque bridges, solar-powered streetlights, and leisurely sidewalks. In sum, marginalized populations would be transformed into citizens through urban planning, a transformation accompanied by the enjoyment of aesthetic comfort, infrastructure, and leisure time facilitated by the imagined technical expertise of the state.

In the face of the significant suffering that national reconstruction brought to thousands of Angolans, it is both tempting and easy to dismiss these kinds of arguments and their accompanying images as disingenuous. The images in the architect's and many other public presentations of Luanda's remaking, after all, sidestepped the violence that these transformations entailed. However, to criticize the plans without acknowledging the genuine desire to transform the city for the better that captured the imaginations of many of those involved in redevelopment initiatives would be unfair and misrepresent their expertise and aspirations. While there is no doubt that political and economic elites cynically used national reconstruction, oil money, and urban development to enrich themselves, the politics of aesthetics and construction is not limited to elite machinations. During my time researching Luanda's remaking, I encountered many people who were strongly invested in making the city a better place for its inhabitants and who genuinely believed in the necessity of fundamentally re-creating the built environment. Many were frustrated with state projects and private investments that they believed flouted regulations and ignored broader social needs. Others were firm believers in large-scale "requalification" projects. Their imagined pathways to a better life often necessitated demolition. This tension between violence and care characterized discussions about and the implementation of redevelopment projects.

The contradiction between the desire to help and the violence that accompanied assistance was perhaps best represented by the very word that was often used to broadly describe urban redevelopment: "requalification" or *requalificação*. While "requalificação" could be translated as "redevelopment," this would fail to capture the local nuance of the word, which came to have emic connotations related to "order." Sílvio, the architect who had me wade through his PowerPoint slides, defined requalification as "improving the quality of life in precarious areas" (architect Sílvio, interview, Alvalade, 19 January 2012). In contrast, an IPGUL employee defined it as "to encounter disorder and to give it order, a rule, discipline" (employee at IPGUL, Carlos, interview, Ingombota, 7 June 2011). Both the element of care and discipline were inherent to the term and to the state's discursive constitution of national reconstruction. Understanding the coexistence of these impulses requires looking beyond oil-boom construction as simply an act that dazzles a vulnerable public or that is limited by the desires of rapacious elites. Such an approach fails to understand why and how people invest in fantasy, and therefore how these projects can be mobilized for political purposes.

Michael Watts (2012) argues that although oil wealth is a prime facilitator of real estate development, state centralization, and mass consumerism, one should avoid crude "commodity determinism." The forms of investment, wealth, and inequality produced by oil economies emerge in the midst of each location's and moment's specific "oil assemblage" (Watts 2012)—the complex network of state institutions, private agents, and material constraints that

shape the uses, imaginaries, and flows of oil and money. It is necessary to ana-
lyze what spectacle actually does, and why, in a particular oil assemblage, specific kinds of objects and images are able to mobilize particular aspirations and
critiques. In the case of Luanda, where the population had long felt that state
neglect had caused the city's gradual disintegration and in which an authoritarian ruling party needed to mobilize oil wealth toward building its legitimacy in
a postwar environment, care and violence marched hand in hand.

The intersection of care and violence and the curious ways they were bound
together in everyday discussions was evident not only in the publicity and official documents of planning that accompanied Luanda's redevelopment but
also in ordinary engagements with the public regarding requalification and
demolition. In May 2011, I attended a community meeting in one of Cazenga's
neighborhoods, organized with the assistance of a local NGO. The meeting
was set up to invite representatives of various public service institutions in the
city, such as the Luanda Public Water Company (Empresa Pública de Águas de
Luanda), the Luanda Electricity Company (EDEL), the police, and the commune administrator, to hear the neighborhood's concerns and needs as well
as to explain why certain services were not being delivered in the area. While
the action was admirable, I arrived feeling it might be futile. It had taken us
nearly an hour and a half to reach the destination, although it was just a few
kilometers from the city center where we had begun our journey. The roads
that approached the meeting area—the yard of a local primary school—were
thick with mud and practically impassable without a 4×4. Vehicles wound their
way carefully along the street, attentively following the path of the car in front,
exploring which parts of the thoroughfare could be safely traveled. The poor
infrastructure spoke to decades of neglect and structural abandonment. It was
not clear that a one-off meeting with local service representatives would resolve this.

Residents had carefully set up rows of white plastic chairs in the primary
school yard, about ninety seats in total. These all faced a table for the invited
guests, which had been decorated with large white cloths and festive red rib-
bons. As I took a seat, men in suits and long-sleeved shirts and women in *pano*
(African-style cloth) gathered. After waiting more than an hour, the organizers
explained that they were running late because they had hoped to begin with
the commune administrator, but he had not yet arrived. Eventually the decision was taken to continue without him. The floor opened and people began
to address their concerns to the representative from EDEL, taking him to task
for electricity issues and the lack of public lighting.

During this back-and-forth, the commune administrator, wearing dress trousers and a Nehru-style shirt, arrived and took a seat at the table. After a brief engagement with the police representative, the group's attention turned to the administrator. Unlike the audience, each of whom stood up to address the representatives, the administrator remained seated, signifying his power through the ability to remain relaxed in his chair. Without waiting for questions, he began to speak, explaining that he was there in an "unofficial" capacity, as he had not yet received authorization from the municipal administrator to attend. After listening to the residents' complaints, he moved swiftly to address them, explaining that many of Cazenga's problems emerged from the fact that it was the "most populated" municipality in the city. With a smile, he enthusiastically told those assembled that the government at last had a solution to this: "We are going to reduce this number. We're going to move lots of families to other zones as part of the requalification that Cazenga will undergo!"

Instead of discussing the details of demolition, the administrator focused, as did so many advocates of government policy, on the infrastructure provision that removals would enable, promising improved roads and indoor plumbing rather than shared water stands. For this to be delivered, however, destruction was necessary. "We will have to get rid of some areas. . . . We'll demolish, and then once the area has been requalified, people can return." He stalwartly ignored the muttering rising from the crowd and outlined a new rubbish disposal system that would be operated by vehicles that could enter the neighborhood when it rained, new water stands (despite having promised indoor plumbing), and rehabilitated stormwater drainage. All of this would be enabled by demolition, with the administrator promising the crowd, "We are going to demolish all the houses that we need to. We are going to demolish lots of houses!" The administrator seemed oblivious to the concerned murmurings of his audience. He ended his speech by exclaiming that he was extremely "satisfied" with his visit.

The plan the administrator was referring to was the plan for the requalification of Cazenga, later renamed the "reconversion" of Cazenga. The renaming followed after it was determined that "requalification" had accrued negative connotations and failed to capture that the redevelopment plan would involve the return of residents, not simply their removal (Dias 2020). At the time of my research, Cazenga was, as the administrator had stated, considered the most densely populated municipality in the country. Residents claim that the area derives its name from a migrant from the Congo, Miguel Pedro Cazenga, who settled there in the eighteenth century and purchased sizeable portions of land in the area. Although originally conceived of as a *bairro indígena* (native quarter) with social housing for Africans who were forcibly removed from the city center as Luanda expanded in the twentieth century, by the late colonial period in the 1960s and 1970s, Cazenga was an expanding industrial area. It was home to working-class African and white residents employed in factories and the neighborhood's growing local economy, who lived in modest state-built housing, alongside areas of informal construction (Development Workshop 2010, 8–9). As with many other areas of the city, services declined rapidly in the postcolonial era. Deepening the municipality's problems, the war, as well as the brutal effects of the introduction of free market reforms in the late 1980s into the 1990s, led to the collapse of industrial activities in the area.

By the time I conducted my research in the 2000s, Cazenga, while being a municipality with prime property potential because of its proximity to the city center, was viewed as an area of intractable obstacles. Factories that in earlier decades had produced packaged food and household commodities had been transformed into warehouses that sold the imported goods that inundated the country's ports. Its roads flooded regularly in the rainy season, making it difficult for cars to pass, uncollected rubbish mounds towered over its landscape, infrastructures had ceased to function, and the wartime housing shortage combined with the postconflict scramble for land had led to an acceleration in informal construction with few accompanying services. As a central support base for the MPLA, being the neighborhood where the urban armed anticolonial struggle began in February 1961, Cazenga was a key site for both intervention and astute politicking. It is not surprising, then, that it soon became a site for imagining the city's future, even if the existing residents were left outside of this reimagining.

In 2011, although members of the neighborhood residents' committees had been informed of the plan for the requalification of Cazenga, much of the population was oblivious to its detail except for an understanding that they would be removed and then supposedly be allowed to return. The plan—or rather multiple plans—for its redevelopment exemplified the intertwining of the aesthetic discipline, violence, and care inherent to the logics and public image of national reconstruction. The first official sign of the project for Cazenga's remaking could be traced to 2008 with the publication of a Presidential Dispatch 30/08 of 12 November in the *Diário da República*. The dispatch announced the formation of a working group of state agencies, private interests, and civil society led by Aguinaldo Jaime, then the head of the National Private Investment Agency (ANIP), to cooperate on the "Project for the Requalification of the Cazenga Municipality."[18] Reflecting the continuing links to the Presidency and the personal relationships that ran through Luanda's remaking, Dar al-Handasah, the company charged with managing the Zango project, was tasked with being both the project's consultant and its primary designer. Civil society was represented by the Cazenga Association of Intellectuals (Associação dos Intellectuais do Cazenga), an organization that had attempted to have the president nominated for the Nobel Peace Prize during the 1990s, the most brutal years of the civil war (Muvuma 2013).

Initially the project was shaped by a larger strategy that had been elaborated by Dar al-Handasah in 2008, the Integrated Plan for the Urban and Infrastructural Expansion of Luanda, which was formally gazetted in 2011.[19] This plan encompassed the Luanda metropolitan region as a whole and sought to streamline and bring coherence to a variety of urban dedensification projects that had broadly shaped urban policy since the 1990s, while also attending to the city's pressing infrastructure needs (Dias 2020). This first phase would be constructed in the Cazenga-Antenas land reserve, which had already been identified as a land reserve for the development of new urban projects.[20] In 2010, greater coherence was brought to the project with the establishment of the Technical Office for the Urban Reconversion of Cazenga, Sambizanga, and Rangel (GTRUCS). Architect Bento Soito, who led the office, while being guided by the 2008 Dar al-Handasah plan, sought to move beyond it and provide a more comprehensive scheme for Cazenga as a whole, not just the areas delimited as land reserves (Dias 2020). It was on the basis of this desire that Surbana, a Singaporean company, was recruited to design a master plan for Cazenga, Sambizanga, and Rangel (Dias 2020, 108).

The public face of the plans mooted by Surbana reimagined Cazenga as a space of dense vertical real estate and lush green spaces, a far cry from the mix of crumbling colonial-era workers' housing and newer self-built homes, crisscrossed by predominantly dirt roads that flooded in the rainy season. It seemed almost impossible to reject such a vision. These images had been drawn from studies that compared Luanda to Singapore, Shanghai, Mumbai, and São Paulo, seeking an Angolan solution based on the examples of those cities. The photoshopped people in the images always looked happy and healthy. The images showed pristine skies and sometimes rivers and ducks, indicating a clean environment and the technological innovation and capacity necessary to construct high-rise buildings. These images were like countless others produced by public offices linked to planning, which focused on the introduction of the grid design and the elimination of the musseques as an act of care that the government was bringing to the population. In image after image, Luanda's prevailing

Figure 1.7. Street scene in Cazenga, 2012.

Figure 1.8. Advertisement for the redevelopment of the Ilha hung on the wall of the shelter of someone who had been expelled from there, 2011. The community had been moved to the outskirts of Zango, its members now living in tents and corrugated-iron residences. The text reads, "We support the revitalization of our Ilha."

informality was eradicated. In its stead developers presented not only images of "African urban fantasies" (Watson 2014)—as the visual renderings of these kinds of projects have been referred to—but performances of technical expertise. Images showed plans of grids, aerial shots of future cities still to be embraced, and interviews with technicians and experts about their drive to make the city "world-class." The imagining of the future city was an opportunity for the state to enact its expertise and reassert its capability to a population long exhausted by what is referred to in Angola as *confusão* (confusion).

Images such as the ones representing the "reconversion" of Cazenga or the transformations found in Sílvio's PowerPoint presentations elided the actual process of construction that required not only the eradication of the existing neighborhoods but the temporary, if not permanent, removal of residents and a radical shift in lifestyle for many. Such actions were justified by the fact that, as the president of the residents' committee in one Cazenga neighborhood explained to me, requalification was "welcome because there will be beauty, well-urbanized buildings, regular electricity, and regular household water" (president of residents' committee Vamos Andar, interview, Cazenga, 16 July 2012). He acknowledged that some people would have trouble adapting to the vertical construction, expressing concern that older people might develop joint problems from walking up stairs and that warehouse owners would lose their sources of income when these were knocked down. Small business owners would lose out because they could no longer run businesses from their yards or rely on foot traffic from the street. It was not clear where the existing occupants of Cazenga would live. Recounting what he knew of the plan to me, he claimed that there would be "low-income" houses for some but was vague about who could access them. Nevertheless, he supported Surbana's vision for the municipality. He had rejected one of the plans, which had envisaged working with the geographies and aesthetics of the existing city in shaping Cazenga's future, saying that he was "tired of the city that already exists."

The social costs of remaking Cazenga and many other parts of the city disappeared in assessments of its redevelopment. Treated as a kind of collateral damage, loss of employment and home were papered over in the name of infrastructural promise. This narrative configured the state as a provider, as reemergent and caring after a period of prolonged absence. Through construction it would provide a salve to the suffering city. Through the "promise of infrastructure" (Anand, Gupta, and Appel 2018)—inasmuch as it allowed for the imagination of the state as a provider—the violent remaking of the city could be reconfigured as an act of care.

The Caring State

Oil spectacle does not dazzle without reason. In Luanda, the state's fantasies drew on the deep desires of many residents for a better resourced, more comfortable city. To understand the political stakes of national reconstruction, it is necessary to frame the aesthetic economy it created as a space of encounter in which the state and political subjects were forged. In Luanda, construction, buildings, and infrastructure were explicitly politicized by state institutions, part of the aesthetic dramaturgy widely associated with modes of domination in much of sub-Saharan Africa (Mbembe 2001; Ndjio 2005). Luanda's bricks, pipes, walls, and wires became the immediate instantiation of the state and its policies, further embellished by a series of publications, billboards, and television advertisements that mobilized the projects of national reconstruction as proof of government largesse and the redistribution of the profits of the oil economy. However, the politicization of the built environment by the MPLA-state through oil spectacle, and the instrumental mobilization of infrastructure, care, and the sensorium, ultimately provided the basis for political discussion and contestation.

A cynical observer of Angola will point to the fictive, even outright deceptive, nature of the government's aesthetic promises. In 2008, human rights organizations protested the UN celebration of Habitat Day in Luanda, arguing that, "rather than build a 'harmonious city' that addresses acute needs for decent shelter and the human right to adequate housing, the government of Angola instead has carried out mass forced evictions, prioritized urban development projects, including the construction of luxury housing and 'beautification' projects at the expense of tens of thousands of people, living in poverty" (Amnesty International 2008). By 2014, Angola's concrete politics hardly appeared to be "solving the people's problems." Apartment blocks in the satellite city of Kilamba remained out of reach of most Angolans, who could not afford the $400 a month needed to purchase them. Given this, it would be easy to dismiss the kinds of images portrayed on government billboards as crude propaganda. However, such a move ignores the political work that a particular configuration of oil spectacle does and with that the conversation and debates it provokes. Luanda's oil spectacle, in the form of rapid construction and runaway consumption, was central in the postconflict moment to understanding how the Angolan state crafted its relationship with citizens and engendered a distinct imagination of urban and national belonging.

In a city broken by war, the projects of national reconstruction, along with accelerating private investments in the real estate market, held out a promise of sensorial citizenship and, with it, a state that could provide. These projects fed not only the elite and middle class but also marginalized populations' desires for inclusion. These forms of inclusion were, however, fragile, subject to contestations about the limits, failures, and violence that enabled them. The investments of national reconstruction were phantasmagorias of care—their technoaesthetics sought to enchant, thereby eliding the social conditions of their making. They manufactured a world of politics, contest, and fantasy that encompassed much of everyday life in oil-boom Luanda and sought to reconfigure the state's relations to its citizens. Nevertheless, despite the state's efforts to craft its violent interventions as acts of care, alternative registers of material and aesthetic belonging would provide platforms for challenging the politics of reconstruction by revealing the violence inherent to master planning and the building of new cities.

CHAPTER TWO

Musseque City

Indigenous Urbanism in Provisional Spaces

The camera pans over the buildings of Luanda's Praia do Bispo neighborhood. Everything is tinged a muted gray by the dawn light. The perspective then suddenly switches to a close-up image of the coastline: the water is clogged with rubbish, so filthy that it seems like the small boat in the image is pushing desperately through mud. A voiceover starts. Candida Correia, twenty-seven years old, begins to give context. The shots move between Candida and her husband looking lovingly at family photos, images of corrugated-iron and concrete-block houses on the brink of collapse, and goats chewing on garbage scattered among the buildings. Candida explains that where she and her husband had built their life in the city center there was raw sewage, piles of rubbish, and no clean water. She wipes the tears from her face as the camera zooms in. The scene switches to Zango, Angola's largest rehousing zone, showing her husband and children planting flowers in their new garden. Images appear of the family watching television and taking a leisurely stroll in the neighborhood. Her children laugh as they run into their new home and turn on water taps. Candida explains to the viewers, "The government went there, knocked down our houses, and gave us keys. I could hardly contain my emotions when they called my name. I couldn't believe it. And now I have a big house. Here they can play, it is really great, they have their own room. Sometimes they ask me to turn on the shower when they want. I am well. I am happy. I have my house, my family, and I thank God for this house." The alternating images of the MPLA election number,[1] an image of President dos Santos, and the MPLA logo floating in the top righthand corner of the screen, however, suggested to the viewer to whom else her gratitude was directed.[2]

While the musseques' aesthetic distinction has acted as their most powerful diacritic, as the above footage (from the MPLA's 2012 election campaign) suggests, it is exactly this aesthetic distinction that has generated the arguments that dismiss their material, spatial, and historical contributions to the city.

Katherine McKittrick (2006, x) describes the kinds of representational practices engaged in by the campaign material, in which dominant aesthetic, material, and geographical imaginaries delegitimatize the "physical and material configurations" of Black life as processes that render people, place, and history "ungeographic." In this case, representations of musseque architecture and materials as poor quality and lacking durability, alongside images of poverty and dirt, made it difficult to locate the histories of change, skill, and design that inhered in them. Despite the fact that, as Marissa Moorman (2008) has argued, musseques are imagined as the birthplaces of Angolan nationalism and the primary location of contemporary urban identity, they are not seen as fundamental to the city's spatial, architectural, and material heritage.

This rendering of the musseques as "ungeographic" was notable in the curious inability of the broader population to mourn their destruction. The demolition of musseques was framed as a civil and human rights issue due to the loss of basic shelter. While individuals might grieve a disappeared life and the broader public reflect on the value of the cultural forms and practices that emerged from musseques, their ongoing destruction during the oil boom failed to elicit widespread outrage.[3] Unlike that of colonial-era buildings in the planned city center, such as Kinaxixe Market and the Elinga Theater, the destruction of the musseques failed to provoke impassioned writings from the city's cultural elites or campaigns to protect them. If the plan to transform the city's promenade led to the formation of the Associação Kalu (an organization focused on the protection of urban heritage), no similar movement emerged to argue that the musseques should be protected because they embodied a unique aspect of Angolan material culture. Musseques were witness to some of the oldest histories of urban place-making in Luanda. They were commonly understood as the birthplace of contemporary national identity, but they were not seen as worthy of mourning.[4]

This denigration and invisibilization of the musseques' material, aesthetic, and spatial contribution to Luanda reproduces what AbdouMaliq Simone (2010, 282) describes as "a constitutive paradox to black urbanism in that in many parts of the world blackness informs what it means to be 'urban' in a cultural sense but still struggles for recognition as a critical factor in the production of urban space." In response to this, this chapter argues that historical practices of occupation and construction in musseques constitute an Indigenous Black urbanism, one that calls into question the aesthetic consensus of the new Luanda. This conceptualization of Indigeneity and Blackness can extend to but is not primarily used to describe the inhabitants of the musseques per se, for, after all, the majority of the population of Luanda's cidade and other formalized areas are both Black and Indigenous. Instead, it references spatiality, place-making traditions, and construction processes that not only situate the musseque as a forerunner of the cidade but also produce a logic of urban autochthony in many of its inhabitants. Framing the musseques in this way requires writing against the processes that have rendered them "ungeographic" by rethinking the very ways their materiality has been understood. This especially necessitates questioning the discourses of provisionality that have run through not only popular representations of the musseques but also scholarly analyses of similar areas across the African continent. As the material inheritors of enslavement, musseques embody a history of fugitive planning and politics that emerged in relation to the practices of racial subjugation and expulsion that shaped Luanda's history. While descriptions of musseques may not always explicitly use the language of race, race need not always be named in order to be present—its logic abounds in the structural processes of urban belonging and exclusion with which Luanda's residents must grapple. As such, the chapter argues that musseques can be located in the long history of fugitive urbanism that runs parallel to the settler-colonial tendencies of normative urbanism embodied in the formal city.

Musseque Histories

The word "musseque," drawn from the Kimbundu *museke*, meaning "sandy place," is a window into the contested histories of place-making in Luanda. Most scholars of contemporary Angola, and Angolans themselves, translate the word as "slum." This popular definition, however, is recent and hides more varied historical mobilizations of the word. From the eighteenth century into the first half of the nineteenth, Luandans used "musseque" to describe large country estates of wealthy merchants who were not only European but often African or "Luso-African" (Martins 2000; Mourão 2006, 95; Oliveira 2022). Ilídio do Amaral (1983, 298) argues that the term might occasionally have been used to describe barracoons (which were sometimes located on these estates) but later transformed to refer to areas of African settlement (both enslaved and free) in the city center that were architecturally distinguished by their "huts." Jill Dias (1986, 309) found the term used to describe smallholdings owned by free Africans on Luanda's periphery. While it is often suggested that the reference to "sandy place" indexes the condition of the spaces to which Africans were expelled after forced removals began in the second half of the nineteenth century, the heavier significance of this meaning only seems to have emerged through shifts in understandings of space, race, and belonging that accompanied the gradual process of abolition and the eventual emergence of more obviously identifiable forms of twentieth-century racialized colonial planning in Luanda.

António Tomás (2022) argues that the original limits of belonging in Luanda were produced through enslavement, a fact that was materially and spatially marked on the city. The city was heavily reliant on not just the economic profits of the Atlantic slave trade but also on slave labor, with approximately one-third of the urban population being enslaved (Oliveira 2022, 21). The distinctions between the free and the enslaved shaped the city. While the initial colonial constructions of the sixteenth and seventeenth centuries used whatever local materials were at hand, these were eventually replaced by stone and wood sourced from Brazil and Portugal, until the first local quarries were established in 1669 and 1676 (Martins 2000, 143–44). Luanda's elite soon began to construct homes of stone and lime. With time, the wealthy began to build and live in houses referred to as *sobrados*. These were large, two- to three-story homes built from wood and earth as well as from lime and mortar extracted from seashells (Tomás 2022). The ground floors of these homes were used for commercial purposes, while the second (and occasionally third floors) served as residences for the homeowners (Martins 2000, 158). Attached to the back or sides of the homes were barracoons, known locally as *quintais* (plural), where the enslaved were kept. The geography of enslavement shaped the city, with barracoons not only being attached to houses but also found along the edges of the city and the beachfront (Tomás 2022, 46; Miller 1988, 390; Mourão 2006). "Unconfined slaves" (*escravos soltos*), who constituted the primary labor force of the city, mostly lived in *senzalas*, settlements made up of what were referred to as *cubatas* (huts) made of wood, clay, and thatch (Caldeira 2013, 85; Ferreira 2013).[5] While some senzalas were located on the owners' estates (the word was commonly associated with slave quarters), many were found in other parts of the city where free Africans built their homes among the stone constructions of the wealthy.

The end of the slave trade and the coming of abolition in 1875 was accompanied by significant shifts in understandings of race, place, and belonging. Portugal officially abolished the slave trade from its colonies in 1836, although the actual abolition of slavery in Angola took close to another forty years. After abolition was announced in 1875, slavery was quickly replaced with systems of indentured labor.[6] During this period, new trading goods and agricultural investment gradually replaced slavery as the primary source of wealth in the colony. In parallel with this shift in the colony's economics was a change in the attitude to African presences in the city. In the eighteenth and early nineteenth centuries, Luanda's racial and economic hierarchies were generally more varied than the forms of racial domination that became increasingly explicit in the twentieth century. While the enslaved were African, the city's elites came from a variety of racial and cultural backgrounds. This was largely due to the prominent role of what the literature has referred to as "Luso-Africans" in the slave trade. This group was constituted by people of mixed African and European descent who were key in managing the transport and sale of the enslaved to the coast (Miller 1988; Oliveira 2022). Many were themselves invested in transporting slaves to Brazil and other parts of the Americas and enjoyed leading roles in the city's social and political life (Oliveira 2022). Their status was reflected in their ownership of large homes and estates. In the aftermath of abolition, however, not only did their economic status come under pressure as one of their historical sources of income came to an end, but shifts in colonial racial logics threatened many of them. For most of Angola's history children of Portuguese men had been classified as "white" regardless of their mother's heritage or their skin color. From the 1850s this shifted as colonial officials revealed growing concern with racial purity. Those of mixed heritage were now classified *pardos* (Oliveira 2022). These reclassifications were followed by increasingly aggressive administrative and legal attacks on this group's urban land and property holdings from the early twentieth century, formalized in the 1926 Estatuto do Indígena (Native Act). This legislation divided the population into "citizens" and "natives." All people of African heritage were classified as "natives" and subjected to discriminatory regulations including forced labor, a poll tax, and limits on movement in the colony (Birmingham 2016, 64–65). People of African heritage could apply to be reclassified as "citizens" and become *assimilados* (assimilated) by undergoing a series of tests that included showing mastery of Portuguese, eating with a knife and fork, and living in what was viewed as acceptable housing (Birmingham 2016, 64–65; Morton 2013, 721–2). These historical elites then increasingly found themselves under pressure to prove their status. It is the dislodgement of this elite from not just their social positions but also the accompanying spatial positions, as they were displaced from Luanda's downtown and into the city's historically Black areas, that David Birmingham (2006, 87) argues laid the foundation for the emergence of twentieth-century anticolonial nationalism in Luanda.

The gradual transformation of geographic and racial imaginaries not only took place at the elite level but also was a broader pattern in Luanda. In this process, the quintais and senzalas transformed into musseques (Moorman 2008, 32; Tomás 2022, 78). Maps of musseque areas in the 1800s referred to them by the names of the original quintal owners (Mingas 2011, 38). The term ceased being used to describe country estates and instead came to refer to areas of African urban occupancy. This change was particularly noticeable in the wake of the first large-scale forced removals of Africans from the city center in the mid-nineteenth century, a process that became increasingly common as racialized urban planning gathered force in the twentieth century (Monteiro 1973; Pepetela 1990; Mingas 2011). The meaning of "musseque" as "sandy place" was said to describe the conditions of the areas to which Africans were forcibly removed. Over the next 100 years racial stratifications "were mapped onto urban geography" characterized "by a series of oppositions molded in local discourse—between the *baixa* (lower city) and the musseques (periphery), between the asphalt city and the musseques (sandy places), and between the white city and the musseques (African townships)—and described the socioeconomic, racial and cultural divisions of the city" (Moorman 2008, 32).

These distinctions, however, were arguably primarily expressed not spatially but materially, particularly through aesthetic assessments of materials, notable in colonial descriptions of constructions in musseque areas as "provisional." Provisionality in many ways became a proxy for talking about a racialized "native" presence, used as a framing device in Portuguese colonial legislation to delegitimize the African urban presence. In 1912, the Portuguese colonial state introduced laws that imposed restrictions on the kinds of materials that could be used to build homes in urban centers, most notably in the planned new city of Nova Lisboa (Huambo). It was forbidden to use wattle, grass, daub, and thatch, which the legislation claimed was typical of "native" construction (Roque 2009, 55; Neto 2012, 135). Bans on the construction of "uncivilized" housing in planned European areas were subsequently instituted in Lobito. By the 1920s, while blaming *indígena* ("native") settlements for urban sanitation problems, legislation was passed determining that new *bairros indígenas* ("native" quarters) should be constructed on the peripheries of Luanda and other cities (Roque 2009, 57). The legislation insisted that only "civilized" Africans could live in the city center in European-style housing and that all new housing in the bairros indígenas had to be of a "permanent character," forbidding materials such as adobe, grass, and thatch (Roque 2009, 57). Most of this legislation was not implemented and was difficult if not impossible to enforce (Neto 2012). In Luanda, cubatas were scattered across the city (Mourão 2006). Nevertheless, the obsession with trying to eradicate "native" materials from the urban highlights how aesthetics associated with "nativeness" were rendered "unurban."

This racialized logic of materiality became ever more notable from the mid-1940s until independence in 1975. Urban planning initiatives increased, strongly shaped by segregationist logics that characterized colonial urban planning across southern Africa during that time (Tomás 2022). It was during this period that most of what constituted the formally planned areas of Luanda until the early 2000s was constructed (Amado, Cruz, and Hakkert 1992). This construction boom was characterized by the arrival of the "age of concrete" (Morton 2019), as this new material enabled architects and engineers to reach vertically in unprecedented ways. Luanda, until then an urbanscape of largely single- and two-story houses, suddenly transformed into a space of concrete towers. In contrast, musseque homes remained single-story dwellings built from "traditional" materials as well as an increasingly eclectic mix of wood, corrugated iron, cement-block, brick, and whatever else residents could afford or salvage (Moorman 2008). The meaning of "musseque" as a "place of sand" took on poignant weight, indexing the infrastructural deprivation of these areas when compared to the asphalted roads of what was referred to as the *cidade de cimento* (cement city), the officially planned areas of white and other elite settlement. "Musseque" suggested sand, informality, and provisionality; "cidade" suggested cement, formality, and permanence, inhabiting normative understandings of colonial urban modernity.

As the city expanded, white immigration quickened and demolitions accelerated, pushing musseques and with that, Black Angolans, ever more to the urban edge (Birmingham 2006). In many cases, however, rather than radically forcing all Africans out of the city, the new brick single-stand homes and concrete mid- and high-rises of Luanda's construction boom rose up awkwardly in the middle of musseque areas, surrounding "thatched huts" or trapping musseques between them, so that they appeared to be "islands of huts surrounded by concrete" (Mendes 1988, 23). In this intertwinement of musseque and cidade, Moorman (2008, 33) argues, "musseque" was sometimes used to refer to "a form of housing—huts—and not a place per se." These architectures weaved through planned blocks and neighborhoods understood as sites from which "authentic" urban Angolan culture, but not material form, emerged (Figure 2.1).

Even as they disparaged the materials from which musseques were constructed, studies positioned them not as survivals of precolonial practices but as entirely new sociological phenomena. In Luanda, the emic category historically associated with precolonial historical continuity was *praia* (beach), a category used to refer to settlements of the AxiLuanda, the area's Indigenous inhabitants (Duarte de Carvalho 2008). José Cortez (1960), in his study of AxiLuanda housing in Luanda's Ilha area, describes them as senzalas, not musseques. Monteiro (1973) noted this distinction in his studies of Luanda's musseques and was careful to distinguish AxiLuanda settlements from other

Figure 2.1. Musseque squeezed between houses in central Luanda, 2011.

kinds of constructions. For him, AxiLuanda homes represented cultural resistance to colonialism, while musseques represented the rise of the waged urban worker and, although not necessarily assimilation, at least "detribalization." Similar distinctions seemed to be made by residents. When the acclaimed Angolan anthropologist Ruy Duarte de Carvalho (2008) conducted research with a beach community in Luanda in the 1980s, he recorded complaints from its inhabitants, who stated with dismay that their settlements were "becoming musseques," connoting in their minds breakdown, disorder, and chaos. The AxiLuanda were identified as the harbingers of any "tradition" that urban inhabitants might have. This was evident in discussions over forced removals. While I rarely heard concerns about the futures of demolition victims outside of activist circles, the residents of the Ilha, often assumed to be AxiLuanda because of their trade in fishing, were an exception. Almost everyone I spoke to argued that people from that area had an "authentic" fishing culture that was being erased by demolition. This was in stark contrast to the relative silence regarding other areas of the city, which were usually framed as characterized by squalid living conditions, with supporters of government policies suggesting that residents benefited from removals.

Even as the musseques' architectures and materials were being mobilized to discredit their existence as sites of legitimate urbanism, however, the very social scientists studying them produced information that suggested that musseques offered a complex material challenge to the colonial city. Starting in at least the 1960s, colonial ethnographers began to claim that self-built Luanda musseque houses indexed a new kind of Black urban Angolan. These new Angolans had shaken off the strictures of "tradition" and ethnicity and begun to remodel themselves and their environments according to European urban norms, immersing themselves in urban anonymity (Redinha 1964; Monteiro 1973). In his work on "traditional housing" in Angola, José Redinha (1964, 33, 36) represented self-built houses in Luanda as their own category, the "detribalized house," arguing that they shared a "common pattern," which included being "frugal due to an extremely utilitarian spirit and for reason of economy," that they made few references to any rural or ethnic origin and instead were closer to "European" housing forms in structure and material.[7] Redinha went so far as to suggest that Luanda's musseque residents constituted their own new ethnic group, "the Luandans" (Marcum 1969, 20).

Musseque architecture began to suggest the making of Indigenous urban architectural practices and spatial forms that often defied state attempts to control them. The evidence for this was the progressively standardized musseque house (Redinha 1964; Monteiro 1973). By the 1960s and 1970s, construction materials varied, with residents having generally abandoned thatch roofs for zinc and walls usually built from wood or *pau-a-pique* (wattle and daub). While materials differed, the house nevertheless had specific features: it was rectangular, had a fenced yard (*quintal*), and often annexes (*anexos*) that were used for cooking, ablutions, and additional rooms for family members or for renting out. The house and quintal combination was the unique and defining feature of Luanda's vernacular architecture, evidence, ethnographers argued, of a rising desire for privacy among urbanized African populations as they began to explore leisure and relaxation in their new roles as salaried wage workers (Redinha 1964). Musseque housing and spatial design also suggested attempts to protect inhabitants from colonial securitization and surveillance. Fernando Mourão (2006, 317) argues that musseques "constituted themselves . . . as fortresses against the external environment and in the only way possible for an urban life." He notes that as authorities systematically attempted to penetrate musseque areas by opening larger roads and mapping water sources within them, residents raised the heights of their quintal walls and built "secondary exits" from their properties that were not easily noticeable. Roads were designed to run parallel to the primary arteries, in what he describes as a "labyrinth system" that was difficult for outsiders to penetrate. These ethnographies provide little insight into musseque dwellers' personal assessments of the architectures and materials that surrounded them, and claims that Africans desired to emulate European aesthetics should be interrogated (Magubane 1971). However, they do track the emergence of an urban vernacular architecture in Luanda, one with recognizable forms and aesthetics that were building the conditions for an urban materiality and imagination that was intertwined with, and yet also separate from, the formal colonial city. These were sites of an emergent Indigenous urbanism, marked by racialized precarity as it navigated the contradictions between the aspirations to permanence that new forms of construction engendered and the denial of these aspirations that political conditions of racialized exclusion imposed.

Permanent Provisionality

The attempts to render African presences provisional was not unique to colonial Angola. Despite the evidence emerging from colonial researchers that Africans were producing new forms of urban life and design, official discourses across Africa sought to deny the contribution of Black place-making to African cities. Colonial city planning only begrudgingly accepted Black presences, viewing Africans as necessary for labor purposes while refusing to recognize Black settlement as permanent. This racialized disavowal took place through the intentional underfunding of infrastructure and prejudicial allocation of land and housing in planning initiatives, as well as other controls over African settlement, labor, and construction (Gandy 2006; Rakodi 1986). These concrete measures were accompanied by descriptions of African urban presences as "unruly" and constructions as "provisional" or otherwise materially inadequate (Bissell 2010; Moorman 2008; Wright 1991).

While colonial governments have long officially decamped, racialized assemblages of planning and disavowal continue to wind a path through contemporary conceptualizations of African cities. Appeals to the supposed flimsy construction of "musseque" housing, descriptions of it as "disordered," "anarchic," and lacking significant construction expertise, all serve to undermine musseques' contribution to city making, as well as the political possibilities emergent from their making. Such trends are evident in cities across the continent, where, for many decades, informality was treated as evidence of economic and policy failure. Contemporary scholars have attempted to overcome these framings by showing how logics of organization and possibilities for survival emerge through informal interactions and practices (de Boeck and Plissart 2004; Simone 2004; Koolhaas et al. 2000). Rather than being signs of failure or chaos, informality and the ephemeral and makeshift relations and opportunities through which cities work are now seen as the redemptive means through which African residents maintain and re-create personal opportunities in the face of the implosion of state capacity and significant economic obstacles.

As important as the above literature has been for reimagining African urbanism in the last two decades, the celebration of the ephemeral not only has had a tendency to center "the city's ability to sustain a market . . . [as] the sole signifier of its health" (Gandy 2005b, 52) but also has failed to adequately grapple with the erasure of African material and spatial practices inherent to colonial framings of cities. This is because, while exposing the fallacy of equating informality to disorder, it has done little to question the presumptions that underlie the dismissal of the materiality of neighborhoods such as musseques, presumptions that often hinge on a statist imagination of order and control at odds with the historical growth of these areas (Agha and Lambert 2020). As seen from histories of Luanda's musseques, many of these assumptions hinge on aesthetic judgments of what constitutes a provisional versus a permanent construction. Formality and informality, provisionality and permanence, however, are not opposed conditions. Permanence is constituted through a palimpsest of everyday practices rather than being an ontological condition, and provisionality is therefore constitutive of but also in tension with it. Rather than approaching permanence and provisionality as shifting conditions on a continuum, I borrow from Susan Gal's (2002, 79) insightful analysis of the private-public distinction, in which she argues that the perceived dichotomy does not "describe the social world in any direct way; they are rather tools for arguments about and in that world." In her view, dichotomies such as "public-private," or "permanent-provisional," are terms that gain meaning only from contextual usage. As Ato Quayson (2014, 241) reminds us, "Nothing is ephemeral or concrete, but framing makes it so." As one moves scale, location, or brings new objects into comparison, entities and processes that might have been viewed as provisional in one context become permanent in their new one.

It would be useful, then, to see the provisional, informal, and ephemeral as framings that produce certain visions of the city, while simultaneously foreclosing other imaginations that nevertheless coexist as potentialities in space and time. In any one instance there are "multiple processes of formalization and informalization that interpenetrate in particular settings" (Bolt 2021, 3). As such, descriptions of constructions and places as provisional or claims to permanence mobilize deeply rooted historical understandings of place and materials, while acting as powerful political vectors inasmuch as they force an interpretation of a particular assemblage of people and objects. The point is not that all conditions are permanent or provisional but rather that we can note provisional qualities coexisting in tension with a sense of permanence and rootedness, a tension that lies at the heart of the emergence of political claims rooted in musseque materiality in Luanda. Even as musseques' material formations disrupt dominant understandings of space and material value, the salvaging of informality in contemporary literature has often been at the expense of a critical engagement with the materiality of informality. African urban residents are generally seen to survive *in spite of* the material world that surrounds them.

The unofficial material world in urban Africa has often been elided in contemporary studies precisely because of its seemingly malleable nature, part of a larger trend in scholarship about post–Cold War urban Africa "whose cumulative effect is to emphasize a certain kind of formlessness" (Degani 2022, 7). Danny Hoffman (2017, 24–25), for instance, reflecting on the broader literature's analysis of the African urban, describes African cities as largely "dematerialized," inasmuch as they are "urban environments made up of spaces, not places, neither one thing nor another. Unformed spaces can be worked and reworked endlessly." Hoffman holds this view despite his exquisite study of the ruins of *formal* construction in Liberia and their ability to limit and shape political imagination. These kinds of evaluations of the material insignificance of the informal are concerning because they reiterate the "ungeographic" tendencies of colonial descriptions of African place-making. They leave dominant readings of space intact by emptying materials and construction of their political significance.[8]

The materials of musseque construction and practices of building have been central to the development of a sense of belonging and Indigenous place-making in Luanda. This centrality shifts into focus if one frames many of the material sites and structures studied by scholars as characterized by patterns of durability and as providing senses of regularity to residents (even as they are rendered provisional in other framings and moments). David Morton (2019) has done this important work in the context of Maputo, showing how processes of construction and design in the city's *caniço* were the product of long histories of expertise, investment, and place-making. In such a telling, the term "informal" becomes decidedly emptied of its ability to capture the enduring urbanity of these neighborhoods. In focusing on the histories of making and claiming of Indigenous urbanism that the musseques represent, rather than provisionality, what emerge are elided structures of feeling and understandings of belonging rooted in long-standing practices of sociality, exchange, construction, and investments in futures. These practices may be provisional and informal inasmuch as they are characterized as beyond the reaches of the state (although they are often complexly bound to state institutions) and are demonized by official institutions, but they are permanent inasmuch as they have deep histories of formation and reproduction that emerged out of the demands of making place under conditions of structural exclusion. The sections that follow highlight the rootedness of these practices. They show how musseque construction produces a fugitive Indigenous urbanism, rooted in a political consciousness of urban autochthony, that moves in anticipation of the formalizing cidade.

Housing as City-Forming

As we emerged from the dirt road that wound its way through a lightly forested area, a vast neighborhood hidden from the freeway stretched out in front of us. I was visiting a neighborhood called Mundial that Walter, my friend who was driving, described as a "bairro em construção" (neighborhood under construction). Hundreds of houses in various stages of completion dotted the hills in front of us, bordered by piles of sand, cement, and concrete blocks that indicated investments in ongoing processes of construction (Figure 2.2). Residents christened the area Mundial because they traced its official establishment to 2010—the year of the soccer World Cup, or "Copo Mundial" in Portuguese. Walter had already built a house in Benfica, about a thirty-minute drive from Mundial, but purchased land in 2009 from *camponêses* ("peasant" farmers) who were cultivating in the area as he speculated on future urban growth. Given that few Angolans trusted the country's banking system, land and housing were viewed as the most reliable form of saving and financial security even in the face of weak property rights. As Nuno, a member of SOS Habitat, explained to me, construction materials were "dinheiro que não estraga" ("money that won't go bad"), a nod to the fact that, unlike money that could be trapped in a bank or subject to runaway inflation, housing and land could be converted into other forms of capital, either financial or social. With the acceleration of demolitions in the postconflict era, however, the certainty in the safety of investing in housing had been slightly shaken. Walter had therefore sold a part of his land in Mundial to someone else looking to build and waited to see if the administration would send someone to demolish the purchaser's home. When, after about a year, no demolitions occurred, he and his brothers began to build. One of his brothers had already completed his house, while Walter

Figure 2.2. Construction in Mundial, 2012.

was still building, with the intention of moving there the following year with his wife and young daughter. The area would be a base from which to expand his fledgling minibus taxi business.

The process of incremental city building revealed itself in the materiality of the area. Heaped next to half-built homes or piled on empty plots were mounds of concrete-block bricks, small stones (*brita*), and sand, symbolizing the owners' dreams one day to have a *casa de bloco* (concrete-block house), the object on which much money and effort was expended. New arrivals to the city occupied vast areas of land alongside long-standing urban residents in search of more space, speculating on plots, rebuilding after suffering demolitions elsewhere in the city, or escaping rental housing. Across Luanda, the same pattern repeated itself: unofficial demarcations, the establishment of informal markets selling construction materials, and kilometers of houses-in-process, awaiting the next flood of income from their owners to add a room or roof, or to plaster the walls. This process of saving and gradually building was reiterated every day as thousands of people pushed forward the urban edge (Figures 2.3 and 2.4).

The actions of Mundial's residents were not unique to Luanda. Autoconstruction is arguably one of the primary, if not *the* primary means of accessing

Figure 2.3. Land occupations in Cacuaco, 2011.

Figure 2.4. Constructing a neighborhood in Cacuaco, 2012.

housing in much of the Global South. Teresa Caldeira (2017, 5) has termed this form of city building "peripheral urbanization," arguing that such areas should be understood as "spaces . . . always in the making" inasmuch as residents are engaged in ongoing, incremental transformations of the material and spatial constituents of their environment. While, as Morton (2019, 22) shows, the use of the term "self-built," or in the case of Angola "autoconstruction" (*autoconstrução*), is inaccurate as most residents hire carpenters, masons, and other experts; the houses (and arguably neighborhoods) are "custom-made to the owners' specifications" and are continually added on to, never seen as complete. Most significant, such areas are generally not predeveloped by private institutions or the state. It is residents themselves who build and transform them according to the limited openings available in the economic and political orders with which they are confronted. Musseques hold in tension the conditional nature of their formation inasmuch as they are in a perpetual process of incremental construction, with the historic durability of these practices and the political significance of their materials and architectures.

While slow processes of accumulation, the mobilization of fragile support networks for labor and finances, and the jostle over purchasing land on the informal market highlighted the ongoing significance of networks of improvised relations in the process of construction, the homes themselves gradually gave residents a sense of fixity and certainty (also see Holston 1991a). Walter's investments in various properties and businesses (he worked for an NGO as a driver), in minibus taxis with his brother, his plans to open a *cantina* (small shop) in his yard, and his practice of regularly bringing food purchased from relatives in rural areas into the city to sell, were hedges against the uncertainties of life in Luanda. They were a means of accumulation and assuring a future. As with autoconstructors across the continent, Walter was investing in concrete, imagining a life of permanent settlement, and guarding his financial savings through construction. The concrete-block house was the primary indication of this (Gastrow 2017a; Melly 2017; Makhulu 2015).

If planners, government officials, and people who spent the majority of their time in the cidade only saw decay and provisionality in the musseques, musseque residents had keen eyes for various material marks of construction quality, indicating internal distinctions in financial status and urban belonging. As we walked through Mundial, Walter meticulously pointed out signs of cheap or inadequate construction, which he read as evidence of financial constraint that owners might be subject to. He explained that some people did not use iron bars to reinforce the support pillars of the house or had not used enough crushed stones to strengthen the foundations. He believed these houses would wash away in three to ten years. In contrast, he spent much time highlighting the effort he had put in to purchasing better quality supports for his house. Those who built musseques thus had a stronger understanding of the distinctions among materials and their meanings than the people who sought to eradicate them.

The most notable example of the conflicting readings of materials at the heart of understandings of these spaces was that of concrete. While observers described all musseque houses as poor-quality construction, residents distinguished between *construção provisória* (provisional construction) and *construção definitiva* (permanent construction). The former term was used to describe houses constructed of wood, zinc, or corrugated iron (*chapa*), while the latter was reserved for houses made of *bloco* (concrete block) (Gastrow 2017a). During the civil war, internally displaced people had come to understand the construction of a *casa de bloco* as proof that they had successfully established themselves in the city (Robson and Roque 2001). Contrary to government expectations that people would return to rural homes (which in many cases no longer existed), when the war ended migration to Luanda continued as Angolans sought to improve their fortunes. The casa de bloco was the symbol of this improvement. A casa de bloco indexed financial stability and urban belonging, while wood and chapa, which in previous decades might have had a higher standing, were now considered markers of poverty and backwardness (Gastrow 2017a). Although musseque construction was often seen by developers as poor-quality construction, emic notions of material value distinguished between bloco and chapa, granting value only to the latter (Gastrow 2017a).

Luandans building homes, like thousands of people across the continent, did not seem to feel the city was endlessly liquid or immaterial. Not only was the loss of a casa de bloco experienced as extremely traumatic (see José Maria's story in Gastrow 2017a) but people also had developed intricate knowledges of housing quality and construction in order to secure their place—to fix themselves, that is—in the city. While Luanda could no doubt be read as dominated by the provisional, necessary questions when asserting this would be what one understands by the category of "permanence," why some objects and spaces are understood as provisional and improvised, and what one misses when, to draw on Quayson (2014), one chooses to frame certain forms and actions as provisional rather than permanent. Just as colonial ethnographers classified Luanda's musseques as characterized by the "provisionality" of the materials used for construction, and associated brick with a move toward permanence and Europeanness, it seems many contemporary ethnographers may have imported definitions of solidity and visibility that draw their power from idealized assumptions about the formality and fixity of Euro-American cities and planning practices. Rem Koolhaas et al. (2000), Filip de Boeck and Marie-Françoise Plissart (2004), and Danny Hoffman (2017) all see the implosion of modernist planning as the moment of the move to provisionality and the emergence of a city of constant improvisation, self-organization, and unpredictability. However, these kinds of assertions overlook the fact that even during the colonial period, many (if not most) African cities had already been primarily constructed by informal means; informal means that encompassed histories, predictability, and skills (Morton 2019). Celebrating informality without recognizing the predictable and permanent nature of its material formations risks, as Okwui Enwezor (2003, 116) argued, reproducing an "erotics of chaos and gigantic flux." In doing this we are in danger of eliding an alternative historical process of place-making, a subaltern tradition of spatialization that provides the means for rethinking the city. We miss the fact that Luandans see bloco as permanent, not liquid or invisible.

When Walter, his brothers, and thousands of others constructed their homes, they were participating in a long-standing urban tradition of building, even if one defined by practices of fugitivity, incremental construction, and unpredictable possibilities of emplacement. While the independence government tried to convince people to abandon the practice, those who could not access housing left behind by settlers generally had to resort to building their own homes. Unofficial land occupations, either through invasion or purchase, became the primary means through which people established themselves in the city. When couples married or people arrived needing somewhere to live, they would try to find a plot through family connections or friends. If necessary, they would travel to the urban periphery and inquire among camponêses if any of them were looking to sell.[9] These processes were not always amicable. Knowing the value of land, police might begin to sell off camponês plots without their owners' consent. Sometimes those in search of land simply invaded (Orlando, interview, Luanda, 26 November 2015). This put pressure on camponêses to sell their land or face its occupation without reaping any financial benefit.

Once land was procured (whether by force or purchase), the new owner would swiftly erect a corrugated iron house to mark ownership. Those who had the means might erect a perimeter fence and even ask a relative to live in the corrugated iron home to make sure that no one would try to occupy the plot. Then the slow process of purchasing bricks, cement, sand, and rocks began. The basic house with which most people started consisted of two rooms and a sloping roof to enable rainwater to wash off. The initial investment to build this was considerable. In 2011, when I interviewed a *pedreiro* (mason) about the cost of building a poor-quality two-bedroom concrete-block home, together we arrived at an estimate of about $6,000, which excluded the cost of the land (Andre, interview, Benfica, 24 March 2012). Once the basic unit was built, those who could would gradually add on to their houses. This process could take years, and, in reality, often continued through an individual's life. Economic success was signaled through extensions and improvements such as plastering the home, tiles on the floor, and building a "cantina," which could open to the road through a window in the yard wall.

This building process gave form to lifecycle and kinship relations, situating the house as a site in which hopes for social reproduction were invested. This was partially because of the association of housing construction with marriage and because people tended to try to live in areas where they had kin.[10] The family was central to the actual construction of the house, even though those who could afford it hired a pedreiro to assist with the initial design and foundations. If possible, they would pay others to dig and build for them under a pedreiro's supervision. Nevertheless, family labor was key to the process of house construction, so much so that a UN report from the 1990s described the Luanda family unit as "little builders" (*pequenos construtores*) (UNDP 1999, 63). Kin typically volunteered to help make concrete blocks (although these could also be purchased), cart water, dig foundations, and build walls (UNDP 1999, 63). But it was not only the family that produced the house; the house also produced the family, providing the means for its everyday reproduction. Once a basic house had been built and the yard fenced, the yard became a space that provided opportunities for economic reproduction as well as the central site of sociality. People regularly cut windows into the walls of their yards and sold drinks and snacks from them. Others built additional rooms and rented them out to new arrivals who were also looking to eventually build. Yards could accommodate small businesses and schools and were also a place for relaxation or sleep on hot summer evenings. Guests were invited to sit in the fresh air of the yard rather than the heat of the home. The house, and especially the yard, became the site through which the everyday texture of the city emerged. The musseque house assembled family, life-course, urban belonging, and financial stability into one object. It also laid the foundation for the expansion of the city.

House construction extended economic networks and activities into new areas as emplacement acted as a catalyst for the emergence of the larger network of economic activities, informal infrastructures, and practices of governance that when knitted together suddenly resulted in Luanda having expanded. In Mundial for instance, once a critical number of people had settled, they grouped together and contributed 2,500 kwanzas each (about twenty-five dollars at the time) to pay someone to bring bulldozers and earth-rollers to flatten out paths where the principal roads for the area were going to be. Many of these roads crossed still undeveloped land, marking out where residents imagined their neighborhood would grow. The presence of accessible roads and population density meant that *candongeiros* (minibus taxis) and *kupapatas* (motorbike taxis) began to circulate, linking the new area to the network of neighborhoods that made Luanda. Cistern trucks began to enter neighborhoods to sell water to residents. Those who had built large water tanks in their yards, a common household investment, would in turn sell small quantities to their neighbors, acting as the infrastructural conduits through which water moved in the absence of plumbing. Markets began to spring up to serve the construction and everyday needs of residents. Individually, the houses of course indicated a transnational economy that converged on the musseque. During a walk through any construction material market, one could see bricks and balustrades bought from Chinese wholesalers, Cubans waiting with water cisterns, Senegalese stores advertising lighting and tiling options, and Angolans selling everything from door handles to toilet seats. As a nod to my nationality, Walter told me that the principal suppliers of brita (the small stones used for filling foundations and primary support pillars) were South African. Within musseque yards, schools, traditional medical services, and auto repair operations were set up, pulling goods and money into and out of the home by providing a space for the ceaseless reproduction of the city's financial basis. Long-established practices of housing construction and design marked the self-built musseque house as an urban tradition, rather than a provisional act. The casa de bloco was arguably the elementary unit of the city.

Architectures of Autochthony

If it was possible to track the historical rootedness of the musseques and their production of the urban through patterns of construction and planning, the political significance of this became evident in residents' narratives of settlement and occupation. Residents' stories revolved around identifying the construction of neighborhoods as preceding any kind of state presence, thereby claiming an autochthonous first-comer status for musseque inhabitants and their buildings. In doing this, they implied they had constructed an urban space that predated state-imposed versions of the city, rendering demolitions an attack on Indigenous urban space and architecture. Thus, for instance, residents of Bairro 3 who had faced several demolitions to make way for the Nova Vida project adamantly insisted to me that the state had arrived after they had built.[11] Explaining that they had purchased the land from camponêses, they argued that "the state has its projects, but it found the people here. It is [now] damaging the rights of citizens" (Samuel and Jonas, interview, Bairro 3, Kilamba Kiaxi, 28 March 2012). While musseque residents did not use the word "autochthonous," they often spoke of the musseques as being home to the "próprio angolano" (the real Angolan), testifying to a sense of cultural authenticity rooted in the materiality and sociality of musseque life. This was in addition to the assertion that they had settled and developed the area prior to the arrival of a state presence. These expressions of urban Indigeneity, while occasionally echoing the politics of "insurgent citizenship" (Holston 2009) inasmuch as they were sometimes mobilized to claim rights to property and legal protections (see chapter 3), diverged from these since they called not for incorporation into the aesthetic norms of the cidade but for a recognition of the material and aesthetic constituents of an Indigenous musseque urbanity. Key to this was a sense of an urban autochthony that emerged out of narratives of settlement and construction but did not deny the existence of other inhabitants of the land (see also Rijke-Epstein 2023). Musseque residents' accounts portrayed them as having created the city from the wilderness or "bush" with the blessing of the original inhabitants of the land—camponêses—or having reclaimed it from usurpers—colonialists. They produced a connection to the land through construction as a historical process of urban place-making.

This sense of the musseque dweller as the original inhabitant of *the city*, if not the land per se, was evident in narratives of occupation that framed the land where neighborhoods now existed as rural, abandoned, or undeveloped prior to the arrival of autoconstructors. A member of the residents' committee of Mabor-Sonef in Cazenga, for instance, explained that when people began to arrive in the area around 1978–79, all that existed were a few farms that had belonged to the *colonos* (colonists), but everything else was *capim* (grass) (residents' committee member, interview, Mabor-Sonef, 27 September 2011). People had to *capinar* (clear grass) themselves until they began to build. When I inquired if anyone from the state had attempted to assist, he laughed at me. "There wasn't any guidance from the state!" He explained that it was "the people" (*o povo*) who had laid the roads, demarcated the blocks, and created the area. "There was no one to manage the process!" While the details of this account might have differed from area to area, what was noticeable was the language used to describe these neighborhoods prior to the construction of houses, which tended to focus on their "wildness." Thus, Marisa, who lived in Bairro 2, also next to Nova Vida, stated that she had lived in the area since before independence because her grandmother had a small holding there. However, she argued that when she arrived there it was *mato* (bush) (Marisa, interview, Bairro 2, 5 March 2012). A resident of the demolished Bairro 3 explained that he had arrived in the area in 1999 and negotiated with the *donos* (owners), whom he referred to as the camponêses, not the state. Once he and others had been ceded land and began to build, he explained that the area ceased to be *campo* (fields) and became a bairro (neighborhood) (resident, interview, Bairro 3, 1 July 2011). Again, Raul, a schoolteacher in Vamos Andar in Cazenga and one of the first residents to live in his particular section of the area, explained that when he had arrived there as a child with his father, "there was bush around this neighborhood" (Group discussion, Vamos Andar, Cazenga, 27 April 2011).

Several similarities stand out in these legitimizing narratives of first-comer status. It is common to admit that land was purchased from, or ceded by, camponêses identified as the original owners of the land. Translated literally as "peasant," "camponês" is more accurately used to refer to small-scale food producers. It emerged out of the colonial period when virtually all agricultural producers who were Black came to be labeled as "camponêses" by the colonial state, thereby flattening out class divisions among Africans in rural areas. During the independence period, political leaders in Angola and Mozambique continued to use the term as a means of socialist mobilization, built on the idealism of a "worker-peasant" alliance, which represented the "camponês" as the backbone of rural production (Castel-Branco 2021). In Angola, the notion of the camponês as the original occupant of land continues to hold sway and became a means for autoconstructors to re-create themselves as the first-comers of the city, if not the land per se. To do this, autoconstructors distinguish between the farming activities of the camponêses, which are grouped in the same category as *mato* (bush) and *capim* (bush/grass), versus the construction of housing and the making of *bairros* (neighborhoods). The camponêses in this story hold the ambiguous position of providing a legitimating anchor in proving that autoconstructors were ceded land from the *original* inhabitants but are grouped as closer to "bush" than "bairro" in order to distinguish the centrality of construction to the making of urban status and rights.

Pushing camponêses out of the category of bairro allows autoconstructors to present themselves as the "autochthons" of the *city*, if not necessarily the *land*, thereby contesting state actions against them. This was notable during a conversation I had with a resident of Bairro 1 in which he explained that Nova Vida had compensated some of the camponêses in the area but not the people who had built housing.[12] Given that the 2004 Land Law did not necessarily recognize sales by camponêses to third parties, I asked if, in the view of the company, it might be possible that they did not think they were obliged to compensate him and others, given that they had already compensated the camponêses who were, legally, the only people who "owned" the land. He vigorously disagreed, explaining that they had to be compensated for their houses, even if they were not compensated for their land. The house became the anchoring point for legitimation, the thing that transformed precarious occupation into first-comer status. This highlights the second aspect of the narrative, which was precisely the transformation of "bush" or farmland into urban space. Residents claim that it was they who did this; in their view, for the state then to suddenly appear and claim the right to the land was ridiculous.

In cases where it would be difficult to claim that there was nothing but "bush" in the area, an alternative narrative of urban Indigeneity focused on rightful appropriation from departing settlers. As Nito's brother Samuel argued, "Agostinho Neto mandou ocupar as casas para não estragar" (Agostinho Neto ordered people to occupy the houses to prevent them from going to ruin). This right to first-comer status through occupation was evident in the tale of Pedro, who, at the time of our interview, had lived in Cazenga for fifty-four years, even prior to independence. In the 1960s, the colonial state forcibly removed people to Cazenga from Miramar, a neighborhood that today is home to diplomats, the former private residence of Angola's second president, José Eduardo dos Santos, and a popular hamburger restaurant.[13] By independence, Cazenga boasted factories, warehouses, and large farms as it became a magnet for late colonial industrial development. These, Pedro explained, had been left behind by the Portuguese, some of whom sold and others who simply abandoned their properties. Pedro had purchased his 75-by-120-meter plot from a departing Portuguese man. He had constructed a house, offices, and annexes on the property and was now thinking about building a clinic. When I asked if he and others who had occupied or bought land at the time had registered it with the state, he said they had not. At the time, he explained, when you occupied land, you typically put up a sign with your name on it and needed to "be clear" that the land was yours. If residents' committees were present, they could give someone a document stating that they could occupy land, but there was no need to go to the municipal or provincial administration like there was now (Pedro, interview, Cazenga, 27 September 2011). A corresponding story of occupation was elaborated by an old man in Hoji-ya-Henda, a neighborhood in the municipality of Sambizanga (Mais Velho, interview, Hoji-ya-Henda, 2 September 2011). He had come to Luanda in 1979 from Malanje, where he had worked as a driver. His cousin was living in a house that had been left to him by his white employer who had fled Luanda in the run-up to independence. His cousin was interested in moving to Malanje, so they swopped houses, with Mais Velho taking unofficial ownership of the house, where he still lived in 2011. When he moved into the neighborhood there were some settler homes and some wooden houses that had been built by Angolans, but everything else had been constructed subsequently. At some point, a member of the neighborhood commission took him to officially register the house, after which he had to pay rent each month to the Ministry of Construction and Housing.

These narratives of settlement, unlike colonial ones that portray land as empty or barely touched (Pratt 1985), recognize the previous owners of the land, whether legitimate (camponêses) or illegitimate (colonial settlers). They do not claim to be autochthonous to the land but, similar to the Comorian migrants to coastal Madagascar described by Tasha Rijke-Epstein (2023, 189), by building houses and crafting kinship and social relations to the original (legitimate) inhabitants of the land, they "created their legitimate status as those who belonged to the soil of the city." In this sense, they echo legitimation myths that are characteristic of political ideologies across much of Equatorial and Central Africa regarding "first-comers" versus settlers. As Kairn Klieman (2003) notes in her study of precolonial Bantu-speaking groups and Batwa interactions, Bantu settlers represented themselves as legitimate rulers of lands they had usurped from Batwa communities by creating mythic histories that positioned them as creating civilization from wilderness. Bantu settlers created fictive kin relations to Batwa but simultaneously "symbolically 'deculturalized'" Batwa by arguing that their settlements were "precivilized" and wild, thereby portraying Batwa as "forest" rather than "village" people (Klieman 2003, 77). As such, Bantu settlers became the harbingers of civilization and makers of meaningful territorial presence that legitimated their first-comer claims in relation to other groups and the colonial state. Liisa Malkki (1995) noted similar tropes of "mythico-history" narratives used to root first-comer claims for political positioning among Hutu refugees in Tanzania in their descriptions of their relations to Burundian Tutsis and Twa. While Tutsis were portrayed as usurpers of Hutu land, Twa were described as equally autochthonous but inferior because they had failed to embrace "civilization." While these are partially stories of conquest, to frame them purely as agonistic or to suggest radical separation between groups reinforces colonial mythologies that focus on segregation between Africans rather than noting the forms of interaction and collaboration that produced contemporary senses of Blackness and Indigeneity (Canham 2023). They speak to complex histories of antagonisms, recognition, and negotiation.

Foundation myths create an order for the world that explains and legitimizes action and experience. Musseque residents' discussion of their land's being ceded or sold by camponêses portrays them as having a link to the original owners of the land, whom, in most cases, they continued to interact with. Their descriptions of occupying colonial housing represent them as reclaiming spaces that colonists usurped. T. J. Tallie (2019, 202fn15) rejects the use of the term "autochthony" for Africans, using it only to refer to settler claims to indigeneity, so as to distinguish between settler attempts to re-create themselves as indigenous through settlement practices, as opposed to African claims to belonging. While the distinction Tallie makes is useful for many contexts, the complexity of city making in Luanda requires the terms "autochthony" and "Indigenous" to hold multiple positions in tension. Luanda's musseques are Indigenous, their residents being urban autochthons. Drawing on understandings of settlement and relationality present in classic political ideologies across much of West and Central Africa, musseque residents position themselves as the legitimate autochthons of the city through their acts of building and construction. They are autochthonous inasmuch as they construct a "first-comer" urban position through their building practices. That moment of first-comer claim-making stands in opposition to the settler-colonial claims of the formalizing city and those who drive its extension. It also exists in conversation with camponêses, whom musseque residents at times poached land from but at other times collaborated and enjoyed relations of mutuality with. Musseques forged a relationship with land and imaginations of belonging shaped by long histories of Black place-making that emerged through ambivalent relations to the cidade. This became especially apparent when discussions of state encroachment into the musseques emerged.

Generating Governance

Housing generated not only a material city but an institutional one. Across Mundial small placards divided the area into "sectors" (*sectores*) and "blocks" (*blocos*) (Figure 2.5). When I asked who had placed the signs there, Walter commented that it was likely the local *comissão de moradores* (residents' committee). The unofficial institutions through which most of Luanda's musseques are governed, residents' committees are neighborhood-based, mostly aligned with the ruling party, and active in many of Luanda's musseques. Their existence dates to the late 1970s, when, in reaction to the attempted ousting of the Agostinho Neto government in May 1977, the MPLA imposed them on urban areas as a means of monitoring neighborhoods and strictly controlling local governance (Gastrow 2021).[14] This process took place in step with the gradual dissolution of their predecessors, the People's Neighborhood Commissions (CPBs). The CPBs were neighborhood political cells that had emerged during the struggle for independence and were linked to but partially independent of the MPLA. They were suspected of supporting the uprising and thus were either disbanded or purged (Mabeko-Tali 2001).

Faced with the absence of any functioning land registration during the immediate postindependence period and the weakness of what did exist in subsequent years, members of people's commissions, and later of residents' committees, were called upon to witness sales or provide oral testimony in the case of conflicts, a practice that continues today (Toni, interview, Cazenga, 2 September 2011). Over the years these committees have taken on roles that would ordinarily be filled by local government. These include, but are not limited to, approving construction plans before they can be submitted to municipal and provincial officials, resolving neighborhood conflicts, issuing documents such as proof of residence papers needed to apply for an identity card or bank account, mediation of interactions with police, and coordination of public health campaigns such as polio and human papillomavirus vaccination rollouts. Residents' committees also fielded requests for financial or social assistance, linking neighborhood members to organizations or individuals who could assist. In areas where residents' committees were strong, members monitored the activities of blocks and buildings, transmitting information about new inhabitants and emerging problems to the residents' committee of the quarter (*quarterão*) and, if deemed necessary, to the municipal administration.[15] They are one of the key institutions through which the state and the MPLA reach into the city's neighborhoods.

Despite the ruling party's imposition of residents' committees, their official status remained vague for many years. Occasional local regulations were passed and then forgotten. Authorities were ambivalent and their status ebbed and flowed with changes in administrations. Since the end of the civil war, however, there has been a rejuvenation of these organizations across Luanda, both to tighten MPLA presence in the city but also, given the absence of elected local government in Angola, to provide stronger representation of people's needs to municipal government (Tomás 2014; Croese 2015).[16] This was reinforced through official legal recognition in 2016, which resulted in the formal delimitation of their duties.[17] The legislation gave them extensive powers

Figure 2.5. Sign identifying block and sector in Mundial, 2012.

even though they are still defined not as state institutions but as nonpartisan voluntary organizations. It was over the unofficial divisions of sectors and blocks that I saw in Mundial that residents' committees, themselves unofficial at the time, governed.

Governance, however, followed construction, not the other way around. Toni, an elderly gentleman, worked for a community organization, Amigos da Cazenga, assisting people with land and housing registrations and disputes, as well as collaborating with larger NGOs in campaigns and projects around service delivery.[18] The office was based in Hoji-ya-Henda, where he also lived. He explained that although there had been some farms in the area prior to independence, the emergence of much of Hoji-ya-Henda was a "people-driven initiative," with many original residents being returnees from what was then Zaire who had reentered Angola in the late 1970s when a peace deal was signed between the MPLA and the FNLA. Although people occupied land, as far as he knew, no one was registered, and no one had proper documents. When I asked him why, he laughed: "Ninguem vendeu com documentos" (No one sold with documents). During this time, not only was there no official market in urban land, but, as he argued, "governação é uma coisa que evolui" (governance is a thing that evolved). The government was not there when people arrived, he explained, so they had to occupy without the state. He believed that, at the time, the government had neither the interest nor the capacity to register land, as the people in key positions were party members, not necessarily skilled functionaries. There were now laws for registering land, he explained, but the process took forever. He was skeptical as to whether anyone in the provincial government was even looking at the applications (Toni, interview, Cazenga, 2 September 2011).

In a related story of arriving without giving any heed to state institutions, a representative of the residents' committee in Ilha de Madeira, an area within Cazenga, explained that in his neighborhood, people had simply arrived in the 1980s and begun occupying land. When I asked if they had bought the land, he emphasized that the area had been established through occupation, not purchase. All you had to do at the time was clear the land and mark it as yours. This depended on your personal "force" (residents' committee member, interview, Ilha de Madeira, 27 September 2011). There was no top-down planning for the area. When people marked out their plots, they spoke to each other to decide where roads should go and how the area should be demarcated. After that, people used the sand in the area mixed with cement purchased from Cuban troops (who had siphoned it off from state construction projects), to build their homes. When I inquired how the occupation process was managed, he bluntly told me that it was not. Although the municipality was technically responsible for the area, it had not intervened; it was only in 1982 that a residents' committee began to function. In 1987, the administration insisted that a survey take place to determine how many people were settled in the area. The survey was meant to help legalize occupation and enable the neighborhood to elect a coordinator to liaise with the administration. Since then, there had been further substantive attempts to formally register land and housing.

Mundial was only one concrete instantiation, then, of a long-standing pattern: with the exception of musseque areas where people occupied housing that had been abandoned by colonial settlers, people occupied and built with little or no input from formal state institutions. In some instances, entrepreneurial individuals bought land from camponêses, declared themselves a residents' committee, and began to sell off the subdivisions. On balance, though, residents' committees were formed when a critical number of people in an area decided the neighborhood needed formal recognition from the municipal administration; typically, this required setting up a residents' committee. It was only after houses and plots had been established that institutions such as residents' committees and MPLA party cells or party action committees (CAPs) emerged, that water and electricity connections were extended, and neighborhoods were officially recognized as being part of the city. It was the people who called "the state" toward them through occupation and construction, rather than accepting incorporation into already designated and planned areas. Musseque houses—the elementary units of the city—generated infrastructure, economic activity, and governance institutions. They expanded Luanda both materially and institutionally. They called the city into being and with it generated a material experience of Indigeneity that became the grounds for political dissensus during the oil boom.

Demanding Recognition

"But it can't be like this! I want a car. I have land, sure, and I want a car, so I have to dance to the music of the car's owner. That's how it works. So, we're here, they found us here, so, they want this site, they have to negotiate with us. They have to accept our proposal. So, I, in this moment . . . think that my house is not worth $400,000 and something. . . . Because of this they want to send me to Zango? But it should be like this. . . . For my house, I should get the price that I want. So, if they if they want my house, seriously, they have to give me a house for a house, or they have to dance to the music" (woman 2, interview, Bairro 1, 8 June 2011). The angry outburst came from a resident of Bairro 1, a neighborhood on the edge of the state-subsidized Nova Vida housing project, whose concrete-block home had been demolished to make way for the project. Seven years later, she was living in a corrugated-iron house, waiting to be rehoused, caught between the machinations of the provincial government and Imogestin, the company that managed Nova Vida. As with thousands of other Luandans facing forced removal, she was outraged at the state and private developer's elision of her existing status on the land. In her mind, she had not encroached on another person's land. Instead, the developers had *found* her there. She was the first-comer, the owner, and with that came certain rights.

Work on the informal and provisional in African cities has recognized its centrality for the reproduction of everyday life, but its critical material politics is often discounted. It was precisely the disparaged materialities of musseques, however, that became reservoirs for the production of alternative imaginations of the urban and with that political belonging. As sites that are recognized as having produced Angolan national symbols, as being neither rural nor precolonial, but also not normatively urban, the musseques trouble existing understandings of urban modernity. Even as they are disparaged for their supposed material inadequacies, their precarity points to layered histories of fugitive settlement and construction that reach back to the early colonial encounter, providing the grounds for a Black modernity that questions contemporary elite presuppositions regarding what constitutes the desirable urban. These elite visions refuse to recognize these spaces as already urban, as coeval in both time and possibility; they relegate musseques to a less desirable, less developed present and past (Fabian 2002). In contrast, while musseque residents were frustrated with the material conditions and forms of abandonment they experienced in their neighborhoods, they nevertheless often believed that construction catalyzed first-comer claims, transforming musseque residents into urban autochthons inasmuch as it generated an "intimate aboriginal connection with territory" (Jackson 2006, 98).

Musseque residents saw themselves as the source of an Indigenous urbanism, building a city in advance of the state. As such, musseques act as spaces from which the aesthetic and therefore political consensus over what constitutes the desired urban subject or citizen can be challenged. They make visible an African urbanism that puts the destructive remaking of Luanda in question. Residents contested what constitutes the urban when they asserted the legitimacy of their areas even while lamenting their poor living conditions and government neglect. Destroying the musseques, without adequate compensation in the form of housing or money, became framed as an attack on the "true" inhabitants of the city, a population increasingly frustrated and angry at the state's sudden incursions into neighborhoods that were for so long overlooked.

CHAPTER THREE

Beyond the Law

Demolition, Belonging, and
the Moral Economy of Materiality

S enhor Mateus was a member of the residents' committee of Bairro 2,[1] one of the many musseque areas that encircled the state-subsidized housing project of Nova Vida (New Life). He had settled there in 2002 after being demobilized from the army. Some members of his family knew the camponêses who farmed in the area, and they negotiated for him to access a plot. He soon began to build his home. His efforts, however, were crushed when, at 2:00 p.m. on 28 September 2004, without any warning, police surrounded Bairros 1 and 2 accompanied by employees from the Angolan and South African construction companies that were building Nova Vida. Over the next few days, the demolition team destroyed 340 houses, leaving approximately 1,180 people homeless. Police arrested those who protested. With nowhere to go and the project not immediately exploiting the land, many residents rebuilt in the exact locations they had been removed from.

The demolition was the first of a cycle of expulsions that took place in 2005 and 2006, each accompanied by a heavy police and private security presence. Residents were shot at, arrested, and beaten. In between larger demolitions, police and the project's private security regularly tore down new structures and confiscated construction materials, frustrating attempts at rebuilding. The violence of the interventions was so intense that Senhor Mateus told me that he felt the state was trying to "Shelltox" the residents, a reference to the name of a widely used insecticide in Angola (Senhor Mateus, interview, Bairro 2, Kilamba Kiaxi, 1 July 2011). Project representatives justified these actions by claiming that the residents were illegally occupying land. Senhor Mateus, however, was not convinced. "An occupied area has a fence," he said. "It has a fence, it has a sign, it has a placard that says the area is occupied. When we came here it was bush and then we lived here." Although the project had deployed aerial photography to show that it had already delimited the area before the population arrived, the images, he argued, showed signs of settlement that belied the developer's statements. While he acknowledged that land might belong to the state in a legal sense, this was not the only or even the most important means through which he understood ownership and property rights to accrue: "Nowadays they say the land is the property of the state, but now, only when it is empty and not being used. Since the state is the owner, the law is on its side, but this land had someone who lives there, so the state has to respect this. The people are part of the state as well. . . . So, it cannot arrive here and destroy people, without notice, without compensation, and make people live for about seven years . . . this September it will be seven years living in these conditions."

While Luanda was considered a space of relative safety during the war, the majority of fighting taking place in the interior of the country, in the post-conflict period it became a site of instability and uncertainty. Although official statistics concerning the number of people who were forcibly evicted under the auspices of national reconstruction do not exist, in 2012, an employee of Odebrecht, the Brazilian company in charge of much of the construction in Zango, estimated that at least 200,000 people had been removed to the area (Odebrecht representative, interview, Zango, 23 July 2012). Zango was only one of at least four rehousing areas, including Panguila, Sapú, and Projecto Morar, in the Luanda region.[2] There are no statistics for the number of people who had their homes demolished and were not rehoused, although the archives of SOS Habitat suggest that these figures are also in the thousands. Instead of numbers, the record provides us with a list of neighborhoods: Boavista, Soba Kapassa, areas of Benfica, parts of the Ilha, Cidadania, Gaiolas, Wenji Maka, Cambamba I, Cambamba II, Banga Wé, 28 de Agosto, Areia Branca, Mayombe, Mbonde Chapé, Iraque-Bagdad, Chimbicato, Chicala. Many of these neighborhoods no longer exist, although some of their former residents still refer to themselves as belonging to these areas as, more than a decade since being expelled, they continue to await rehousing (José 2023). These names only represent the more prominent demolitions, with numerous smaller ones having taken place on a regular basis during the oil boom.

Ananya Roy (2017, 2) has argued that eviction offers a powerful point of entry into "the urban land question" inasmuch as it reveals "who owns land and on what terms, who profits from land and on what terms, and how ownership, use and financialization of land is governed and regulated by the state." In the case of Luanda, demolition drew attention to the existence of a moral economy of materiality, a shared belief that rights to housing, emplacement, and urban belonging accrued through processes of construction. This belief informed the "the production, distribution, circulation, and use of moral sentiments, emotions and values, and norms and obligations in social space" (Fassin 2009, para. 37) that mediated interpersonal, administrative, and even legal institutions' interactions when the questions of housing, compensation, and rights were discussed. While this moral economy emerged through the process of musseque construction, it had infiltrated official institutions and processes through which state recognition of belonging and status were determined. For this reason Senhor Mateus, and many others in his position, believed that their claims to housing trumped the state's formal legal right to the land. Demolition unmasked the rising tensions between the moral economy of materiality through which the majority of the population had historically enjoyed unofficial property rights, and the increasingly aggressive use of law to strip them of their homes.

In the rest of this chapter, I follow Roy's insight and show how demolitions revealed the ways official and unofficial recognition of property had long implicitly rested on a moral economy of materiality. I focus on the demolition and compensation experiences of three neighborhoods surrounding Nova Vida—Bairros 1, 2, and 3—to explore rights and recognition as material and aesthetic conditions, registers of belonging that lived both parallel to and within official laws and bureaucratic systems. Running alongside the conventional analytic sections of the chapter are text boxes that briefly present the lives, experiences, and views of a selection of demolition victims. Throughout my research, those who had lived through demolitions insisted that I should emphasize to a broader public that the "new Luanda" was built on the destruction of lives, families, and futures. Impressing on readers the personal devastation that demolition inflicted on individuals, especially in a context of deep inequality and widespread poverty, in which social status and financial stability relied on the kinds of material investments that housing represents, at times feels almost impossible. By presenting personal narratives describing experiences of demolition, I hope to provide a clearer understanding of the profound loss experienced by those who found themselves forced from their homes.

The Limits of Legal Abstractions

In late 2011, a YouTube video about Kilamba, the newly inaugurated satellite city on the edge of Luanda, went viral ("Hitler: Os apartamentos do Kilamba" n.d.). The video showed a clip from the German film *Der Untergang*, which depicts the final days of World War II played out through imagining life in Adolf Hitler's bunker. The scene showed Hitler arguing with his generals about how to protect Germany from Allied invasion. The makers of the video had placed Portuguese subtitles in the clip, supposedly translating Hitler's conversation.

The subtitles made it seem as if Hitler were berating his generals for failing to secure him a five-bedroom apartment in Kilamba, the new satellite city on the edge of Luanda. His generals explain that only MPLA members can acquire apartments. After expressing his frustration with the situation, Hitler accepts defeat and instructs them to "call the fatty of the MPLA, Bento Bento. Tell him that Hitler is asking for a two-bedroom in Kilamba. Before you do it, I will register with the MPLA CAP in Kilamba. I will only get a house in Kilamba if I fall in line with the MPLA."

The clip highlighted the ambiguous status of official institutions, and indeed legal definitions themselves, in determining belonging and accessing property. Its humor pivoted on Hitler's frustration with the impossibility of circumventing the ruling party to access state-subsidized housing, thereby highlighting the gap between the empty appeal to a normative Weberian state that was found in official documents and law, and the everyday experience of emplacement and ownership. The *partidarização* (generally translated as "partisanship" but indexing a strong sense of specifically political party influence) of official and unofficial institutions is a common feature of Angolan politics, where the division between ruling party and state is tenuous. People often mentioned being asked at interviews to produce party membership cards or being forced by local officials to participate in MPLA marches and events. The clip underscored what Angolans knew but was kept out of official public discourse: ownership was not simply a matter of following the law. Indeed, given the difficulties at the time of registering land and housing, it was virtually impossible for most people to meet the official legal requirements of property ownership. Notwithstanding their historical weakness in shaping understandings of urban property, legal considerations were, however, not moot. To the contrary, during the oil boom formal legal recognition of ownership gained significance as state institutions and private investors increasingly mobilized legal arguments to justify expulsions. The arguments of those who ordered expulsion often had official backing, because at the time Angola's legislation at best ambiguously recognized good faith occupation of land, generally rendering empty land claims that fell outside of the narrow official forms of recognition. The 2010 Angolan Constitution declares that all land is the original property of the state (Article 15.1), although customary land rights in rural areas are recognized (Article 15.2), as is private property in certain circumstances (Articles 14 and 37). The Constitution grants the state the right to expropriate land for the "public good" (*utilidade pública*) but insists that a just and prompt compensation as defined by legislation must be provided (Articles 15.3 and 37). Article 85 of the Constitution explicitly recognizes the rights of citizens to housing and "quality of life." While the Constitution traces broad guidelines regarding land and property, Angola's legislation provides additional detailed information about tenure and property rights.[3] The salient legislation in this regard is the 2004 Land Law. This law generated significant controversy when it was passed. When the intention to create a new land law was announced in 2001, the Angolan government declared that it would engage in broad consultation. Several NGOs, community groups, and nonprofits undertook research and actively engaged the government to contribute to a law they believed would represent the current situation on the ground regarding property and land tenure in Angola, as well as protect the poor (Cain 2010). At the last moment, however, the Presidency forced a law through the National Assembly that ignored these contributions and barely accounted for the vast number of people who owned land and housing through unofficial mechanisms in the country. Instead, the legislation placed strict emphasis on difficult-to-meet bureaucratic requirements for the official recognition of land rights. Most notable was the 2004 Land Law's explicit rejection of the possibility that rights could be acquired through acquisitive prescription (*usucapião*), whether in good or bad faith (Article 6.4).[4] In order to not leave any ambiguity regarding the question of good faith occupation, Article 8 declares that all methods of acquiring land that do not adhere to those contained in the law have no legal standing.

It is difficult to not interpret the action from the Presidency and the content of the law as an act of lawfare against the general population. During Angola's turbulent independence and civil war, many state institutions were gutted of capacity, including the office tasked with maintaining the province's cadaster. As a result, most property in Luanda that had been settled since 1975 was attained through ad hoc occupation. Immediately postindependence, protocols for land registration were almost nonexistent. Although regulations were gradually instituted in subsequent years, the requirements for registration were extremely onerous. Applications could take years to be processed and approved. As I have described, Luanda thus expanded through the ad hoc negotiation of access to land, with little formal registration of ownership (see also Robson and Roque 2001). Although outside of the formal confines of Angolan law, urban dwellers by and large recognized these purchases and occupations as legitimate. This recognition was forthcoming because these sales were often sanctioned by residents' committees (and therefore implicitly by the MPLA) and because, as Walter explained in the previous chapter, no other state institution stepped in to prevent construction. For many people, this implied tacit recognition of their occupation rights. Given Luanda's history of land occupation, then, the majority of Luandans do not possess title deeds

(Cain 2007). This absence of formal registration was widely acknowledged, and yet the Land Law failed to adequately take account of it. Instead, it exposed urban residents to greater legal vulnerability.

Rather than recognizing the fact of informal occupation, the law attempted to destroy it. After significant pressure from civil society, a three-year window (2005–8) was opened to allow people to register their land in accordance with the Land Law. Given the overwhelming number of the applications, however, and the incapacity of the province's bureaucracy, this was barely enough time to make a dent in the system of informal ownership. Those I interviewed who had applied to legalize their land were still waiting for an official response, leading many people to not bother initiating a registration process. The incapacity of state institutions even to manage properties that were technically officially registered was revealed when an employee of the Luanda Provincial Housing Office (Direcção Provincial de Habitação), the agency in charge of managing the rental and sale of pre-2002 state housing in the province, told me they had no idea how many properties they actually managed (Provincial Housing Office representative, interview, Luanda, 10 January 2012). It is no surprise, then, that people would angrily point out that they were accused of illegally occupying land when there were no other options. Equally shocking was a section of the law (Article 83) that retroactively revoked tenure security under specific conditions. Rights to urban land acquired before 1992 could be annulled if the owners had not regularized their claims in accordance with the 1992 Land Law (Amnesty International 2007). But the 1992 Land Law (Law 21-C/92) did not explicitly address the question of how to legalize informally acquired urban land, and the 1990s are widely considered the most devastating years of the civil war, when many state institutions functioned only in name. The hostility to informal occupation was reiterated in the Land Law regulations, which, in Article 9, stated that tenure through acquisitive prescription and good faith occupation was prohibited. In its attack on informal property holding, the Land Law came into conflict with Angola's Civil Code, which recognizes acquisitive prescription in specific instances.[5] While this does not apply to housing or property easements, Article 1528 of the Civil Code recognizes the possibility of acquiring surface rights through long-term occupation. The legal confusion produced by the conflict between the Land Law and the Civil Code potentially nullified the land claims of many, if not most, Luandans (see also Cain 2010).

The existence of confusing and seemingly antipoor laws is not unique to Angola. However, unlike many other contexts in which law has become a tool that the marginalized wield against the powerful (Holston 1991b), the structure of power, wealth, and law in Angola has made the courtroom a place that those who experience expulsion generally avoid. In fact, Tomás (2022) has argued that given the power that the Land Law invests in the state (which remains the ultimate owner of all land in Angola), all of Luanda's residents could be considered "squatters," as their rights to land and housing can be revoked at almost any time. This analysis would feel devastating were it not for the fact that how most people negotiate tenure and rights in practice bears little relation to formal legal regulations. Property claims in much of Africa, as Sara Berry (1993, 132) has powerfully shown, are less rooted in legal abstractions than in social and political relations, making access to land "contested and negotiable." The fact is that in Luanda few people rely on official legal mechanisms to assert property ownership in their everyday lives. Pétur Waldorff (2016, 2) has characterized Luanda's land tenure system as "two-tiered," a situation in which a small, usually wealthy and politically connected group of people are able to legalize their land and property according to the law, while "the vast majority only has access to the informal land market and informal or quasiformal tenure documents." He notes that "despite being considered illicit by the law, land titles issued informally continue to be the norm and are widely accepted in contemporary Luanda" (Waldorff 2016, 2). A 2011 World Bank study in four areas of the city found that although 85 percent of respondents considered their land rights to be protected, only 8 percent of those surveyed had any form of documentation that officially proved ownership (World Bank 2011). While overestimations of tenure security could simply suggest a lack of legal knowledge, it might also reflect the fact that residents have historically not been asked to produce official proof of ownership. The same study did show, however, that since the introduction of the 2004 Land Law and the rise in urban demolitions there had been a notable move toward using formal and informal institutions in the resolution of land disputes, rather than family and neighbors. This still begs the question, however, of what residents believed constituted legitimate forms of claiming property.

De facto, rather than de jure, tenure was usually negotiated not through the courts but through neighborhood relations and local bureaucracies. The most prominent institutions in this regard were residents' committees, which provided not only a localized form of tenure recognition (see chapter 2) but also the impression that there was MPLA and therefore state recognition of ownership. While the MPLA is formally represented in neighborhoods through CAPs, in several areas people serve on both the CAP and the residents' committee, and they often have offices adjacent to each other (Croese 2015). Notwithstanding the Land Law's insistence that only official procedures be followed for granting tenure rights, the entire system of land registration in the musseques relied on the residents' committees, which issued documents and observed agreements that the law at the time did not mention. To formally apply to have a plot legalized or to construct a house in a musseque area, a person had to get a "neighborhood declaration" (*declaração de bairro*) from the residents' committee stating that the committee had authorized the said person to legalize their plot and live there. In addition, the applicant had to attach a *croquis de localização*, essentially a map of the location where they intended to claim the plot or build. The map of the neighborhood was available in residents' committee offices. Residents' committees also acted as witnesses to the sale of land. The document that arose from this process was known as a *compra e venda* (purchase-and-sale). Both seller and purchaser signed the document, which then had to be officially notarized. But it did not on its own hold legal weight, except to show that the property had passed from one person to another. Yet, within the neighborhood, such a document, especially one that had been approved by the residents' committee, held considerable weight in instances of disputes (such as, for instance, if a plot had been sold to more than one person) (residents' committee member, interview, Mabor-Sonef, 27 September 2011). Residents' committees regularly adjudicated boundary and construction disputes between neighbors, even occasionally managing payments between residents for certain infractions (residents' committee member, interview, Vamos Andar, 16 July 2012). Recognition from the residents' committee was important, as it stood in for tenure security in lieu of official ownership documentation. Although outside of the confines of Angolan land law, Luandans often acknowledged these acquisitions as legitimate not only because they were recognized by residents' committees but also because state institutions did not step in to prevent construction. Absence of demolition implicitly recognized the occupant's legitimacy in residents' eyes.

Many Luandans believed that the establishment of a CAP in their area offered protection from eviction as it indicated MPLA recognition of the neighborhood.[6] On more than one occasion, people who had been subject to demolition emphasized that there had been a CAP in their neighborhood. Representatives of the Iraque-Bagdad community brought me photographs of their former CAP to prove to me that they had official MPLA recognition as a neighborhood, making it unthinkable, in their eyes, that they were subject to demolitions resulting from claims that they had illegally occupied land. As one of the former residents of Iraque-Bagdad bemoaned to me, "There was collaboration between the community, in terms of the residents' committee, with the commune and municipal administration and the provincial government.

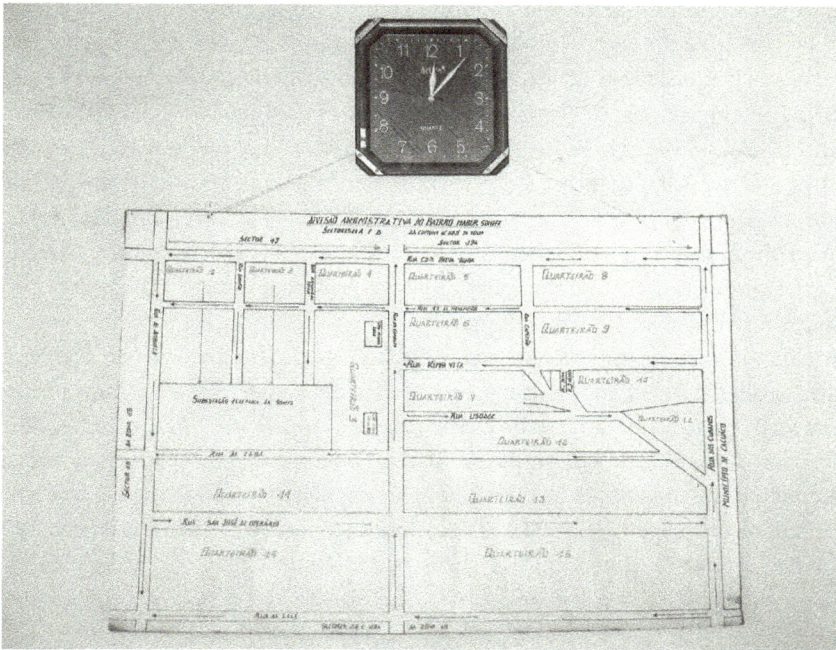

Figure 3.1. Neighborhood "croquis" on the wall of a residents' committee office, 2011.

There was also collaboration with members of the MPLA, there was already an MPLA office there, and the party, every time that there was an event, like 11 November, our Independence Day, they always invited us. We participated in events linked to the Angolan nation, as well as events of the party in power, such as 10 December, the day of the founding of the MPLA. The members of the CAP were always there participating. This is to say that it was clear that this was a recognized neighborhood" (lraque-Bagdad community representative, interview, Wenji-Maka, Camama, 16 August 2011).

While the law might be exclusionary, one could argue that the problem in Luanda is not the law per se, but, as Christine Messiant (2001, 289) so astutely noted of state structures in Angola, "the power which occupies it." As the active engagement with residents' committees and CAPs suggests, Luandans, as with millions of other people throughout the world, make claims on the state and demand recognition through a variety of extralegal, symbolic, and administrative processes rather than the formal regulations of an imagined Weberian state (Chatterjee 2004). While the general scholarly imagination of statecraft in Angola has long privileged a vision of a hegemonic and overbearing party-state that uses the law to impose its will, a burgeoning body of work produced over the last decade indicates that power and sovereignty are far more fractured and vulnerable in Angola than previously imagined (Croese 2015; Blanes and Samussuku 2022; Buire 2018). If nothing else, the overly reactive use of laws and security agencies against ordinary Angolans speaks to the ruling party's deep fear of the population's potential (Roque 2021). In Luanda, as the YouTube clip suggested, rather than legal land ownership, the quotidian basis of recognition was thought to partially emerge through unofficial political relations. Political and urban belonging were products of the multiple modes of recognition that operated in everyday life, sometimes in conversation with, but often parallel to, official legal systems. As David Harvey (2008, 23) reminds us, the struggle for the right to the city is primarily about not law but rather "the freedom to make and remake our cities and ourselves." The law, as enacted in Angola, has increasingly hindered people's capacity to realize their quotidian urban visions of the good life, but it cannot completely halt this. It is precisely for this reason that the right to the city is an object of struggle, a struggle that plays out not only in courts but also in the everyday production of space.

Demolition and Material Properties

While local forms of state and party power played a significant role in providing quotidian legitimacy to settlements, in the aftermath of demolition a different aspect of unofficial recognition came to the center of discussion—the aesthetics of the home. This should not be surprising; after all, residents viewed the concrete block house as the cornerstone of urban autochthony claims and the means through which the city came into being. What is unexpected, however, is that state institutions implicitly worked using similar assumptions showing that historical practices of recognition rooted in construction, a moral economy of materiality, even if not having official legal weight, had infiltrated administrative institutions and shaped bureaucratic decision-making. Ironically, it was in the aftermath of the mass demolitions between 2001 and 2015, and the negation they expressed of officially recognized belonging and rights, that the moral economy of materiality was revealed to still be shaping decisions.

Demolition and expulsion have long been tools of urban planning in Luanda. The first recorded evictions took place in 1864. Claiming that African living conditions were responsible for the spread of disease, colonial authorities destroyed the predominantly African neighborhood of Coqueiros, the oldest settlement in the city, and expelled its residents to the zone of Maculusso, at that time considered to be on the city's extreme periphery.[7] The demolition of musseque areas, largely inhabited by Africans, would become a staple of urban expansion in the late colonial period. As Luanda experienced significant urban growth, rising numbers of African neighborhoods were destroyed to build elite, predominantly white, residential zones, making the city an ever-changing and uncertain space for Black residents (Pepetela 1990).

Despite apparent conflicts over land and housing throughout Angola's civil war, most Angolans I spoke to argued that demolitions and mass expulsions were not a feature of urban life in the postcolonial period until the early 2000s. The archival record bears this out for the first two decades after independence. Newspaper articles and interviews revealed that a variety of state institutions were either ambivalent about undertaking evictions and demolitions due to political circumstances or, in other cases, simply lacked the institutional capacity to do so (see chapter 1). Nevertheless, the threat of demolition hovered over musseque residents and existed in official policy approaches to planning. Sebastian Kasack (1992, 93) describes how the Cuban planners who worked with the new socialist government in the 1970s and 1980s viewed urban development as a process of slum elimination through demolition and rehousing in "modern" apartments. When Kasack undertook his PhD research in the Sambizanga area of Luanda in the early 1990s, residents worried that he and other researchers were there to facilitate the demolition of their homes and their forced removal to the municipality of Viana.

In the early 1990s, residents' concerns might have seemed strange to onlookers given that at the time the state made almost no coordinated effort to remove people from urban land. But they turned out to be well founded. From the mid-1990s, there was a clear shift in state policies and attitudes regarding land and housing in Luanda. While land occupations had previously gone unchecked, the formal introduction of a market economy following the abandonment of socialism generated renewed interest in opportunities for speculation and accumulation through urban property. The first indication of this was demolitions undertaken to implement the Luanda Sul project (see chapter 1). The project heralded an official return to colonial-era practices of expulsion. In January 1999, EDURB destroyed the homes of a number of families in the Samba municipality ("GPL atira cidadãos a rua" 1999). Later that month, the GPL authorized the removal of more than 2,000 people from the municipality of Kilamba Kiaxi ("GPL continua a desalojar" 1999). Despite these growing incidences of removal, for most Luandans, the act that symbolized the formal

Oswaldo, Bairro 2, 5 March 2012

Oswaldo was born in Malanje and joined the People's Armed Forces for the Liberation of Angola (FAPLA), the MPLA military, in 1983, when he was twenty-three. He had been studying when he joined the army, but, as he described it, from then on, "studying was just the gun." In 1992, he was demobilized and traveled from Menongue, in the far southeastern province of Cuando-Cubango, to settle in Luanda. Shortly afterward, however, he moved to Cunene, on Angola's border with Namibia, to set up a business. In 2003 he returned to Luanda. While looking for somewhere to build, he was put in contact with Senhor Miguel, the coordinator of Bairro 2, and introduced to Mama Manuela, the *camponêsa* who owned the land on which Bairro 2 was built. A year later, when he had just finished erecting the walls of his home, the demolitions began and were repeated in 2005 and 2006. It was now 2012 and he was still living in a *casa de chapa*, unconvinced that the government ever actually planned to rehouse him or others.

Believing the demolitions showed that the government was more interested in catering to the market and foreign interests than serving the "real Angolan" (see chapter 5), Oswaldo felt that the government was failing to treat Angolans with the dignity with which they treated foreigners. "We have a right to everything. A right to a house and electricity. Everything that they have. The rights they are giving to foreigners, as owners of the soil [*donos de terra*], we deserve them."

When I asked him if he had tried to find land somewhere else, he mocked the idea: "But *senhora*, I found a piece of land already. Do you see our government's problem? When this was bush the government never thought of putting a project here. But it sees a place where the population put its shacks to live, and the government comes, it spies, when it realizes that it is a good location, this is when it comes to knock down houses. Those people, those people are left out in the cold, like us now. Now, am I going to leave here where they already forced me out, already destroyed my house, find another place to go, to run even more? No. It has to be here, they have to feel this, that Angolan [the president] has to give what I deserve. I'm not interested in looking for land, just so he can implement his project."

return of mass demolition as a tool of statecraft in the city was the destruction of Boavista in 2001 (see chapter 1).

During the oil boom, under the auspices of national reconstruction, Luanda become a site of mass displacement. While demolitions appeared arbitrary to those subject to them, many (but not all) were part of a state architecture of removal that had its roots in the urban planning initiatives of the 1990s. The GOE had had an internal rehousing division since its creation in 1998. However, in 2007, this division was separated from the main organization and transformed into a special office, the PRP, which was meant to oversee the surveying, relocation, and rehousing of people to make way for national reconstruction initiatives.[8] There was a direct institutional link, then, between projects tied to national reconstruction and forced removals. The PRP answered to the GOE, which itself answered directly to the Presidency. Although the Program for Social Housing (PHS), a provincial level office, was technically in charge of rehousing people who lived in what were classified as "high-risk zones," it lacked the human and financial resources to do this. As a result of the challenges faced by the PHS, the PRP also took over some of its duties, working with the Provincial Office for Social Reintegration (Direcção Provincial de Reinserção Social) and the Ministry for Social Assistance and Reintegration (Ministério de Assistência e Reinserção Social) to rehouse people (PRP representative, interview, Praia do Bispo, 3 November 2011). The PRP coordinated the demolition and rehousing process among companies looking to build, the institutions that managed the rehousing zones, and the contractors that built the social housing (PRP representative, interview, Praia do Bispo, 3 November 2011).

While demolition and removal processes were thus rooted in an established bureaucratic and legal framework, the actual process of eviction and compensation revealed that aesthetic assessments determined decisions about rehousing and compensation. Once an area had been identified for demolition, the PRP sent a team there to perform a survey. While they included information such as the number of families living in an area and the property rights of those to be affected, the primary means through which compensation was determined was aesthetic. A representative of the PRP explained that teams primarily looked at the size of the home when determining compensation. Those with large houses would receive more than one house in the rehousing area. This was because, unlike the homes people were coming from, the houses in the rehousing zones were generally all one size;[9] he did not think it fair that someone with a large house should receive the same compensation as someone with a small house (PRP representative, interview, Praia do Bispo, 3 November

2011). Ad hoc forms of evaluation underpinned rehousing decisions, typically based on materially defined perceptions of age, quality, and size rather than formal rights (Dias 2020). An individual associated with one of the companies involved in rehousing explained to me that compensation was determined by measuring the size of the existing house and judging whether it was larger or smaller than the house in the rehousing area. If it was larger, the owner might receive more than one house. If it was smaller, then they might only receive financial compensation, or nothing at all (Xavier, interview, Ilha, 28 March 2012). People were then assigned a house (or more than one house) based on the assessments of the survey team (representative of municipal administration in Cacuaco, Milton, discussion on visit to Panguila, 10 June 2011). On the agreed upon day, fleets of trucks and buses would arrive to transport families from their current homes to the rehousing areas. Using lists drawn up based on survey data, people were assigned a house and waited in the rehousing area for their name to be called and to receive a key. They were then instructed to walk through the rehousing zone and locate their new home. Some people received a *guia de entrega* (proof of issuance) for the house they received. Throughout this process, those affected were rarely, if ever, asked to produce documentation showing that they had formally owned their now-demolished homes. Material and aesthetic considerations were more significant than legal ones in shaping statecraft in these instances.

In practice, even official demolitions were messy. People were often given little warning of their impending eviction. Sometimes surveys were performed years before the actual removals, resulting in notable discrepancies between official lists and the actual demographics of the neighborhood. Many people tried to profit from the system. Several people told me that police involved in the removals often put their names down on the rehousing lists in order to access properties. Within the messiness, however, some sought to profit from the fact that, in the wake of demolitions, material rather than legal concerns shaped practices of recognition. Both António Tomás (2012) and Sylvia Croese (2013) have shown how people who were aware that surveys were about to take place and understood that assessments turned on, among other features, the size of the house, quickly built small structures in areas marked for demolition, or added rooms so that the surveyors would mark them down for additional compensation. In some cases, individuals managed to manipulate cycles of demolition to be awarded several houses, which they then rented out to other people.

The opportunism of some, though, does not diminish the real suffering of many. As the program of mass demolition unfolded from the late years of the war into the oil-boom period, thousands of people were expelled with no rehousing. Some were transferred to tents in which they remained for years, with no clear sense of when they might be rehoused. Others were left with nothing, forced to seek shelter with friends or family while they attempted to rebuild. Schooling was disrupted and neighborhood bonds ripped apart. Children had to be scattered between households to ensure they had a roof over their heads. People rehoused far from where they worked (or not rehoused at all) often found it impossible to keep their jobs. Some developed health problems as their lack of housing exposed them to disease and dangerous environmental conditions. Some developed severe depression. Many communities reported spiraling levels of alcoholism and suicide following demolitions.

Official demolitions created an atmosphere that enabled a variety of private and public actors to exploit the destruction to extract money from, abuse, and expel urban residents. Local administrators and state employees used the threat of demolition to demand payments from residents who were building their homes. In a settled neighborhood in Cacuaco, the northern-most municipality of Luanda, where, in 2012, a sizeable amount of land remained available for settlement, the *fiscal* (economic police) insisted that residents pay yearly rates of 10,000 kwanzas ($100 at the time) to maintain a corrugated-iron home in the area, and 60,000 kwanzas ($600) for a concrete-block house (neighborhood residents, discussion, Cacuaco, 19 May 2012). Similarly, private individuals manipulated demolitions by using their links to state institutions to force existing residents off desirable land.

The most drastic demolitions, however, continued to be those performed for private companies or public-private partnerships invested in real estate development, primarily because, unlike many of the officially state-sanctioned evictions, they ignored the moral economy of materiality. Not only were these often unannounced, accompanied by extreme violence, and resulted in little or no compensation, but, in a context where private capital was often linked to the politically powerful, victims were left little recourse to legal assistance or justice of any kind (SOS Habitat 2012). Drawing on official definitions of land ownership, while ignoring the other registers of negotiation through which property was historically recognized, companies pointed to residents' illegal status as justification for their removal. Homes were suddenly defined as *construções anárquicas* (anarchic constructions) and citizens were transformed into *anárquicos* (anarchics). These descriptions had chilling effects on Luandans, who found them ironic given their belief that corruption underlay most elites' wealth, resulting in elites' being as much in breach of the law as those they were attempting to remove. As Bernado of SOS Habitat told me with frustration, "When they need these lands, they ask, 'Where is the document?'

Bibiana, Bairro 2, 5 March 2012

Bibiana was born in Kwanza Sul but moved with her family to Luanda when she was fifteen, following the disputed election result in 1992 that reignited the civil war. The family was placed in a *centro de recolhimento*—a government camp for internally displaced people—until officials managed to locate her relatives. She ended up living with a cousin in the neighborhood of São Paulo. She subsequently began a relationship with an older man and moved into his house in Praia do Bispo. The relationship became abusive, and one day she found herself homeless. Her partner had beaten her so brutally that she had to be hospitalized. Resolving not to return to him, she began to look for another place to live.

A woman who sold manioc flour in the road where Bibiana had previously lived advised her that camponêses were selling land on the southern edge of the city. The woman referred her to an *intermediario* (intermediary) who sold Bibiana a piece of land from one of the *donas de lavras* (female owners of the farms). She began to live in the area in 1996. She first built a house with corrugated iron, and then began to construct with concrete blocks, but, in 2004, before she could complete her construction, the neighborhood was demolished. She was outside of Luanda at the time, visiting her mother in Kwanza Sul. When she returned, her home was gone. She felt overwhelmed, mostly because she had no idea what to do with her four children. In Luanda, she explained, it was difficult to convince someone—even an aunt or cousin—to take you in with children. In the end she had to split the family up, leaving each child with a different relative in Luanda so that they could study and be cared for in conditions that she found acceptable. Other women who did not want to be separated from their children, she explained, tried to live on the streets or in a corrugated iron house a bit longer, but this was not sustainable. Her aim now was to build another house with concrete blocks.

They accuse you of being anarchic. But they never say how they acquired their wealth, because their wealth is also anarchic. . . . They drive big luxury cars. They have huge luxury cars, big cars and luxury houses. . . . They have never accounted for how they acquired these. But you manage to get a small house where you live with your family, where, when you go to work, your heart is

The Fortunato Family, Kilamba Kiaxi, 15 September 2011

Miguel Fortunato moved to Luanda from Uige in 1992, escaping the resumption of Angola's civil war. He initially lived with his brother in Boavista. It was in Luanda that he met Sylvia, who had grown up in Luanda's Petrangol neighborhood. When they met, she was working as an assistant to her uncle in a local clinic. Although she had no formal medical training, her experience in the clinic meant that she undertook many of the basic jobs of a nurse. After they married, the couple moved to Cazenga and then to Calemba II, living in rented housing. In 2007, they finally managed to purchase land in Iraque and began to build. Two years later, however, their new house was demolished. Finding themselves homeless, and with few options, the Fortunato family "walked the city" until they found an area that Sylvia described as "bush." There they cleared the grass and other plants for construction and built a corrugated-iron home.

A year later, the *fiscal* (economic police) arrived with a man who claimed that his mother, Dona Filomena, owned the land and told them that they had seventy-two hours to leave. When the son returned and saw they had not left, he negotiated with the Fortunato family and some other families who had arrived since 2009 and granted each a plot of between 100 and 150 square meters to build on. About six months later, the woman who claimed to own the land appeared with police and military officers. The Fortunato family went to the military police to request assistance, but the military police simply gave them a cell phone number and told them to call should more police appear. Soon afterward, Sylvia received a call from the woman's daughter telling them that they needed to leave. Sylvia refused, asking how it was possible that the woman's son had told them they could stay but the daughter was telling them they had to leave. They resolved to stay.

(continued)

A few months later, the woman's daughter sent a group of young men to pull down the Fortunatos' home and intimidate them. Sylvia argued with them and called the police, which got the men to stop. The Fortunatos approached the police and the fiscal about the intimidation but were ignored. They contacted Radio Despertar, the mouthpiece of UNITA in Luanda, which put them in touch with SOS Habitat. As soon as SOS Habitat was involved, however, the woman who claimed ownership reappeared, now with documents that she stated proved her claim. She and her son, who now described her as his aunt, began bringing prospective buyers to the area and threatening Sylvia and her family with representatives from the military and police. Given the endlessly changing account of the young man's relation to Dona Filomena, and his inability to present original documents rather than copies, Sylvia became suspicious of the papers' authenticity and believed that Dona Filomena may have bribed the fiscal to secure recognition of the land under her name.

They now lived in a corrugated-iron house that they were renting from a man who lived in the neighborhood of Palanca but had occupied land in the area for speculation purposes. Their previous homes lay in a mangle of ruins a few meters from their current residence, with bits of broken corrugated iron strewn on the ground. Eyeing the emerging constructions of her neighbors, whose plots had been ceded to them by camponêses, Sylvia explained that, in hindsight, she wished they had bought land from the "owners of the farms"—the camponêses—rather than simply occupying this one, which had appeared at the time to lack an owner. Reflecting on the many previous and possible future displacements her family faced because of the difficulties of claiming space in the city, she expressed her disillusionment with the postconflict settlement: "With all of that confusion of the war, sometimes people lived more, had more peace. That thing of struggling but having a fixed abode. But now, a lot of these things, these demolitions, are happening. Even the police, the work they are doing . . . a few days ago they destroyed houses here, they destroyed houses. They destroyed houses and no one understands why."

"Concrete-block houses!" Miguel exclaimed in disbelief. "Yes, concrete-block," she sighed.

at peace because you left your family there, you, unfortunately are 'an anarchic.' An anarchic" (Bernardo and Nuno of SOS Habitat, discussion, Maianga, 5 May 2011).

Despite the increasing fragility of materiality and aesthetics as a means of claim-making, negotiations over compensation in the wake of demolition revealed that a moral economy of materiality has remained key to understandings and practices of emplacement and recognition. As in many other parts of the world, ownership claims emerged and solidified over time as people established themselves in a place and incrementally built relationships and dwellings that performed their claims (Smith 2019). These actions and contestations created their own "geographies of property"—landscapes constitutive of and constituted by the material effects of property norms, such as fences and gates, that perform the ideologies of access and exclusion characteristic of particular property regimes (Blomley 1998). In Luanda, while in theory these material markers had no formal status, in practice they shaped legal and administrative decisions. They did not legalize settlement, but they could be mobilized to demand recognition of place and rights from state and private actors. For this reason, civil society organizations working in the immediate aftermath of demolitions created registers of who had built using what kinds of materials and when possible supported these registers with photographs. Lawyers who represented demolition victims asked not only for documents but also for other kinds of material proof, such as water or electricity connections, proof of cultivation, and photographs of housing (lawyer at Mãos Livres, interview, Luanda, 20 February 2012). These kinds of "proof" did not legalize ownership in the formal sense, but they often led to some form of compensation, implying that even when, as Tomás (2022) points out, the state was able to render someone a "squatter" in the abstract, the person nevertheless could be recognized as deserving compensation through other processes and markers. Actors' ability to negotiate between attachments rooted in bricks and local informal agreements as well as abstract recognitions rooted in law enabled them to negotiate and remake possibilities for emplacement and belonging in Luanda.

Material Negotiations

The sight of a wooden house perched on the remains of the foundation of a destroyed concrete-block home has always been one of the starkest reminders for me that violence is marked on landscapes. It materially symbolizes the conflicts between the moral economy of materiality and those forms of value and power emergent through legal abstractions. Bairros 1, 2, and 3 each lay on

Abilio, Bairro 1, Kilamba Kiaxi, 24 February 2012

Abilio was born and raised in Prenda, a mixed-income neighborhood in the heart of Luanda. In 2000, after getting married, he moved out of his brother's home, where he had lived all his life, and rented a house in Prenda for fifty dollars a month. He was earning a steady income from his job as a driver for Macon taxi and began looking for land where he could build a home. Having no faith in the government to grant him land, he traversed the peripheries of Luanda, trying to find a *camponês* who would sell him a desirable plot. In 2002, he managed to purchase a plot of land from a camponês for $350 in what became Bairro 1. By 2003, he and his wife had built their home. In 2004, however, Group 5 suddenly appeared and began to extend the Nova Vida project toward them.

"We never though it would reach," Abilio said. "But you know, now that everything in our country, and especially in Luanda, is a business, the project resolved to eliminate our living space so that they could do their business. That's how, in 2004, they decided to demolish the residents who lived here or who still live here."

"What happened on this day in 2004, the day of the demolition?" I asked.

"Okay," he replied, "2004, we were here, this was around 4 a.m., at 4 a.m. we realized the neighborhood was surrounded by police. We hadn't received any warning about negotiation or that they would demolish residents' homes. They arrived with the soldiers, and the police emerged with their bulldozers. They said they were here because we had invaded the space, and they began to demolish the houses."

"With the bulldozers?"

"With the bulldozers. After the demolition they posted guards from a private security company, Visgo, that belongs to the current vice president of the Republic, Nandó [Fernando da Piedade Dias dos Santos]. This was to prevent anyone entering with corrugated iron to rebuild what they had destroyed. During the time that they kept the security there we lived in the open, in the open without even having a roof. This was practically how this table is." He points to the table where we are sitting. "We lived here just to be able to lie down and not have the rain fall right on top of us. Here, everything was in the open."

"People didn't look for other spaces to live?"

"Well, no one left to look for another space, we stayed here by the neighborhood until they decided to negotiate."

"They negotiated?"

"They . . . That wasn't a negotiation. They arrived with a proposal. They said they could give us land in a neighborhood called Fúbu, where they had set up a site. They would give three or five piles of sand to those who were interested in building."

"What was the reaction to this proposal?"

"Well, some residents, the weaker ones, ended up giving in and received fifteen sheets of corrugated iron, a kilogram of nails, and eight slats of wood. After those people left, we saw that this was never a negotiation, it was an expulsion done in the way they wanted. So those of us who had not given in, we began to resist here in the neighborhood. Two or three years later we heard the vice president, or minister, it was Prime Minister Nandó, say in an interview that the people who were here in the Nova Vida project were here because of negligence because they had already been compensated."

"How did you feel when you heard this?"

"We felt really hurt, really hurt by the way the prime minister of the nation spoke."

different edges of Nova Vida. These areas were once growing musseque neighborhoods, with the same landscapes of expectation described in chapter 2. When I went there in June 2011, they had been transformed into collections of wood and corrugated-iron houses with none of the piles of sand or concrete-block that indicated aspirations for permanent settlement. Residents feared that concrete blocks would provoke violent reactions from private security and the police. The inhabitants of these neighborhoods were representative of most Luandans. Some drove taxis, others were teachers or zungeiras (ambulant traders), and of course some were unemployed. Most had landed there in the last decade of the war in search of a permanent home. The camponêses who sold the land to residents carried on farming between the settlements, their cassava plants mixed with the residents' gardens along with fields of vegetables for household use as well as for sale in the city's markets. They also felt undermined by the project, which had offered them meager compensation for their land that it continued to encroach on.

The land where Nova Vida was situated was technically owned by the Casa Militar (the Presidency's military cabinet), although this was contested since camponêses had been settled there since at least the 1930s. In the late 1990s, it had been earmarked for development by the Military Works Construction Brigade (BCOM), with the idea of constructing housing for demobilized soldiers.[10] This plan later transformed into one for a state-subsidized housing project—Nova Vida—aimed at providing housing for what an Imogestin representative described to me as "lower-middle-class" or "middle-class" civil servants. At the time of the project's conception, members of the government felt that civil servants should not have to live in musseques (Daniel, interview, Nova Vida, 1 December 2011). Bricomil/BCOM, ENSA, and Banco BAI became shareholders of Imogestin, the company that would oversee the construction and management of Nova Vida. The first phase of the project was launched in 2001. It was completed in 2005, with subsequent phases expanding the project. It was during the first phase that the project's expansion came to the awareness of the residents of Bairros 1, 2, and 3, such as Senhor Mateus, whose homes stood in the way of its growth.

The violent demolitions of 25 September 2004 prompted residents to approach SOS Habitat to help them negotiate with state and project representatives for financial compensation or rehousing. SOS Habitat quickly began the process of re-creating the neighborhoods in a set of registers that would enable the state to recognize them as negotiating partners. The first step was for the neighborhoods to constitute new residents' committees by dividing the areas in quarters (quarterões). Next, they undertook a careful survey of the number of families affected by the demolition and carefully listed whether they had a "casa de bloco" or a "casa de chapa" (corrugated iron house). Then they began to write to the management of the Nova Vida project, the Angolan National Assembly, and the local administration explaining that residents' rights had been violated and demanding a solution to the conflict between residents and the project. In arguing for the illegality of demolitions, which was central to their activism, they appealed not only to domestic laws regarding the right to housing and just compensation but also to regional and international human rights law (Gastrow 2013–14).

By the time I began research with residents of these three neighborhoods, they were in a stalemate with the Nova Vida project. In 2007, in the run-up to the 2008 election, members of the MPLA government, the Nova Vida project,

Figure 3.2. Wooden house built on demolished cement brick foundation. Bairro 1, Luanda, June 2011.

and community representatives held a meeting during which it was agreed that the residents would be rehoused. Following this, demolitions ceased. However, this agreement also put the residents into a kind of material stasis. If concrete blocks became the basis for claiming urban status and belonging, then moving back to corrugated iron symbolized a reversal of this process of urban incorporation, a move back to marginality, precarity, and impoverishment. Demolition victims described living in chapa as being equivalent to being in jail, or held hostage, being unable to develop, as evidence of the state's considering them as being part of a "lower level" and forced into an embodied state of constant discomfort because the material exposed one to heat, cold, flooding, and disease (Gastrow 2017a). In addition to fearing reprisals if they began to build with concrete blocks, inhabitants of Bairros 1, 2, and 3, having been promised that they would be rehoused, also did not want to invest in the expense. They felt stuck in corrugated iron (or wood), unable, in their view, to progress or make more of their lives because of their material conditions.

Even though demolition had resulted in a deep disillusionment with the MPLA among many residents of these neighborhoods, the ruling party's unofficial centrality to the workings of the state meant that many were nevertheless tempted to negotiate with local party representatives for assistance.

While Bairros 1 and 2 avoided extensive dealings with the MPLA, residents of Bairro 3 sought them out, slowly distancing themselves from SOS Habitat. The other two neighborhoods mocked them for purchasing a shipping container and painting it with MPLA colors to gain the party's approval. Nevertheless, Bairro 3's actions appeared to bear fruit when local authorities built a public water stand there. Much to the chagrin of the other neighborhoods and SOS Habitat, Bairro 3's residents' committee avoided the organization, failed to communicate information to residents, or blatantly defied them to curry favor with members of the MPLA. SOS's Bernardo believed that such actions undermined attempts to collectively mobilize communities, but he was powerless to prevent them and often warned people not to place too much hope in the ruling party to resolve their problems.

Nevertheless, by 2011, there was still no sign that rehousing was imminent. This experience of material inertia was making residents restless and frustrated. In June 2011, residents of the three neighborhoods threatened to stage a protest to contest the lack of action from the municipality and province. Soon afterward, the municipal administration invited members of SOS Habitat and neighborhood representatives to a meeting. Requesting that they not protest, the municipality furnished them with an official document signed by the provincial governor, which pledged to rehouse them between September 2011 and April 2012. In return, residents cancelled the planned protest. Unfortunately, by January 2012, there was no sign of their being rehoused, leading to the adoption of a new strategy—rebuilding.

In January 2012, the Bairro 1 and Bairro 2 residents' committees called neighborhood meetings to discuss what should be done. To compel the administration to respond to their condition, they agreed to begin rebuilding with concrete blocks. This emulated a strategy employed by other neighborhoods around the city in the face of demolition. By continuing to build while negotiating with the provincial government, they created better-quality housing in case no demolition occurred. As a resident of Bairro 1 stated, "We, that is 'the people' [o povo], thought to do it in this manner of reconstructing and urbanizing the neighborhood so that we could pressure the government to give us a response. If the government doesn't respond, then, God willing, we will build and remain here until the end" (resident of Barrio 1, interview, 24 February 2012). Bairro 3 residents felt that rebuilding was too confrontational. Although they continued to negotiate with the administration, the residents' committee also began to actively engage MPLA structures as an official strategy. The other two neighborhoods did not negotiate with the party but were worried about what the administration's inaction suggested. Samuel, a member of Bairro 1's residents' committee, was concerned that it was an electoral strategy. He felt that by not demolishing the housing in the buildup to the 2012 election and leaving residents in a position of negotiation, the MPLA showed it believed it could win over voters. He thought that once the election was over, the MPLA might contract a force to "limpar tudo" (eliminate everything). In the moral economy of materiality that ran through public considerations, the demolition of corrugated-iron houses would not elicit meaningful public outrage. Seeking to avoid such a situation and thereby put pressure on the administration and the Nova Vida project, residents began to write letters to state institutions, the media, and organizations abroad informing them of their intentions. They saw this as providing fair warning and a minimal amount of protection, as they could not be accused of having carried out their actions in secret.

In March 2012, over several weekends, men in the two neighborhoods worked together to lay out lots in Bairro 1, driving small iron rods into the earth to mark out where future properties would be. A plain iron rod with blue plastic tied to it indicated the border of the plot with another plot. A rod that was painted white marked where a road was meant to be. Because some of the existing houses would have to be knocked down in order for the plan to be realized, neighborhood residents had begun laying out plots in a part of the neighborhood that had less construction, so that only one home would have to be dismantled to allow for the first houses to be erected. In Bairro 1, residents planned for seventy-two plots built in a grid pattern that echoed aesthetic visions of desirable urbanism. The grid was made up of nine blocks of eight plots each, with each plot being twenty-by-twenty-five meters. Within this grid, plots had been reserved for a committee office, a school, a market space, a church, and a children's play area. All entrances from the yards would open onto the principal roads, ones wide enough for cars to pass, rather than constructing alleyways between the houses. Jorge, one the members of the residents' committee, showed me the neighborhood plan, explaining that it allowed for all of the houses to have identical walls that faced the road, so that they could align with their wealthy neighbors' and the state's understandings of "organization." He thought that they could escape being branded a *bairro desorganizado* (disorganized neighborhood), an oft-used term in official parlance that indexed both legal (in the sense that residents lacked title deeds) and aesthetic (informal construction) disorganization. "They," Jorge explained, "normally say that we build without logic, but with a wall, a house looks different" (data from participant observation, Bairro 1, 27 March 2012).

This mode of linking the possibility of recognition to a specific aesthetic register revealed the ways the moral economy of materiality continued to factor into people's actions, even if this was under extreme pressure. As Morten Nielson (2011) has shown in the case of Mozambique, urban residents on the margins of legality often try to mimic what they believe are the forms and practices that index state preferences to gain legal recognition of their claims. Residents use materials and planning designs and create institutions to "call" the state toward them in specific ways. Similar processes were taking place in Bairros 1 and 2, evident in the aesthetics of the neighborhood plans as tools of negotiation, which mimicked official visuals of urban requalification circulated in newspapers, television media, and government publications that dwelt on the "before" and "after" aspect of the move from informal "disorganization" to "formal" organization. Residents came to identify these urban designs as being the condition for state recognition of occupation as legitimate, if not necessarily legal.

These sentiments were reiterated a day later by another residents' committee member, Samuel, who told me that Bairro 1 had partially chosen to build according to a grid, and with standardized housing, so that the residents of Nova Vida would not think that there was a "disorganized neighborhood" alongside them. He hoped this would avoid any possible problems. Explicitly indexing state-driven notions of urban development, he argued that their project was a form of state-directed self-building, as the design of the houses meant that access to roads and services would not be blocked.[11] In this way, he argued they would be no different from what he referred to as the "luxury musseque" that bordered the other edge of Bairro 1. In that area, lots were laid out by a private-public consortium in the 1990s and sold to the emerging middle class before infrastructure was built. "They've done the same as we are doing here," Samuel said. "We are building roads, so, in the future, the government can come and put in infrastructure" (data from participant observation, Bairro 1, 28 March 2012). As I walked through the demarcated area, Samuel and his friend pointed out where the plots and the roads were. They could envision the layout and geography of the bairro before it officially existed, conjuring their future homes into existence through words. "Here is the road," Samuel told me, pointing at one of the white markers, "and there, see where it is, that is where it ends. All the houses will only have access to one road. They will have their backs to each other, just like in the project."

The residents of Bairro 1 attempted to make claims to the legitimacy of their emplacement, although not necessarily the legality of their land ownership, by repeating the forms of aesthetic standardization promoted by state visuals of urban and housing projects. In making their claim to belonging one about the architecture, materials, and layout of the neighborhood, they conjured recognition as based on an aesthetic standard. Such forms of recognition were subject to political caprice and fragile, but they had historically proven to be some of the few factors that urban residents could mobilize against a hostile legal structure. Drawing on registers of negotiation that intertwined the legal, unofficial, and material as means for the recognition of rights to place and property, Bairros 1 and 2 reaffirmed the centrality of aesthetic concerns and the moral economy of materiality to understandings of belonging in Luanda.

Material Outcomes

Bairro 1's and Bairro 2's plans to rebuild would never be realized. In September 2012, Nova Vida, with the support of the provincial government, offered them, and the residents of Bairro 3, housing in Zango. Negotiations ensued. Initially, it appeared that Bairro 3 would be rehoused first. However, after Bairro 2's election of a residents' committee president who was a vocal MPLA supporter, they were rehoused first. Residents were moved to Zango in 2013. Members of SOS Habitat said that the residents' committee's president personally went to speak to someone at Nova Vida whom they believed to be a party member. Bairro 1 was rehoused in 2014. Bairro 3 was rehoused four years later, in 2018. I asked a resident of Bairro 3 why he thought that they were rehoused last. He responded that he believed that Bairro 1's and Bairro 2's threat to rebuild had concerned Nova Vida and the government. When I asked the same question to a member of SOS Habitat, he replied that Bairro 3 had forgotten the saying "Não é do MPLA quem quer, mas quem merece" (You don't get into the MPLA because you want to but because you deserve to).

In Luanda, the material world was a means of claiming belonging and demanding recognition in the face of a legal system that was a tool of elite power rather than a source of justice. This moral economy of materiality, while in theory having no place in the official considerations of Angola's legal system, had nevertheless infiltrated it. In a context of diminished state capacity to manage a cadaster or register property, aesthetic considerations had historically been a means for officials, courts, private companies, and bureaucracies to make decisions when faced with a lack of official documentation (also see Ghertner 2015). This does not mean that claims rooted in these considerations were always successful; laws could easily be used to undermine them, especially if this was in the interest of a powerful institution or individual. However, when, in the act and aftermath of demolition, companies and state institutions suddenly refused to consider this moral economy, they stoked strong emotions and anger.

The trauma of demolition lay not only in abstract rights being violated, but in the incursion into the material and tactile experiences of belonging through which accommodations with the state had been forged over the years. Demolition brought into stark relief that existing tacit modes of recognition were under pressure. The remaking of Luanda was resulting in the creation of a swathe of people who, left exposed to the caprices of powerful political and economic actors, were caught in cycles of expulsion as they struggled to have their previously seemingly settled claims to place recognized. However, even in the context of rampant land speculation and removal, the use of material markers to determine compensation suggests that they continued to provide a parallel and powerful space of negotiation between state and citizens, an emergent moral economy of materiality based in histories and processes of Indigenous city building.

CHAPTER FOUR

The Aesthesis of Class

Infrastructure and the Politics of Comfort

The importance of the musseques in anchoring claims to urban belonging and generating dissent with the aesthetic claims of the state should not distract us from the living conditions that residents decried. Lack of infrastructure and social services were facts of life that plagued musseque residents. These frustrations are widely felt across urban Africa, with demands for quality infrastructure having been identified as one of the primary drivers for new forms of enclaved privatized urbanism on the continent (Silver 2023). These demands point to the appeals and ambiguities of the aesthetic promises that inhered in oil-fueled national reconstruction. The aesthetics of belonging were felt across multiple registers, including not only assessments of design and materials but also the embodied experience of the promised new cities. These registers often came into conflict, revealing the fraught and unstable nature of aesthetic politics and hence the constant grappling with it as a site through which to imagine and enact belonging. While residents rejected the material and symbolic violence that inhered in demolition and questioned the negations of Indigenous urbanism and belonging that accompanied expulsions, they were attracted to the comfort promised in state spectacle (see chapter 1), located most powerfully in the embodied experience of the home.

State institutions' and private developers' discourses about national development tried to sidestep the overt conflicts generated by the visions of normative urbanism they promoted by appealing to many Luandans' deepest desire: a comfortable home. A *casa condigna* (decent home) or a house with *condições* (conditions) were the housing dreams that people most often elaborated on when discussing their hopes for the future. The terms largely referred to the presence of infrastructural connections that could facilitate everyday activities and create the ambience of comfort and modernity that urban residents strove for. The promise of care that stood at the heart of state propaganda and hopes for legitimation was therefore defined by an appeal to the embodied "promise of infrastructure" (Anand, Gupta, and Appel 2018, 8). While megaprojects and consumerism featured prominently as tools of regime legitimation, these were effective only because they contained an appeal to quotidian experiences such as driving one's car on a paved road and flushing human waste down a working toilet. The promise of comfort, achieved by rendering less stark the differentiation in infrastructure provision between the haves and have-nots, lay at the heart of the appeal of national reconstruction, as well as the contestation of it. Unfortunately, however, through the process of infrastructure and housing construction, residents began to understand that some people's aesthetic comfort was considered to be more important than others'.

In Luanda, the decline of infrastructural provision as one moved away from wealthier areas was notable as roads began to fray and sanitation services petered out. The insight that infrastructure is a marker of inequality is not a new one. Several studies have identified variances in infrastructural provision as a key indication of economic inequality and urban segregation (Appel 2012; Graham and Marvin 2001; Rodgers and O'Neill 2012). Equally, infrastructure highlights political inequalities. As one of the primary material instantiations of state provision, arguments over infrastructure are never simply about the practicalities of physical connection but always also political connection, inasmuch as they shape "the very definition of community, its possible futures, and its relation to the state" (Larkin 2018, 189). It is little surprise, then, that in an era when the rights of citizenship are increasingly being winnowed away by the supposed demands of "the market," infrastructure has become a primary site of contestation and negotiation. Demands for water and electricity sit at the heart of the pushback against the official and unofficial privatization of the state, as marginalized urban residents attempt to claim rights and recognitions they believe they have been excluded from (Anand 2011; von Schnitzler 2016). The architects of national reconstruction appeared to be at least implicitly aware of the symbolic significance of infrastructure, with part of the spectacle of national reconstruction involving the launch of infrastructure projects such as Água para Todos (Water for All) and Vias de Luanda (Luanda's Roads) as a means of performing state provision and care. In doing this, the Angolan state attempted to capitalize on the political expectations of inclusion that inhered in infrastructure. It is the nature of these desires and expectations, however, that struck me during my time in Luanda. It was not surprising to me that in my interactions in musseque areas, person after person expressed desires for better water, electricity, roads, public lighting, youth centers, and heath care facilities. However, the terms through which these desires were expressed suggested a realm of the political that moved the question of infrastructure to the sensuous. For those I spoke to, inclusion was not simply about having a connection but also about the aesthesis of infrastructure, with the home being the object in which these desires came together.

"Aesthesis," a term that describes the historically cultivated sensory experience of the world, lay at the center of arguments over infrastructure and belonging exhibited during a training about urban rights organized by a local NGO in Vamos Andar, a neighborhood in the municipality of Cazenga.[1] The event was held in a large hall that served as a nightclub on weekend nights and a community center during the day. The residents' committee offices were in the same building, on the second floor. In the middle of the empty hall, a projector, a computer, and a printer had been set up, although, given the lack of electricity, their presence could be described as aspirational. Plastic tables with yellow cloths covering them had been arranged in a semicircle, with the participants sitting at them and the NGO workers, all of whom were Angolan, sitting at the front. The participants consisted of thirteen men and two women, among them a primary school teacher, a tailor, and a member of the residents' committee. Patricia, one of the NGO workers, stood up and explained to everyone that the role of community-based organizations and NGOs was to advocate for better social conditions, such as improved access to water and better roads. Hugo, the most senior of the NGO employees, clarified that he and the others were there to help the participants identify the problems in their neighborhood. This was because no one knew their own pain as well as "the patient" did, he said, so, similarly, "the community" were the ones in the best position to identify what their neighborhood needed. However, he advised them that sometimes a patient had a pain in their hip, but the ultimate cause of the pain was something else in the body, so participants needed to think carefully about what constituted a cause and what constituted an effect. After distributing pieces of paper, he asked each participant to write one serious difficulty they believed their neighborhood faced.

The two top responses were "a lack of electricity" and "a lack of water." The latter point generated some discussion. When the statement "a lack of water" (*falta de água*) was first made, Hugo asked if it was accurate to say there was no water in the neighborhood (which would imply a *falta*) or if the issue was that there was a shortage (*escassez*). The answers to this question were mixed because they were contingent on where in the neighborhood a person lived. While people who lived close to the public water standposts agreed that one could say there was a shortage, those who lived farther away insisted there was a lack. Eventually, the group decided it was probably accurate to say that there was a shortage of water rather than a lack. But when Hugo asked one of the participants, Moises, what he had identified as the neighborhood's central problem, Moises loudly stated, "a lack of water." Hugo corrected him, saying that there was a "shortage," not a "lack." Moises, who had been visibly uncomfortable with the discussion about lack versus shortage suddenly blurted out, "Lack of water in my house! A lack of piped water!" Hugo paused for an instant and asked the group what they thought would happen if everyone had piped water in their homes. Moises replied that people would save money because water would be cheaper,[2] people would sleep more because they would not have to waste their time fetching water, and they would be able to dress better because it would be easier to wash clothes. He argued, drawing on tropes of musseque incivility, that some people would be careless with water, and, noting questions of materiality, that the construction of housing in his neighborhood, mostly with concrete blocks, might make the installation and maintenance of indoor plumbing difficult. Nevertheless, he argued, to experience "well-being" (*bem estar*), a person needed to have water and electricity so they could wash their clothes and bathe. "A *real* bath, not a bath with a jug," he commented, as the rest of the participants began to laugh (data from NGO training exercise, observation, Vamos Andar, Cazenga, 4 May 2011).

Moises's demands spoke of a world of sensuous and material comfort that would index state care. A clean body and clothes, a restful night's sleep, more time, and the expanding possibilities for consumption spoke to a meeting of aesthesis and political economy that shaped his everyday frustrations. Many people I interacted with described Luanda's musseques as "cheio de poeira" (full of dust). Piped water would provide the embodied experience of cleanliness that promised to lift Moises out of that state; his lack of access to it indexed his marginality. His response turned infrastructure into a question of aesthesis and the exploitative human-object relations that produced differential aesthetic experiences. In doing this it shifted the question of infrastructural violence and urban segregation away from the spectacular visuals of urban division or stark geographical differentiations and toward the quotidian interactions that produce differentiated everyday aesthesis. His argument was a protest against what Hugo took for granted as acceptable: that the toiling bodies of the economically marginalized should walk for kilometers to fetch water, replacing what would have been the leaking but enviable pipes that carried water from the grid into the taps of the economically better-off. To enjoy cleanliness, some people were forced to become literal "people as infrastructure" (Simone 2004), an exploitative, unenviable position in a city whose origins lay in enslavement. Moises's outburst indicated how the politics of comfort emerges at the intersection of the built environment and the political and economic relationships that constitute the possibilities of infrastructural aesthesis.

The provision of infrastructure sheds light on the fact that political recognition and belonging are starkly economically defined, as what were previously understood as classic Marshallian social rights now hinge on one's ability to pay for them (Gastrow 2020b). This is not surprising given burgeoning arguments that under conditions of neoliberalism, the rights previously afforded to those officially classified as citizens are now contingent on economic status, so that the wealthy enjoy rights and privileges that the poor do not, regardless of formal status (Ong 2006). While the forms of privilege and exclusion that emerged in Angola were arguably a product of the political economy of authoritarianism and the processes of neglect that accompanied it rather than explicit neoliberal policies, experiences of belonging were shaped by class and status. Class and status in Luanda were experienced through what was provided by the aesthesis of infrastructure—comfort or its lack.

The key site for understanding the infrastructural intersections that produced these aesthetic discrepancies in comfort was the home. As Louise White (1990) showed in her iconic study of sex work in colonial Nairobi, desires for domestic comfort have long produced their own historically specific economies and socialities. If, in her work, men's desires for comfort were embodied through feminized domestic care, in the form of not only sex but also cooked meals, bathing, and conversations, in Luanda they were starkly attached to the sensorial experience of infrastructure. Gandy (2005a, 28) has described the "modern home" as a "complex exoskeleton for the human body with its provision of water, warmth, light and other essential needs." The ability to access, produce, and maintain this exoskeleton revealed class differentiations in Luanda that were felt through the body. Differentiations in exposure to heat, noise, and smell were significant indicators of economic and political distinction. If demolitions indicated a stark and growing divide between those who could dwell and those to be uprooted due to shifts in the moral economies underpinning property recognition, the question of condições raised a subtle means though which urban exclusion and social hierarchy were reproduced: unequal access to the infrastructures (official and unofficial) that could render one's life "decent." Within this context, rehousing promised to lift people out of the set of provisional infrastructural relations into which they had been inserted and provide them with a casa condigna—a decent house—that would offer not only shelter but an aesthesis of comfort. However, rather than breaking with the existing sensuous distinctions that defined experiences of the urban, infrastructural inequality was built into the new housing projects, fueling complaints among Luandans who saw their continuing marginality reiterated in projects meant to deliver a postconflict era of prosperity and inclusion. Rather than necessarily strengthening affectual relations to the MPLA-state, the politics of comfort brewed anger as it showed how economic calculation defined the grounds for political recognition, something felt in the very everyday aesthesis of those affected. The spectacle of state care that inhered in images of infrastructure delivery was being unmade through the actual realization of this process.

Unofficial Infrastructures and Class Formation

Infrastructural differentiation has been central to shared understandings and experiences of living in Luanda. It is no surprise that the story "Luuanda," by renowned Angolan author Luandino Vieira, an iconic tale of a young musseque-dweller's life in the late colonial period, begins with the principal character listening to the sound of rainfall on the corrugated iron roof of the home he shares with his mother. It is through sounds, smells, tactile properties, and sights that infrastructure is immediately experienced. Nowhere is this more intensely felt than in the home. When summer rains flooded the city, the complaints one heard were not that workplaces had been submerged but that people had had to scramble to protect their personal belongings as water rushed into their residences. An inordinate amount of time and money was invested in trying to create a domesticity of aesthetic comfort. Even those with few resources would save to build a water tank in their yards, and eventually try to pay for an electricity connection (legal or illegal) or purchase a cheap generator. Moving up the income ladder, air conditioners, water pumps, filters, three-phase electricity boxes, air fresheners, and closed windows (to prevent dust from entering) were all methods employed to keep the house a place of aesthetic comfort for the bodies that lived there. The aesthetics of belonging were intimately experienced in the interior of the home, where personal investments intersected with state provision. The lack of capacity to enjoy these comforts was keenly felt. Tracking inhabitants' attempts to create a world of aesthetic comfort, however, revealed that in contrast to tales of enclaved urbanism, which expose a stark divide between those with access to a formal grid and those who are left outside, the situation in Luanda (and for that matter most African cities) is more complex.

Luanda is best described as a "self-service city" (McFarlane 2010), defined by a "back-up culture" (Trovalla and Trovalla 2015) or do-it-yourself urbanism

(Gastrow 2020b). These terms describe cities in which the lack of working infrastructure means that people from all socioeconomic backgrounds must improvise provisional infrastructural networks in order to produce the desired effects of infrastructural well-being. While detailed statistics for Luanda are not available, the 2014 Angolan census estimated that only 50.9 percent of urban dwellers had access to electricity from the grid, 6 percent were connected to the official sanitation system, and at a national level only 17 percent of the population received its drinking water from a tap linked to the public water system (INE 2016).[3] In Luanda, only 46.9 percent of people had access to what the census defined as a "suitable source of drinking water" (INE 2016). Given this context, a variety of improvised infrastructures were necessary to create a comfortable home. Even the wealthy could not escape infrastructural interruptions, as the same fragile grid that supported the poor also supplied their homes. Luandans evoked this as something that had historically bound urban residents during the postcolonial period: no one could escape the difficult urban conditions. The rich and the poor had to use the same potholed roads, suffer the same electricity cuts, and live through the same food shortages and sanitation crises. Infrastructural deprivation created the basis for affective links among residents.

This commonality of suffering had, however, begun to change in the 1990s with the abandonment of socialism and its accompanying ideologies as well as the opening of the country's markets. Generators and water tanks became readily available for private purchase, and new gated communities offered private infrastructure solutions to the city's service delivery shortcomings. The tendency toward geographic and aesthetic segregation accelerated after the civil war as escalating numbers of wealthy Angolans and expatriates moved into the gated communities of Talatona or the closed high-rises of the city center. This was for the most part driven by a desire to access quality private infrastructure rather than for security concerns (Frias and Rodrigues 2018). While these trends reintroduced a dynamic of social and spatial segregation that had not been present since the colonial period (Rodrigues 2012), they still could not free the wealthy from the city's material conditions. Even the shining tower of Sonangol's downtown headquarters and the immaculate lawns of Talatona's condominiums were subject to them. In 2012, a media article revealed that Chevron had instructed its employees living in the Monte Belo condominium in Talatona, a $250 million development, to use bottled water for drinking, cooking, and brushing teeth. Investigations revealed that water in the complex was not from the grid but brought in by tankers and stored in giant vats, often from untreated sources (Marques de Morais 2012). Many of the city's new buildings were running up bills of thousands of dollars a month to fuel their generators, as the grid could not support them. This was not a tale of a stark divide between infrastructural deprivation and infrastructural plenty but a gradated system of privilege based on financial capacity to produce other options. For what was revealed in Luanda was that even the unofficial is not equal. While much literature on African urbanism has celebrated the vitality of people making do, there is a significant inequality in the capacity to do so. Comfort, Charlotte Johnson (2018, 157) reminds us, "sits at the nexus between individual effort and external support or constraint," and where external supports falter in contexts of state neglect, people are left to draw on personal resources.

THE (GENDERED) DISCOMFORTS OF HOME

Without question, the areas of the city most deprived of formal infrastructures were its musseques. Musseque residents simply did not have the same financial power as many in the formally planned areas of the city to create backups and high-quality replacement infrastructure. Improvisations in the musseque, which lacked the intervening support of the grid, usually could not make up for the scarcity of working formal infrastructure, something keenly felt in the everyday life of the home. In my many discussions with residents of musseques about what would be required to make their neighborhoods better, they regularly returned to water, electricity, road access, and sanitation. Discussions with women about their desire for these services in relation to the home best revealed what was at stake.

I had spent many mornings and afternoons visiting Dona Cristina, who had lived in Vamos Andar since the late 1990s, when she moved to her sister's home after separating from her husband.[4] She later moved in with a man from Cabo Verde, whom, she confessed, she had stayed with for financial reasons. She had eventually left him when he wanted them to formally marry. She now lived in a concrete-block home that he had built for her, with a kitchen, indoor washroom, two bedrooms, and a large lounge. People described her as a *mulher forte* (a strong woman). Despite my repeated explanations that I could not help, she used my presence to discuss what she believed the neighborhood needed to improve itself. In her area there was a single public water stand, no tarred roads, and irregular electricity access. The crux of this situation was explained to me, however, in terms of her ongoing difficulties in trying to purchase groceries. As I sat with her and her friends in the neighborhood one afternoon, Dona Cristina recounted that when she had moved to the area a good dirt road led to it and there was regular electricity. In the late 1990s, however, someone from EDEL, the provincial electricity company, decommissioned the substation that fed the area. Since then, electricity supply had become unreliable. While Dona Cristina voiced various concerns about the lack of regular electricity, including a belief that poor public lighting was responsible for crime in the neighborhood, her frustrations focused on the intimate sphere of the home and everyday labor:

> Electricity is a problem, a serious problem. Electricity is life. Electricity is energy. Electricity is health. With electricity you can enjoy a lot of things. With a freezer in your house, you can have fresh groceries, you can sell beer, you can make ice cream and ice, you can do lots of things and we don't have this right. We live from the generator, but we also want to drink cold water. You can buy five liters, leave it [the generator] to work for two hours and the water is cold. You'll drink cold water. But in the case of groceries, you have to go to the market every day, the fish is poorly conserved, the meat is poorly conserved. Those green flies, you ask how much the fish is, how much is the meat, the woman waves the flies away, you will see the fish or the vegetables, and you'll eat that meat, because you want to eat, you'll buy it. Cheap fish, you see a container of fish, but for you to keep it, where will you conserve it? We tried to do this with the generator once . . . we bought the fish to keep in my house, but we were worried because the day we had arranged [to eat it] was delayed. The next day, I said no, if this fish stays here one more day, we are going to have a serious problem, but the generator was working . . . (Dona Cristina, group discussion, Cazenga, 27 April 2011)

Her friend jumped in to confirm the event, "Yeah, we had to buy fuel." "Yup," Dona Cristina continued, "we all contributed." Stating the final word on the matter, her friend sighed, "To sustain that fish for two days. . . . It was a sacrifice" (residents of Vamos Andar, group discussion, Cazenga, 27 April 2011).

Electricity in this case was acutely felt in daily planning. It was the difference between having to go to the market every day or purchasing groceries for the week. It was the difference between having to pay for fuel to run the generator to enjoy a cold drink or taking that drink from the refrigerator without thinking. It was the difference between being able to sell beer and ice from one's yard or losing out on a business opportunity. Dona Cristina felt the lack of infrastructure through the mediums of coolness and warmth, freshness and decay—preserved versus rotting fish, cold drinks versus warm drinks. The absence of infrastructure was acutely felt in the labor—usually gendered—that had to be undertaken to try to attain the standards of life that its absence stole from people. The cost was measured in hours spent going to public water standposts, lugging water home in jerrycans, purchasing diesel, and storing it for the occasional use of a noisy generator. Quotidian gendered labor was keenly determined by the kinds of formal and informal infrastructures that people had access to. Women repeatedly complained of infrastructural short-comings, since they were the ones forced every day to reckon with resolving them in the household. This labor revealed the shifting links to the privileged city. For the labor that musseque residents undertook for themselves in their own homes, they also undertook for the wealthier residents of the city, becoming the human infrastructure that enabled the wealthy to sustain a comfortable home aesthesis in the context of infrastructural breakdown.

PEOPLE AS INFRASTRUCTURAL BACKUPS

In my home, the economic determinants of urban relations created by the intersections of official and unofficial infrastructure became apparent when we were faced with a continuing water shortage. The building was a typical colonial-era modernist mid-rise near the city center, located in the Kinaxixe area, part of the former colonial urban core. At the time of their construction, these apartment blocks embodied the aspirations of an ascendent colonial bourgeoisie, their tropical modernist architecture representing the most con-temporary forms of technology and design. In 2011, as with many of Luanda's buildings, mine appeared ragged on the outside, a perception that continued into the shared areas, with the entrance having no gate or door, and the skele-tons of useless postboxes decorating the ground-floor wall. The trek up to the fifth floor was not always pleasant given that the elevator had long since ceased to work. It appeared this journey was likewise one that the city's water supply found difficult to undertake. My landlady claimed that the reason we had no water was because the new Escom high-rise had powerful water pumps that were pulling all the water in the area toward it.[5] I did not know much about engineering, but I thought this was probably not the case. In Luanda, the aging infrastructure and shortage of supply often means that there is simply not enough pressure in the system for even those living on the ground floor to have water without an electric water pump. When they continued to run during water cuts, water pump's motors often burned out.

In our case we were hit by a triple problem. First, the water pressure was too low to make it up to the fifth floor. Second, our water tank (an infrastructure that many Luandans purchased to store water from the grid in anticipation of future water cuts) had a leak that we learned about only when the grid supply was cut. The water pump burned out while pumping nonexistent water when we turned on the taps. Coordinating the fixing of everything took weeks. In the meantime, the apartment began to reek as the drains dried out. The smell of the bathroom made it a distinctly unpleasant place. Nevertheless, there was a backup in case our existing provisional infrastructural system of tanks and pumps broke down. My bathroom had a large plastic barrel, which the domestic worker filled with water just in case none made it up the pipes that, at present, appeared mostly decorative. The gap between the existing physical official infrastructure and the actual aesthesis of the apartment was a yawning one. The interior of the apartment was beautifully decorated with new tiles, contemporary domestic appliances (washing machine, microwave, iron), and a large flatscreen television with satellite connection. Yet we could not use the washing machine, flush the toilets without scooping water from the large bins in the bathroom, or bathe without the object that Moises had so derided: the jug. With no water flowing, the bathroom water container could not be easily filled; eventually it was empty. The next backup infrastructure was then activated. Hanging out at the ground level of our building was a group of ostensibly unemployed young men. When I had first moved in, my friend's driver had paid them 1,000 kwanzas (ten dollars at the time) to carry my bags up the stairs, their exertions replacing the defunct elevator. Now they became the building's plumbing, going in search of a tap somewhere to fill jerrycans and heave them to the fifth floor. These young men were literally "people as infrastructure," part of the patched-together arrangements that I, my landlady and most people of the cidade had developed over the years to ensure that their sensorial experience of home matched their desired standard of living. My flushing toilet and clean clothes depended on their exertions. Their labor substituted for the formal grid.

AbdouMaliq Simone (2004, 408) speaks of "people as infrastructure" to describe how temporary social relationships forged by those in precarious conditions are created and mobilized in order to support and reproduce the conditions for their survival in the city. His imagination of these connections is largely based on an everyday hustle, and that, indeed, is what the young men in my building were involved in—hustling to get by. These accounts of hustling, however, do not take into account the power relations inherent to the divisions of labor and broader economies that force the production of these provisional relations of making do. The quick steps of security guards lugging groceries up multiple flights of stairs, young men's aching arms as they carted liters of water for wealthy clients, and domestic workers' movements in and out of apartment blocks to check that generators were supplied with diesel not only enabled the reproduction of aesthetic comfort for the wealthy but revealed the deep inequality that lay in the "violence that inheres in the instrumentalization of human life as people become means to ends" (Doherty 2017, 193). Such processes of objectification are arguably inherent to contemporary racial capitalism, which transforms humans into objects to be exploited and valuated (James 1989 [1938]). Nevertheless, these processes are not equally distributed, especially when some people become the replacement objects that enable time and leisure for others. Conditions of improvisation often expose and exacerbate inequality even as they might provide opportunities for some to profit (Desai et al. 2015). The young men who "idled" in the building's entrance became its pipes and plumbing, dragging water up the flights of stairs so that I could enjoy the pleasures of bathing, even if it did involve a jug.

When we highlight the human-object relations through which the comforts of home for some people are the products of the infrastructural labor of others, we are not simply underscoring that cities and the experience of them are shaped by inequality. Rather, this focus on "infrastructure as people" as a form of exploitation stresses that in the existing city, class formation is contingent not only on the visual spectacles of wealth but also on the subtle everyday worlds of comfort enabled by infrastructural access, which is not necessarily provided by the state. We should keep in mind that in "back-up" cities, the public grid forces both the wealthy and the poor into conditions of informality (Naqvi 2018). The cool touch of the air conditioner, the thirst-quenching of cold water, the feeling of being freshly bathed, and the electric light glowing when the surrounding streets were dark, were often more likely to be the result of a generator and jerrycans than of "the grid." They reflect the differential capacity to draw on the market to create a network of human and physical infrastructure to constitute a desirable home aesthesis.

The capacity to mobilize funds to make unofficial infrastructures produce the sensations that people associate with gridded life marked income and status differences and created the embodied feeling of class distinction. While access to "the grid" certainly did index distinction, inasmuch as people in officially planned areas, which were more expensive to live in, tended to be the ones connected to the formal grid, connection in itself did not mean reliable access to the services promised. This is even more the case in the historical cidade, where the ongoing physical deterioration of many buildings led Angola's most prominent political hip-hop star, MCK, to release a track titled "Vertical Ghettos." In this song he describes the infrastructural breakdown of the cidade and mocks its inhabitants for thinking they are better than people who live in the musseques. In this sense, studies that trace the physical distribution of official infrastructure as markers of segregation or inequality are not necessarily capturing the realities of urban distinction. What marked class distinction was urban residents' capacity to draw on a range of unofficial and provisional infrastructures to create worlds of aesthetic flight from the city in their own areas of movement: the interior of the house, vehicles, restaurants, and so on. These informal infrastructures created a geography of classed aesthesis whose outlines could not be captured by the maps of planners, which tracked the formal distribution of services. Official maps could not show the relations that provisional infrastructures created, neither the feelings of shared experience or exclusion nor the everyday interactions that enabled the production of aesthetic comfort for some through the labor of others. Provisional infrastructures revealed the webs through which people's aesthetic lives were determined by economic logics and the urban distinctions that turned some people into others' infrastructure.

Differential provision of infrastructure did not so much divide people as bind them to one another through socioeconomic arrangements of making do. It is the implicit knowledge of one's ranking within these arrangements, I suggest, that indicated to people where they fitted in the urban hierarchy. This, in turn, suggests what lay at the heart of the desire to live in the Angolan state's new housing projects. For, in offering houses *em condições* (with conditions), the Angolan government was promising to use state resources to level the playing field, to create a context where people could be lifted out of these provisional arrangements and into a new world of infrastructural well-being. The failure to provide an equitable home aesthesis, however, revealed that, in the end, the housing policy, while cloaked in the language of state developmentalism, had designed into its very details the existing logic of infrastructural discrimination. As such, it reproduced the economic definition of belonging that lay at the heart of the new Angola and, with that, quotidian experiences of aesthetic marginalization.

Designing Aesthetic Inequality:
Angola's Postconflict Housing Policy

The MPLA's key 2008 election promise, known as the "1 Million Houses" program, marked a shift from the "first phase" of national reconstruction, which had focused on basic infrastructure (roads, water and electrical connections), to the "second phase," which emphasized housing (Soares de Oliveira 2015). Under pressure to deliver a peace dividend to Angolans and show that record oil profits were being well spent, the move was a popular and strategic investment. Although publicized as state housing provision, the PNUH (National Program for Urbanism and Housing), the official initiative under which the 1 Million Houses promise fell, foresaw a mixture of private and public supply. The state committed to constructing 11 percent of the promised housing, while the rest was to be built by cooperatives, private investors, and through site-and-service schemes (Cain 2017a). Even though they constituted only a fraction of the planned housing, the MPLA-state used representations of state-subsidized housing schemes to capture the public's imagination. Featured in government advertisements and MPLA propaganda, these projects came to stand as symbols of state capacity, care, and wealth (see chapter 1). However, the wave of enthusiasm for these new investments was undercut by the inequalities that marked them.

State housing projects were divided into two categories. One consisted of state-subsidized housing that was available for purchase. Nova Vida and the multiple Chinese-designed satellite cities, referred to locally as *novas centralidades* (new centralities), fell into this category. These projects were aimed at what MPLA election propaganda described as those people with "greater purchasing power" and required formal employment or personal savings to qualify for purchase. The type of housing on offer was comprised of apartment blocks and large single-stand residences; prominent developments included social services, such as the flagship new centrality, Kilamba, just outside of Luanda, which had paved roads, parking areas, schools, clinics, and offices where residents could apply for identity cards. Conveniently, both Kilamba and Nova Vida had supermarkets located close to the entrances to the projects. The second category of housing, referred to as "social housing" (*habitação social*), was found in resettlement zones such as Zango, Panguila, and Projecto Morar. These areas had been built to rehouse forcibly removed populations, and while it did not seem that housing recipients would be forced to purchase their new residences, there remained no clarity, when I was undertaking my research, about whether people removed to these areas would eventually be forced to pay rent on the homes.[6] The houses there were typically small, single-level constructions, with no paved roads and decidedly haphazard infrastructure. Initially there were no social services in the areas, although private and public actors subsequently provided schools, clinics, shopping areas, and state administrative offices. As such, postconflict housing policy clearly distinguished between two groups: those who could pay and those who could not.

The division between citizens based on income was reproduced in housing design and further exacerbated by the infrastructural provision made available for homes. Central to the appeal of Kilamba and other new centralities were

Figure 4.1. Kilamba waiting for inhabitants, 2011.

Figure 4.2. Zango 4, 2012.

the promises of infrastructure. The publicity booklet that had been given away for free with the state newspaper, *Jornal de Angola*, the day after the opening of the first phase of the project emphasized this. It proudly stated that "the city of Kilamba is planned with basic infrastructures: such as a road network, the drainage of rainwater and wastewater, ETAR [sewerage treatment plant] for 35,000 cubic meters a day; a water network, ETA [water treatment plant] for 40,000 cubic meters a day, electricity substations and distribution network, telecommunications and public transport terminals."[7] The text was reinforced by visuals displaying these infrastructures, so that people could see what was usually hidden. When the first phase of the project opened on 11 July 2011, it became a new activity to drive to the still-empty city simply to look at what had been built. Schools took students on fieldtrips to Kilamba, where they were allowed to walk around the model apartment, on display so the public could see what the Angolan state was able to provide. The apartment included a fully equipped kitchen and bathroom. Observers walked over gleaming white tiles. Switches, taps, showers, flush toilets, and outlets for appliances promised working infrastructural connections. The apartments featured tiny balconies that could accommodate air-conditioning units. In Nova Vida, a state-subsidized housing project originally aimed at civil servants, special infrastructures such as water treatment plants and power substations had also been installed.[8] In order to ensure the smooth provision of services, the management of water, electricity, sanitation, and road maintenance had been outsourced to a private consortium, which relayed residents' concerns to the relevant state-owned entities (former employee of Imogestin, interview, Kilamba Kiaxi, 19 October 2011). If the "standard of living" has long been a means for states to compete with each other at an international level (de Grazia 2005), in postconflict Angola it was a means for the MPLA to prove the legitimacy of its wartime victory and postconflict rule. By providing infrastructural services to citizens, it engaged them through the register of promised embodied experience, bringing people into the fold through their domestic comfort. State care and political inclusion would be experienced through the splash of water on one's skin, the feel of tiles under bare feet, and the hum of a working refrigerator.

The provision and management of infrastructures, however, simultaneously highlighted the centrality of economic concerns in the processes of inclusion and the impacts of this on the aesthetics of belonging. For, as was made abundantly clear, Zango and similar rehousing areas were not provided with the same infrastructural services that were on display at Kilamba or Nova Vida. In an interview, an employee of the companies managing housing construction in

Zango explained why the infrastructural provision in Zango was so glaringly discrepant. It had to do with the financing of construction and the process of re-housing. The representative stated that although Zango's masterplan included full infrastructural connections (water, electricity, sanitation), when it came to rehousing, it was the client who determined what infrastructure would be built. Clients, typically the company or ministry overseeing a demolition and relocation, would consult the masterplan and then tell the company respon-sible for housing construction which infrastructures they were willing to pay for (representative of construction company, interview, Zango, 23 July 2012). The result was blatantly discordant service provisions, as it remained subject to the whims of the client which connections were deemed financially viable. With residents of Zango not among those with "greater purchasing power," the Angolan state seemed unwilling to provide the same megainfrastructural investments that it had advertised that Kilamba's residents were going to enjoy. In an interview with an architect involved in the 1 Million Houses program, I asked why housing sometimes appeared to be constructed with no matching infrastructure. The reason he provided was explicitly financial. The govern-ment simply could not afford to provide infrastructure, and so it had to build what he termed "progressive infrastructure" in the rehousing areas, adding infrastructural connections when there was money available, and otherwise relying on private investors to construct these in return for access to land or other perks (architect Sílvio, interview, Alvalade, 16 January 2012). A represen-tative of the PRP provided a similar explanation in trying to justify the move toward building what he described as *casas evolutivas* ("evolving houses," or incremental housing). These consisted of two divisions and a bathroom, rather than the two rooms, bathroom, kitchen, and lounge of most existing social housing models. The idea, he explained, was that people could gradually add on to the house over time rather than have the state provide everything. This would cost the state half of what he claimed was the unit price of between $21,000 and $25,000 of the current social housing model (PRP representative, interview, Praia do Bispo, 3 November 2011). As would become clear later, casas evolutivas tended to lack even the basic infrastructure of the existing social housing. The state's housing plan explicitly divided people into socioeconomic hierarchies, not only in size and design but also through imagining what kind of infrastructure they deserved. These decisions were rooted in imaginations of a qualitative difference between musseque residents and those who lived in the cidade, a difference that those affected by this imagination contested, recognizing it as lying at the root of their political marginalization.

Experiencing Classed Citizenship

The immediate impression of horizontal versus vertical living, paved roads versus dust, and social services versus none were stark visual reminders of the discrepant levels of investment that had been made in housing projects aimed at different income groups. However, experiences of socioeconomic distinction and discrimination were often more subtle, and, in many ways, more insidious, resting on assumptions about not only who could afford but also who could cope without the "comforts of home" (White 1990). These sentiments were conspicuous in the frustrations that Diogo, an advertising executive, expressed regarding his search for a new home. Despite earning a fairly good salary, he was finding it difficult to purchase an apartment for himself and his wife in the area of his choice—Talatona. The problem was, he explained, that the government's housing policy and the prevailing housing market was not catering to a "classe média" (middle class). The price of the well-serviced and well-located housing he wanted was too high, and, he explained, unlike the "classe baixa" (lower class), Angola's middle class was not cut out for the demands of infrastructural shortage:

> My concern nowadays is much more with what is going to happen with the middle class, what are we going to do with the middle class. For the lower classes [camadas mais baixas] there is a social aspect, an aspect of expectation, there's an aspect which is complicated to resolve, but I think that the lower class is a class that has, not more resources, but more *skills* to work the system, whether through self-building or other things. The lower class, for example, I'll give some examples: The lower class can manage, if I am in a place with no water, no electricity, I can manage to live because I already lived in Cazenga for twenty years without water and electricity. The middle class can't cope with this.[9] (Diogo, interview, Talatona, 18 August 2011)

In Diogo's account, there were some people—the poor or "lower class"—who simply did not suffer in the same way from a lack of infrastructure, because they were used to doing without. This, of course, ignored the deep aspirations embedded in the promise of aesthetic comfort and the ways these were thwarted by the economic demands of achieving it.

Aesthetic inequality was experienced as an embodied marginalization from belonging. This embodied marginalization was the experiential version of what has long been a hallmark of political incorporation in Angola, that access to citizenship rights is "a sociopolitical privilege and not a universal right" (Martins 2017, 101). This "privilege" tends to be determined by an individual's relationship to the ruling MPLA's centers of power, a relationship that often determines economic status (Messiant 1992). Climbing the socio-economic ladder is often contingent on cultivating personalized networks of influence rather than on merit per se. Economic marginalization therefore tends not only to be accompanied by a relative exclusion from classical Marshallian notions of citizenship but also indexes a marginalization from the personalized relations of power that could move one up the social hierarchy. This systemic marginalization, and the economic production of citizenship— a classed citizenship—that accompanied it, came together in the aesthetic experience and performance of the infrastructured house. Those who were excluded from accessing services in their homes felt it as an embodied political exclusion based on economic hierarchy. They felt their status in the city in their quotidian experience of home that marked the distinction between them and the wealthy. These distinctions, they believed, were being reproduced in the rehousing zones. Negative assessments of government rehousing zones pivoted on, among other things, the question of infrastructure and aesthesis, which became the basis for assessing one's position within an economically determined hierarchy of citizenship.

In June 2011, a group of residents had gathered beneath a tree in Bairro 1, sitting on white plastic chairs or lounging on the hood of a parked car that one of the residents used for his taxi business. The group, who had arranged to meet to provide me with background to the demolitions they had suffered, drifted into discussing the question of rehousing. The women raised objections to the group's promised rehousing in Zango. One of the men lamented that the housing in Zango was not "habitação condigna" because electricity had to be illegally accessed. For him, Zango was therefore simply another "musseque." Pushing back against this description, Bernardo, from SOS Habitat, argued that although the area lacked sanitation, it had electricity connections and was "urbanized," so it could not be considered a musseque.

Augusta, in her twenties and heavily pregnant, was having none of this. She interrupted the discussion to call for recognition of the equal aesthetic needs of urban residents: "If someone asked me . . . where would you like to live? I would respond like this: I would also like to live in the Nova Vida project, because I have the same qualities that any citizen living in the Nova Vida project possesses." The statement elicited laughter and snickers, and Bernardo immediately tried to explain why she was mistaken in her assessment. Nova Vida, he emphasized, was a government project but one with "private ends. It's commercial, like that stall there selling biscuits, this [Nova Vida] is the government's biscuit, it's there to be sold. And what is the price of a house there? Two hundred thousand and something, three hundred thousand?" The group jumped in, discussing prices with the most expensive suggestion reaching $450,000. Triumphantly, Bernardo continued, "Dona Augusta, just to say that you say that you have the same qualities, you don't. Do you have 400,000 kwanzas right now? $400,000?" "Okay," Augusta responded, "but. . . ." "There are people who do," Bernardo said. Suddenly another woman jumped in, "But she is also human!" The rest of the group began to laugh. "She's human in human terms," Bernardo responded, "but in terms of money. . . ." The two women began to argue with him, saying they should be able to express how they felt and that the state belonged to the people. The second woman, Delfina, continued, "People are free, aren't they? I want to live like they live, how they live." Bernardo began to laugh, but Delfina persevered. "I also want a house *em condições* [with conditions], a decent home [*uma casa condigna*]."

As the discussion continued, the women begin to find some humor in the situation. Raising her voice, Augusta chuckled, "It [the rehousing] could also be in a project, in . . . the Jardim de Eden project.[10] I can also go there!" Her friends began to laugh. "I can!" she repeated. One of the men, Samuel, a member of the residents' committee, gravely interrupted: "I have already said . . . this [the Nova Vida project] is for their businesses. This is not for any type of people. Because it is like this: Here, there are people who are considered people and there are people that are not considered to be so. So, a hierarchy exists here. Do you understand? There is a hierarchy. There is level A and there is level B." "And a level C!" another man chimed in. Samuel continued, "This means that Nova Vida is for level A. Those of you who are level B cannot enter." Bernardo exclaimed, "You have to go to Zango!"

Delfina refused to accept this logic: "But the people of level B have the same needs [as the people of level A]. I am still focusing on this because I *can* also live there [in Nova Vida]." Samuel shook his head. "In the city, do you understand, if they take you from an apartment building, they will also put you in an apartment building. Now, not you, who they already found, so to say, you who are . . . in a shack, right? You are in a shack, as far as they are concerned. . . . So, in practice, they put you in something slightly better than you already are, that is, they put you in Zango, which is urbanized, right, but without sanitation." "So, Dona Augusta," Bernardo said, turning to look at her, "we are going to Zango, we are going to Panguila, because our site is there, that is our place."

The conversation underlined how the government's rehousing projects were automatically interpolated into existing understandings of status, income, and political inclusion, communicated through housing and infrastructure. While Augusta claimed she had the same "qualities" as the residents of Nova Vida, Bernardo was at pains to explain that economic resources, rather than a shared humanity, defined "quality." Nova Vida and Zango represented qualitatively different people within an urban hierarchy: the level "A," in Nova Vida as opposed to the levels "B" and "C" in Zango. The future location, design, and infrastructural conditions of the housing itself—small and poorly serviced—symbolized this qualitative difference. The government's move to rehouse them to Zango merely reproduced their marginality. They may have left the musseque, but they remained aesthetically excluded, their desires for comfort unmet and unrecognized.

Contesting Aesthetic Exclusion

On 13 August 2013, commuters stuck in Luanda's early morning gridlock were startled by the appearance of banners, posters, and protesters along one of the city's primary arteries, Rua Comandante Arguelles, colloquially known as the Rua do Prenda. An array of signs and posters bearing slogans such as "Where are my rights?," "The best conditions are in Margoso," and "There should be decent housing" greeted the shocked drivers. One of the city's central musseques, Margoso, had been threatened with removal. Public protest was carefully controlled in Angola with mass expressions of anti-MPLA or antistate sentiment generally met with violence. In this case, however, anger regarding their proposed rehousing had led Margoso's residents to risk state reprisal. Provincial authorities had promised to rehouse residents in Zango 4, part of the Zango rehousing zone. Following earlier discussions between the residents' committee and provincial authorities, neighborhood representatives had visited Zango 4 to view the houses that the government had offered them. What they found angered them. The government was offering them casas evolutivas. These were the houses that the PRP representative had suggested were built to save costs. They were tiny and had no plastering, kitchen, or proper flooring. These basic elements had to be added on to by residents, hence the "evolving" nature of the house.

The residents of Margoso were outraged. Printouts of photographs they had taken of the houses and of the poor infrastructure in Zango 4 were displayed on boards. The large cloth banners included statements such as "Out with Zango 4" and described the government houses as "casebres" (hovels). Images showed people collecting water from a broken pipe, illegally accessed because, it appeared, the houses did not have water connections and were unfinished. The police were brought in. Witnesses reported that upon seeing the images of the housing and accompanying conditions, at least one policeman was so disgusted that he promised the police would not intervene as long as the protest remained peaceful. It did, and by early afternoon, residents had mostly dispersed, although a few posters and banners remained in place.

When I questioned some of Margoso's residents about why they had decided to protest, one theme became clear: They thought the housing in Zango 4 was beneath them. Musseque residents, even if they lamented the conditions of their homes in comparison to the cidade, Talatona, or Kilamba, nevertheless valued the concrete-block houses they had constructed. In addition, in this case the infrastructure in Margoso was superior to that being offered in Zango. Despite difficulties, they had relatively good access to water and electricity and they were close to hospitals, shops, and transport. At the time, Zango 4, in comparison, had virtually no public services, and the houses they were to receive had substandard sanitation and water connections. They criticized the lack of schools as well as the distance from the city center, where most of them worked. In contrast, one of the members of the residents' committee told me that if the government were to promise them accommodation in Kilamba, I would return the next day to find Margoso empty, as everyone would have moved voluntarily. Margoso's residents were making a strong claim against the economic logic inherent to rehousing, which condemned them to small, uncomfortable, poorly provisioned housing that would make their lives even more uncomfortable. They were demanding their right to a "casa em condições," a house with conditions, to be freed from the infrastructural labor and discomfort to which they were exposed.[11]

Key to the protest was, as the discussion about Kilamba revealed, that Margoso's residents were not against demolition per se. This was an assertion that came up many times in my discussions with those who had either experienced demolitions or were facing the prospect of them. What they wanted was to be transferred to housing that had "conditions," even as the government claimed that it did not have the resources to provide these. The house, as one of the architects interviewed had argued, should be enough. This claim, however, overlooked a key reason why the house was central to a sense of well-being, status, and belonging in the city. Not only because it indicated financial stability and urban integration, as the previous chapters have shown, but also because it engendered the "comforts of home," the sensuous experience of well-being that people had gradually invested in over the years, and that they had hoped government housing schemes would provide. The housing schemes did provide this, but only to those who had the money. The rest were left— once again—to retreat into Luanda's backup culture, using their labor, time, and meager finances to try to produce the aesthesis of home that they desired. Rehousing therefore ingrained into house design existing experiences of inequality, generating anger toward the process and products of national reconstruction. It was not only radical acts of segregation and conspicuous consumption but also the subtle inequities of aesthetic comfort produced by the crisscrossing provisional conduits of people, objects, and finances that delineated class and belonging in the city, and with that, a politics of comfort that defined the boundaries of political belonging and recognition.

CHAPTER FIVE

Aesthetic Dissent

Negotiating Worlding from
an African Metropolis

Yvette was an Angolan-Portuguese urban planner. She had grown up in Luanda but had lived outside of the country since she was a teenager, when she moved to Portugal to further her education. With Angola booming and the Portuguese economy in freefall, she had returned, taking advantage of her optimal labor position of being a skilled dual-national. Portuguese companies were desperate to enter Angola to take advantage of the exploding construction market but were hamstrung by visa difficulties, a shortage of individuals with relevant work experience and education, and no knowledge of local business contexts. For them, Yvette was the perfect employee. Her Portuguese nationality made European companies feel at ease with her. She did not require a visa, possessed sought-after skills, and enjoyed extensive local networks coupled with a deep knowledge of the country. Yvette had been able to leverage her unique position for a good salary in a company that also provided housing and transport. For some, oil-boom Angola was a site of unparalleled opportunity.

While sipping a beer at Rialto, a pizzeria overlooking the breathtaking promenade, she explained to me the division of labor in the architecture and planning firm where she was employed.[1] In Luanda, a small team managed contact with clients, worked on small assignments, and oversaw projects under construction. In Portugal, a larger studio coordinated big ventures, designing them there and sending them back to the Angolan team to implement. Despite my only having been in Luanda for about three weeks at the time we spoke, I had already heard complaints that the city was being designed by foreigners who did not understand the environmental, historical, and social contexts of the city. Initially, Yvette did not question the division of labor but noted that it led to the tendency to follow a "Western model." As our conversation progressed into a deeper discussion of Luanda's challenges, she grew impassioned. On the question of mid- and high-rises and whether Angolans liked them or not, a topic I would eventually discover reached back into the colonial period, she paused for a second and then began a long reflection on the failures of the new architectures:

> Look, wait, me, as an architect, as someone who works with architects, wow, the buildings here . . . full of glass. So, you have to think, you make the modernism, the tropical modernism that was built here in the sixties and the seventies, with concrete but with lots of circulation of air. *Epa* it was much more functional than filling buildings with layers of glass, and then you have to think of air-conditioning, and the air-conditioning doesn't work and then you have electricity problems and . . . wow! Really, *epa*, there are some things being destroyed, but the majority of projects are usually done out there . . . then they build them here and they don't work. So, are you really going to learn from this? I believe that there are studios here that need to learn. For example, I work in a building that has the most incredible view of the city. But its interior is an oven, nothing works in there! The building is beautiful, the building is beautiful, but the interior doesn't work.

I tried to intervene, but she continued, ignoring my eager attempts to move the conversation to another topic.

> And then, there is no coherence in the architecture that is being made here, because they order a building from who knows where, from the Egyptians, from the Israelis, I don't know. Then they use arches as if it were Islamic architecture. . . . There is no coherence, there is no coherence in the dialogue, and they are not searching for an African identity you see. Instead of going and looking, because there are, there are some African architects, some already well known in South Africa. . . . So, also, the government and the licensing and the structure that is created and the deals, are not really looking for an African identity, those of us here are hardly ever consulted. . . . Because sometimes the person who . . . does the approval also . . . receives something under the table. (Yvette, urban planner, interview, Marginal, 12 April 2011)

Yvette's vexations echoed stories that I would hear throughout my research about the "foreign" nature of the new Luanda, a voicing of frustrations that demand a reassessment of the politics of aesthetics raised by the building of new cities in Africa and globally. As the building of such cities has become a dominant form of urban planning in the Global South in the last two decades, scholars have highlighted the prominent role of a banal "world-city" aesthetic in the attempted legitimation of these initiatives (Ghertner 2015; de Boeck and Baloji 2016; Watson 2014, 2020; Harms 2012). New cities' designs, it is argued, seek to reference cities and architectures held up as "models of modernity" (Tarbush 2012), especially those of leading Asian and Middle Eastern metropolises such as Singapore and Dubai (Watson 2014, 2020). This aesthetic, coupled with now flagging discourses of "Africa rising," present these cities as material solutions that promise to kickstart economic growth and integration into transnational flows of people and capital. Scholars have referred to these plans as "fantasies" that systematically disregard urban conditions in Africa, as well as foster segregated and elitist urban imaginations (Watson 2014, 2020; Murray 2015; Myers 2015). In promoting a tabula rasa imagination of urban development, they draw funds away from tackling entrenched problems in existing cities and "ignore the very real and very serious social and environmental issues in current and future African cities" (Watson 2020, 42). This is a product, it has been argued, of the rise of circulating policy mobilities facilitated by international engineering and consulting companies that are able to offer ready-made solutions to urban problems, solutions not based on detailed studies of local conditions.

While there is no doubt that many of these plans seem to iterate what Martin Murray (2015) refers to as a "modular urbanism," or Vanessa Watson (2020) calls a "'cut and paste' similarity," such arguments overlook the complex domestic urban histories and ideologies that have resulted in states seeking out these developments. A growing body of literature has shown that while international actors have been central to the conceptualization of many new city projects, these projects are nevertheless deeply rooted in local planning and politics (Korah 2020; Fält 2019). In Angola, Sylvia Croese (2017) and Ricardo Cardoso (2016) have shown how prime urban initiatives such as the redevelopment of Luanda's Marginal and the building of Kilamba have their origins in local planning practices rather than in contemporary orientations to belong to a global village of competitive cities. The recognition of local planning histories points to the need to understand what politics are produced through quotidian grounded engagements with these worlding projects. It also points to the existence of more complicated processes of contestation, subjectification, and agency than are allowed for in analyses that criticize these plans as fantasies.

If Euro-American, and more recently Asian and Middle Eastern, cities have been identified as the sites of normative visions of urban modernity, African countries are now embarking on their own experiments with urban worlding inasmuch as the images and structures they produce "instantiate some vision of the world in formation" (Ong 2011, 11). Such worlding practices at an urban level seek to remake the normative standards thought to define shared understandings of the city at an international level (Ong 2011). In the African case, however, the sense of a lack of ownership over design and process among much of the population has caused consternation, overtly politicizing imaginaries of the urban while placing debates about belonging and inclusion at the heart of design. Luanda's new architectures brought into open discussion the underlying disquiets about autochthony, national belonging, and African identity that the dissensus of the musseques catalyzed in subtle ways.

The ubiquity of comments such as Yvette's, echoing scholars' concerns about the modularity of contemporary architectural initiatives, reveals not only that local planners were aware of problems raised by the decontextualization these plans were accused of but also that her complaints about corruption and African identity speak to situated concerns and politics that often escape even scholarly critiques of these plans. While the designs of new cities may be exclusionary, scholars working on the topic have argued that residents are seduced by the aesthetic promises of these plans (Ghertner 2015; Harms 2012; de Boeck 2011; Watson 2014). Inasmuch as these projects embody aspirations of upward mobility, comfort, and modernity, urban residents embrace them, even while knowing that the constructions could portend inhabitants' future removal and that most city residents are unlikely ever to access their air-conditioned comforts. Such analyses resonate with Frankfurt School arguments about the nullifying power of the aesthetic as well as writings on oil spectacle that portray it as transforming citizens into uncritical spectators of the state (see the introduction and chapter 1). However, as the comments by Yvette and many other people I encountered suggested, Luandans' engagements with the final products of these plans, and their representations in the form of computer-generated images found in pamphlets, short films, and advertisements, constituted a more complex range of orientations to the aesthetic promises of modernity than existing critiques of new cities suggest. While urban residents expressed admiration for the designs of redevelopment projects and the new satellite cities, this veneration was accompanied by an equally strong criticism and at times total rejection of the very same aesthetics. Nothing about expressing desires in relation to certain urban aesthetics at some moments precluded a trenchant critique of the same aesthetics at others. What this indicated was a more nuanced aesthetic politics than the one captured in accounts assuming that designs inspired by imaginations of world-class citiness primarily index local aspirations to be included in an unmarked global, or that they are crude expressions of capital accumulation, or that they constitute foreign impositions on a local landscape. Urban aesthetics are an unstable ground for both complicity and dissent, a site for the opening of political contestation. To understand the political ramifications of urban redevelopment and the building of new cities in Africa, the political instability of aesthetics needs to be recognized and engaged.

In Luanda what I refer to as "aesthetic dissent," the expression of political dissent through a register of aesthetics rooted in evaluations of the design and materiality of buildings, was rife. Luandans from various socioeconomic backgrounds used the aesthetics of new constructions to critique what they saw as the inappropriate pact between international capital and their own government. Aesthetic dissent was a means of expressing anxieties about elite control over the oil economy and definitions of citizenship. New constructions, many knew, did not simply shoot up unassisted. Their existence led back to the complex networks of power, influence, and finance that fed on Angola's petrodollars. They were a material symbol of impunity, constantly invoking aspirations and desires for the good life in their aesthetic promises while damaging the existing material and social worlds of the city.

Disquiet emerged in the bricks and mortar of the city. My interlocutors argued that new buildings were not designed to accommodate Angolan families, made certain informal socioeconomic activities untenable, and were environmentally inappropriate for the city. Critics of national reconstruction often pushed back using the same objects that were meant to index the success of the postconflict polity. Luandans circulated images on social media of new constructions that were already fissuring or had failed in some other way. Many argued that the new city caused the breakdown of the existing one. A university lecturer told me that the construction of the Torres Ambiente, a high-rise close to Luanda's promenade whose penthouse was rumored to be selling for $10 million, had led to cracks in the walls of the neighboring Agostinho Neto University economics building. The circulation of these images and stories constituted a form of dissent from the government's narrative of reconstruction as the panacea to Angola's woes by representing the broken buildings as embodying an immanent material critique of the promised postconflict prosperity. Poor construction indexed the careless planning and corruption that many believed underlay the projects. These arguments about architectural failure and comments about buildings' "suitability" and "culture" spoke to a political realm that did not lie in legal classifications and formal institutions. Instead, it was steeped in the finishings, architectural designs, and visual representations of the city: urban aesthetics to be precise.

The above stories were obviously the stuff of rumor. However, as Quayson

(2014, 241) argues, "Rumors and myths are the transactional glue that hold African urban society together." Texts, narratives, and discourses are the keys to understanding shared notions of urbanism, politics, and sociality, as well as the means by which residents reproduce and take them up. These texts create the city just as much as the built environment does. In Kinshasa, de Boeck and Plissart (2004) argue that the everyday street rumors and gossip, what they describe as "Radio Trottoir" (Sidewalk Radio), not only are the center of urban politics but also are often more consequential in structuring urban space and experience than the city's crumbling material forms. It is precisely through rumor and gossip that the workings of power are explained (White 2000). In Angola, political dissent is often crushed, and the MPLA is widely recognized as promoting a discourse in which any opposition to it is an attempt to stoke a return to war (Faria 2013). Given this context of political repression, these stories become a means for playing with the signs and narratives of state power so as to unsettle the political frameworks imposed from above (Mbembe 2001; de Boeck and Plissart 2004, 51). At the heart of these unsettlings lie the tensions that arise from imagining what the new city meant and for whom it was being built.

In the contemporary African context, careful attention must be paid to domestic politics to understand the stakes involved in state investments in worlding and the local perceptions of their meanings. Most scholarship on Luanda's remaking has emphasized how the MPLA has used the built environment to entrench its power in the postconflict period (Schubert 2015; Soares de Oliveira 2015). The MPLA's relentless advertising of itself as responsible for the visual spectacle of national reconstruction, however, turned out to be a dangerous move. For, as Rafael Marques de Morais, an Angolan human rights and anticorruption activist, has commented, in times of economic crisis and political tension "the magic turns back on the magician" (Rocha 2015). Building on existing political tensions about the relations of elites to "ordinary" Angolans, in which elites figured as more welcoming to foreigners than to locals, many residents perceived the buildings as threatening to undo their claims to urban and national belonging. Discussions about urban aesthetics therefore became one of the primary means of critiquing the project of national reconstruction and, by proxy, the Angolan government. Rather than anaesthetizing critique or merely being desired because they beckon a better future, the aesthetics of world-class citiness (design, materiality, color) became powerful materials for dissent. They not only embodied the actors and processes that urban residents felt were responsible for their dispossessions, but they also, through their design and materials, were understood to displace residents. These concerns sometimes took on xenophobic and especially Sinophobic characteristics, as supposedly foreign design became associated with foreign countries' collaboration with local elites and the elision of ordinary Angolans' concerns. As Luandans grappled with what is meant to world the metropolis from Africa, they raised the question of where national belonging and citizenship intersected with the political economy of urban aesthetics through which worlding was packaged. In contemporary Luanda, rather than erasing politics, the aesthetic field became the one through which long-standing conflicts over national and urban belonging were contested, and the possibilities for reimagining African urbanism were constituted.

Material Critiques and Fighting Dubaização

Luis was sick of Luanda. Having trained at one of Portugal's top architecture schools, his future had appeared secure until the 2008 financial crisis collapsed his job prospects. In his search for employment, he had landed in Angola, one of hundreds of thousands of Portuguese nationals who turned to the country's former colony, now turned benefactor, in pursuit of a new start. Employed at a leading international architecture and planning firm, he earned a good salary and had swiftly integrated into the Luanda social scene. Nevertheless, after many years in the country he was tired of the city, which he described as "a giant sewer," arguing that plans for its redevelopment lacked vision and originality. As we shared dinner at Naquele Lugar, a restaurant in a small courtyard perched near the top of a hill overlooking Luanda's bay, his interest was fixed on his vacation, for which he was leaving the next day. Eager to push past his frustration, I mentioned that the letters of the word "Cuca," the name of the country's national beer, had been removed the night before from an iconic colonial-era high-rise. The high-rise had earned its moniker, "the Cuca building" ("Prédio da Cuca"), from the giant letters spelling "Cuca" that had for decades stood on its roof, visible across the city. The building bordered the now destroyed Kinaxixe Market. A few months before, in December 2010, its residents had been evacuated and rehoused in high-rises near Zango; the emergency arose when engineers declared that the foundations of the building had weakened due to years of neglect and posed a threat to its inhabitants. Luis sighed and remarked that many believed there had been nothing wrong with the foundations. According to Luanda's rumor mill, someone with political power wanted the site for a new construction and had therefore invented a story that the building's foundations had degraded. Luis believed that the foundations were in fact damaged, but not due to natural causes. He suspected that a politically influential individual had sent workers in secret every night to hack away at its foundations until they became unstable. My face clearly expressed my incredulity. He looked me in the eyes, smiled, and reminded me, "This is Luanda—no matter how crazy a rumor is, it could be true."

Luis's tale was one of many that represented the new city as physically attacking and undermining the existing one, in this case literally. Like political accounts of corruption and impunity in much of Africa, which focus on the trope of "eating" resources, these rumors and comments portrayed the emerging buildings as consuming their predecessors. In the process, many people, especially the city's cultural elites, argued that the history and broader identity of the city was being destroyed (see chapter 1). Some saw this as a deliberate action by a government they believed to be corrupted by personal business interests, or as a means of imprinting MPLA hegemony on the city by removing all potential mnemonic references to histories not sanctioned by the ruling party (Schubert 2017; Araújo 2010). The evidence provided for this contention was the state's neglect of the colonial-era city center, where most buildings with official heritage status were located. More than one person told me that the government purposefully let buildings fall to ruin so they would lose their heritage classification, thereby facilitating demolition and paving the way for new construction. The built environment thus mediated beliefs about the privatization of the state and the corruption of politics. New constructions stood as symbols of a political realm gone wrong.

At the heart of these concerns were not simply arguments about corruption but a deeper concern about national and urban identity. This had come to a head early in the process of Luanda's postconflict remaking with the 2003 announcement of the Luanda Bay Project, focused on the redevelopment of the promenade (see chapter 1). The shock over the proposed development, which many saw as an attack on the city, galvanized the formation of civil society groups promoting urban heritage, especially among those who saw themselves, Angola, and the city as intimately connected to a broader world of Luso-Atlantic aesthetics and histories. One example was the Associação Kalu, formed shortly after the announcement of the Luanda Bay Project, to advocate for the protection of urban heritage (Tânia from Associação Kalu, interview, Luanda, 16 September 2011). The organization was active in opposing demolitions of historic buildings such as the *sobrado* that housed the Elinga Theater, at the time one of the few independent arts spaces in the city and home to a much-loved nightclub. It also occasionally held guided urban walks with local university professors to teach a broader public about Luanda's architectural history. Association members used the city's birthday (25 January) to organize events that raised awareness about urban redevelopment and its pitfalls. At the heart of Associação Kalu's concerns and those of many others was the belief that modern urban development would destroy Luanda's identity along with its material history. As Tânia, a university lecturer and active member of Associação Kalu, explained to me, "The past is part of our city, it's part of our identity. We don't want a characterless city" (interview, Luanda, 16 September 2011).

Tânia's concerns spoke to what was often described as the "dubaização" of the city, a term used to describe the obliteration of the city's identity through the imposition of a "world-class city" aesthetic. This was evident in the language used in official petitions against redevelopment, one of which stated, "We are concerned with the almost daily destruction and arbitrary reconstruction that we see, which attack the history, traditions, and evolving identity of Luandans."[2] A 2009 petition protesting the threat to the Elinga Theater's building exclaimed, "What is the reason that Elinga Teatro's space must be destroyed? They say that in its place 'a large and new building' (perhaps Dubai style?) must be erected and that one of its floors will be the 'new' headquarters for the Elinga collective. What an aberration! And the soul of the old Elinga building? And the soul? The soul does not count?"[3]

It was not just that the new buildings were soulless but that their very design was, as Yvette had suggested, inappropriate for Luanda. Discussions of heritage often were accompanied by an environmental appeal to the practicalities of designing and building for "tropical" conditions. Local architects and supporters of the heritage movement typically idealized the modernist high-rises of the 1950s and 1960s, explaining that they had been specially designed for Luanda's climate, allowing air to circulate without the necessity of burdensome infrastructure such as air-conditioning. Even the Cuban buildings of the 1970s and 1980s took this into account, Tânia argued, since they were purposefully limited to four or five stories so residents would not need elevators. In contrast, the new constructions, built on a scale that dwarfed the older buildings, were portrayed as environmentally disastrous, requiring levels of electricity and water supply that were impractical in Luanda's context. They were criticized for being too large for the city, taking up too much space, and creating problems with parking and traffic that heightened pollution and a sense of overcrowding (data from discussion at Associação Kalu celebration for Luanda, Associação dos Escritores de Luanda, 25 January 2012). The reason behind this was not stupidity, many argued, but greed and an obsession with markers of status and class that derived from international world-city imaginations. Tânia described the aesthetic of the new Luanda as a product of the "nouveau riche," who went to Dubai and confused buildings with development. In a similar vein, an Angolan urban planner working for a government office commented that the designs for much of the new housing for Luanda's middle class were inappropriate for the city's climate. Pointing at images of housing on her computer screen as I sat in her office, she said, "These are not suited for the tropics. See those roofs? The house will just get hot." When I asked why they were designed this way, she responded, "People look at China and South Africa and want to be like them, so they build houses that you find there. But these rich people here don't even know how to live in these houses" (data from observation at government office, Ingombota, 15 April 2011). In the eyes of cultural advocates for the city and many planners, the world-city aesthetic was anything but desirable. It was environmentally destructive and undermined Luanda's historical identity, as well as existing senses of national identity and belonging. While many of them attributed this to greed or ignorance on the part of those in charge of the planning processes, for those on the violent receiving end of these developments, the new designs spoke to sinister political pacts shaping the future of Luanda and their position in it.

Foreign Materials and Local Alienations

Late one afternoon, I drove along the main road of Angola's largest state rehousing area, Zango. Next to me sat Raul, a member of an Angolan civil society organization. As we exited the area, turning onto Luanda's ring road, we passed a cluster of new Chinese-designed high-rises (Figure 5.1). The multicolored structures rose up in stark contrast to the surrounding flat landscape. Raul, staring from the window, asked if I thought the high-rises were well built. Fearing that his question was fueled by Sinophobic assumptions about the poor quality of Chinese construction, I told him that I did not know. He paused and then confided in me that he was worried about the apartments. The Chinese, he explained, only had one child. The buildings, he continued, were likely designed with Chinese families in mind; but Angolan families were bigger. He shot me a concerned look and asked if I thought the buildings would collapse from the extra weight (data from discussion with Raul, Zango, 13 May 2012).

Raul's comments were just one indication of a widespread anxiety among urban residents with whom I interacted that both the political-economic underpinnings and actual aesthetic products of national reconstruction were pushing Angolans out of the city. In Raul's case, his concern was that the foreign origin of the high-rise designers might mean that the buildings were not

Figure 5.1. Condominium development near the entrance to Zango, 2011.

suitable for Angolans. However, the fear of displacement did not end there. Raul's comments need to be understood in a context where discussions of aesthetics are laminated onto a complex host of experiences of urban displacement and anxiety about foreign presences in the city. These anxieties show that local interpretations of world-city projects cannot be separated from domestic politics, a politics that might become the grounds for rejection of the project.

The new buildings represented not only wealth and peace but also a more than decade-long process of urban displacement. Ongoing mass demolitions since 2001 had resulted in displacement being one of the most common features of postconflict life in Luanda (see chapter 3). Although the city's devastating housing demolitions constituted the most visceral material form of expulsion, displacement was also experienced through the perceived elision and alienation of the population from the processes of national reconstruction, an alienation paralleled by a rapid increase in the presence of foreign labor in the country. By 2012, an estimated 259,000 Chinese nationals and 113,000 Portuguese people were living in Angola (Candeias et al. 2019; Schmitz

2014). Projects funded by oil-credit lines employed a significant quota of foreign labor as a condition of the loan. The shortage of skilled individuals in key sectors of the economy, as well as the general rush to Angola by individuals and companies attracted by its double-digit economic growth, had brought a rapid increase in the presence of foreign workers in many sectors, from bricklayers to bank managers. This led to a feeling, especially among poor Angolans, that Angolans had been economically excluded from the promises of reconstruction. Tellingly, when I asked Miguel Fortunato from Kilamba Kiaxi (see chapter 3) if he had sought employment at Kilamba when it was under construction, he commented, "Since the Chinese arrived it's difficult to find work. All of Kilamba belongs to the Chinese" (data from discussion with Fortunato Family, Kilamba Kiaxi, 15 September 2011). Well-paid foreigners began to occupy the new offices, houses, and public spaces that were the fruits of postconflict prosperity. On a quotidian level, tensions became notable in instances such as skirmishes between Angolans and Chinese nationals who traded in informal construction markets after Angolans accused the Chinese of engaging in business practices that undercut Angolan ventures (data from discussion with Carlos, Benfica, 12 April 2012).[4]

Foreign workers and investors became increasingly associated with local displacement, both literal and experiential, causing Angolans to question their position in the emerging postconflict polity and the broader meaning of what it meant to be a citizen. These concerns were refracted through the evolving built environment. The association of foreigners with displacement was evident in a discussion I had with Fausto, a resident of Bairro 2. He had been living in a corrugated iron house for seven years, waiting to be resettled, as he watched Nova Vida, in which many expatriates lived, rise on the carcass of his former neighborhood. Following the demolition, when residents tried unsuccessfully to contact Angola's parliament, the government had dismissed their claims by referring to them as "occupants." Fausto rejected this description, implying that it misconstrued who really belonged in the country. "So we are 'occupants.' So are we foreigners, or are we Angolans? If we are Angolans, then these houses that you [the government] are building are for whom? . . . Those houses that they are building are for foreigners and . . . people who have money. But us, we who are here, they are going to take us and dump us in the bush" (data from discussion with Fausto, Kilamba Kiaxi, 1 July 2011). I asked him what he meant by that, because at first I did not understand the term he used for bush, "capim."[5] He responded, "To Zango, really far away, in the bush [*mato*], it's a place that doesn't have a lot of value. They are going to take us there, but here where we are, they are only going to put people who have money, that have money. Or . . . they are going to put foreigners here. But the actual Angolan does not have the right to live in the city."

The references to neocolonial economic intrigues, physical displacement, and socioeconomic marginalization repeat the themes found in many studies of contemporary xenophobia and autochthony. As various scholars have shown, the uncertainties engendered by neoliberal economic policies have a strong correlation with increased outbursts of xenophobia (Geschiere 2009). However, as Jason Hickel (2014, 104) has emphasized, while xenophobia is often catalyzed by a struggle over resources, the ways in which "otherness" is constituted is "experienced in a specific cultural idiom," which must be equally explained to comprehend the expressions that xenophobia takes. Mike McGovern (2011, 99) makes a similar point when he argues that resentment is "not a sentiment" but rather a "social idiom" that mobilizes shared local tropes, narratives, and understandings of behavior to explain the past, present, and hopes for the future in terms of a hostility to those classified as foreign.

In Luanda, the anxiety about foreign presence builds upon long-running political discourses that identify the MPLA elite as "foreign." Early Angolan elites were prominent Black and mixed-race families who had risen to their status during the initial stages of the colonial encounter and had long severed their relations with marked forms of African "tradition" (Messiant 1992; Soares de Oliveira 2015). In the twentieth century, this group joined other *assimilados* (Black and "mixed race" Angolans legally classified as having adopted "Western" ways and therefore qualifying for special legal status as Portuguese citizens) to dominate the independence elite of the MPLA. In moments of disillusionment, critics of the MPLA have mobilized this history to suggest that the party's leadership is antagonistic to "autochthonous" Africans, in the process implying that the leadership is itself of questionable origin. The narrative of a Lusophone coastal elite at odds with an Indigenous interior African population particularly characterized the discourses of UNITA's civil war leader, Jonas Savimbi (Péclard 2012). This included framing the MPLA as the puppet of foreign powers through its affiliations with Cuba and the Soviet Union, as "un-African" because of its socialist ideologies, and sometimes as anti-Black (Brinkman 2003; de Grassi 2015; Pearce 2015). Savimbi mobilized these points to suggest that the MPLA facilitated foreign interests at the expense of Angolans, and that he and UNITA were there to champion the cause of "real" Angolans.

In postconflict Luanda, these currents of thought continued to resonate politically. They often focused on President dos Santos, whom critics conspiratorially accused of being from São Tomé. Copies of the president's birth certificate of clearly questionable authenticity regularly circulated online and were held up by UNITA supporters in their 2012 protest against electoral fraud. But it is in discussions of the city that these suspicions were most evidently expressed. The most commonly cited supposed "proof" of dos Santos's foreign origins was rooted in urban space. Urban rumor claims that dos Santos's childhood home remained unknown, despite his official biography stating that he was born in Sambizanga, one of Luanda's oldest musseque areas. In Luanda, neighborhood identity is the primary means of claiming urban autochthony and identity (see chapter 2; also Moorman 2008). In being unable to establish a concrete urban location of origin, the then-president became a person onto whom people laminated their frustrations regarding the perceived privileges of foreigners and anger at the failures of national reconstruction to provide everyday benefits.

The suspicion leveled against the president was evident in the account by Oswaldo, an army veteran and resident of Bairro 2 whose house was demolished in 2004. In 2012, he was still waiting to be rehoused. When I asked him why he thought the government was treating the "povo" poorly, he responded that he believed it was due to the government's ambivalence as to whether the poor counted as citizens. "It has forgotten about us, it doesn't know if we are Angolans or if we are from somewhere else. . . . When the foreigner arrives here, he finds everything prepared. He has water, electricity, a house, everything. But the Angolan lives like a slave." When I asked him to clarify if he really meant that foreigners lived better than Angolans, he raised his voice. "The foreigner lives much better, he is in command! We should speak with shame about what we are seeing!" When I inquired why he thought the government was giving preference to foreigners, he commented, "If I am a foreigner, I have to put another foreigner there to rule. The boss [the president], if he is the boss, he knows that the Angolan people deserve better; the Angolan people can't be left to be sacrificed like this. No. So, because he is a foreigner, to my mind he is a foreigner, so he gives more opportunities to foreigners, the Angolan is left to suffer" (Oswaldo, interview, Bairro 2, 5 March 2012). The question therefore was no longer whether elites were in alliance with foreigners but whether or not the elite themselves were foreign. In many ways then, anxieties about foreigners have more to do with Luandans' relations to their own elites than to foreigners per se. The critique of the foreign became a critique of Angola's leaders.

Central to the critiques of the new Luanda were quotidian understandings of the intersection of foreign investment, presidential power, and construction. Interlocutors' frustrations with the government became entangled with and voiced as anger at the government's partners, generally referred to as *estrangeiros* (foreigners). Thus, for example, in an article titled "New 'Idiocy' or Preparation for Chinese Colonization?" that appeared on the website *Central Angola 7311*, the mouthpiece of an emerging, largely Luanda-based youth movement, the authors argued that the ground was being laid for a "'Chinese Empire' in Angola." In their eyes, the proof of this was what they referred to as "the case of disposable constructions." Recounting that the government had justified the Chinese presence by claiming that their technical expertise was needed, the authors asked why, then, Chinese constructions were thought to be of such poor quality that they were effectively "disposable." The article argued that the employment of Chinese experts and labor, despite the continuing failure of their buildings, could suggest only one of two options. Either Angolans were "idiots" or "they [the Chinese] are preparing the grounds for a neocolonialism facilitated by our own countrymen who have taken control of power." To illustrate their point, they posted photos of a newly completed car dealership that had partially collapsed after heavy rains (Francisco and Viera 2015).

The statement echoed a larger trend of identifying the postconflict landscape as the product of collusion between neocolonial interests and local power brokers. While it would be easy to dismiss such statements as crude xenophobia, their ubiquity calls for an analysis of why the obsession with "foreignness" features so prominently in critiques of Luanda's redevelopment, and why the materiality of the buildings is so central to these arguments. At issue here is not whether Chinese investors or other foreign nationals really have the influence that critics claim. Beliefs do not need to be accurate to have an impact on the social imaginary (White 2000). In this case, comments about design and materiality critique the economic pacts that underpin national reconstruction. They slot into longer histories of the resentment of foreign presences, presences marked by the destruction of war and the humiliation of colonization. Many Luandans therefore view the new constructions with suspicion as the latest manifestations of foreign presences whose lingering mark will be the buildings they leave behind.

The new Luanda was taking shape within this domestic crucible of anxieties about foreigners, which were, by proxy, the general population's anxieties about their relationship to their rulers. While comments about the president's nationality show how xenophobic sentiments have at times come to stand in for political critique, the discussion of urban aesthetics is, I argue, not only a more subtle but also more pervasive way people are both affronted by and push back against the prevailing political and economic systems. In their rejection of "foreign" buildings, they reject the ruling political regime. The city's buildings have become the terrain through which "everyday autochthony" has taken root (McGovern 2011, 69), expressed, as I show in the following section, in moments of aesthetic dissent.

Displacement by Design

In August 2011, I listened to José Maria, a young Angolan architect who had been educated in Portugal, passionately critique the fact that Luanda's redevelopment had created relatively few jobs for Angolan architects. Although I had heard similar complaints from poorer Angolans, I was surprised to hear them from someone with sought-after expertise, especially since companies always claimed they were desperate to hire well-educated Angolans. When I asked him why he thought Angolan architects were not benefiting from the construction boom, he at first suggested that they were not pushy enough in trying to get contracts. However, he then paused and told me, "Lots of people come from Brazil, Portugal, China, and they [the client] want something fast. . . . They want something *chave na mão*, something fast that already has financing.[6] This is another aspect that works against Angolan architects because these foreign firms arrive with financing, and often with the project, financing, and construction capacity. It's a package, an unmatchable package" (architect José Maria, interview, Maianga, 9 August 2011). The result of foreigners supervising design, José Maria and many others argued, was that the newly emerging structures were unsuitable for Angolans and Angola.

While many of the critiques of the new city that emerged from elites focused on what they referred to as "dubaização," the evisceration of Luanda's history through the destruction of its buildings and their replacement with a seemingly alien architecture, a more fundamental critique, based in design and usage, emerged from both the lived experience and romantic imaginaries of the musseques. A "cultural" critique of urban aesthetics embedded in often problematic assumptions about musseque life and "Angolanness" could be found among various strata of Luandans. If musseques' material and spatial practices were dismissed as undesirable, at moments in which national identity was at stake, the claim to Indigeneity that the musseque house embodied emerged as a site of politics. José Maria, for instance, drew on arguments about musseque domestic spatial practices in his critique of the "new centrality" of Kilamba, which he viewed as the symbol of all that was wrong with the new Luanda. Despite living in an apartment, he felt that the construction of Kilamba was a mistake. Its vertical design, he believed, was ill-suited for the "normal citizen" because "the Angolan likes spaces . . . he likes to be in the shade in big open spaces, to lunch with the family. . . . He prefers a yard [quintal], or a large veranda that is similar to a yard, rather than closed spaces like this living room, like this." This space," he said, gesturing to his apartment's living room, "is not typical for an Angolan."

José Maria's discussion of architecture was premised upon and constructed an idealized traditional urban Angolan, wedded to large open spaces and extended families, and antithetical to apartment blocks. This view reached back to the early postcolonial period, when state sources had argued that the reason for the deterioration of the colonial-era housing stock was the rural and musseque habitus of their new residents (Gastrow 2021). The belief that verticality was antithetical to cultural norms of spatial usage was widespread. Diogo, the advertising executive, held similar beliefs, telling me that foreign architects had failed to understand the cultural values of domestic architecture in Angola. "The annex is more important than the house. The value of the yard, of open air, one's life in the open is more important than life closed, locked inside the house. There are other cultural values that I think architects don't pay attention to" (Diogo, interview, Talatona, 18 August 2011). In an interview with a group of real estate agents, one of them reiterated these views as well as Raul's concerns about the size of the apartments. He argued that the residents of the urban periphery who were mostly poor, "have five, six, ten children and we are preparing apartments that only have enough room for two. It doesn't make sense. Whoever came up with the project thought of Eastern Europe, thought of Brazil, thought of South America, but didn't think about Angola" (real estate agents, interview, Ingombota, 15 April 2011). In the views of many, then, the new constructions were promoting nuclear families and apartment living, something that contrasted with popular-classed imaginations of "Angolanness," rooted in beliefs about musseque cultural life and the material forms this took.[7] The very architectures that were used to critique the musseque were now being mobilized to critique the new Luanda.

While it might be easy to dismiss the discursive construction of these sentiments as the prejudiced utterances of middle-class Angolans, the same ideas circulated among musseque residents. Dona Cristina, a resident of Cazenga, told me that she did not want to be removed to a high-rise because she could "never get used to the height." She argued that if the government wanted to put her in a high-rise, she would need training in how to live in one. When I insisted that she could easily adapt to high-rise life, a friend of hers intervened, "Look Claudia, it's like this. You learned to write in a book with lines. Now, imagine that one day someone suddenly hands you a book without lines and tells you to write in it. Sure, eventually you'll adapt and learn to write straight and correctly without the lines, but until then you are going to write all over the place: up, down, backward. This is what it is like for people who move from the musseque to a high-rise" (Dona Cristina, discussion, Vamos Andar, Cazenga, 24 May 2011). The head of the residents' committee of her neighborhood had similar beliefs. When I interviewed him regarding plans for the redevelopment of Cazenga, he explained in detail the infrastructural benefits that "requalification" would bring. Then, however, he paused and reflected that there would be challenges for people accustomed to living on the ground floor, or those with "camponês" habits of cooking on an open fire rather than in an oven. They would struggle to adapt to a high-rise (residents' committee president, interview, Vamos Andar, Cazenga, 16 July 2012). Design, it seemed, threatened to disorientate.

The design of new constructions in and of themselves then, by disrupting inhabitants' everyday practices, threatened to displace them. The banal aesthetic of the world-city was not simply transposable, it had a sinister quality that erased the everyday life of the majority. The disjuncture between practice and design, but also recognition of the classed nature of these designs, led many musseque residents to believe that the architectures of the new buildings would make their lives impossible and were therefore indicative of their removal. This was evident from the words of Senhor Kuntuala, an elderly man who had moved back to Luanda after spending much of the postwar period in the north of the country, as he studied a glossy state-sponsored leaflet advertising the redevelopment of Cazenga during a meeting of neighborhood representatives in 2012. The cover of the leaflet showed a grouping of glass-covered high-rises with lush green lawns stretching out to a sparkling body of water. These were in stark contrast to the single-story concrete-block homes and dirt roads of the existing neighborhood. Referencing the leaflet, Senhor Kuntuala commented, "The image that it shows is of a luxury villa. Will we continue to live there once they build those? What are the conditions according to which we will get those houses? If I live in an apartment block, how will I cultivate land?" (data from observation of community meeting, Cazenga, 13 June 2012). While many people in the group disagreed with him, arguing that access to new infrastructures might outweigh the lack of access to larger spaces, a colleague of his from a community-based organization stepped in to support him. "I only see disadvantages. In my yard I have a school and a business. If they take me from there, how will I eat? I don't work for the state. It's not possible to mess with a state project. I went to Kilamba, it's impossible. My wife works in front of our house, we can't put a bench to sell food in front of an apartment block.

How will we work and eat?" The comments made by Senhor Kuntuala and his colleague reflected the discrepant understandings of spatial usage between government plans and Indigenous architectures. Miguel Dias (2020, 118) has described the home in Luanda as a "unit of production" inasmuch as the uses that people make of its spaces generally collapse the division between work and domesticity that characterized the new plans for the city. Yards become sites for selling food, running businesses, and renting out rooms. People such as Senhor Kuntuala believed the inability of advertised plans to recognize these uses threatened to unmake urban belonging and collapse financial certainty through the imposition of architectural design.

The concerns about design, practice, and culture reflected anxieties about how existing populations fit into the emerging city, and by proxy the emerging postconflict political order. The supposed "problem" of the architecture was precisely that it derived its aesthetic impetus from a foreign culture to which the majority of Angolans, many of my informants argued, could either not acculturate or felt alienated from. The new structures threatened to displace them not just physically but aesthetically, as the design, they argued, made their current ways of life impossible. The buildings' aesthetics suggested not only that the majority of Luandans could not access them but that they had to transform themselves into something other than themselves. Otherwise, there would be no space for them in the new city. They would have to abandon kinship practices, economic activities, and historical attachments to the city's built environment. They would have to unmake Indigenous urbanism. The world-city aesthetic was neither desirable nor undefined; it was decidedly foreign and aggressive, something to be counteracted even as many Angolans yearned for the promises of comfort it embodied.

Questioning Elite Worlding

In 2009, when I asked an Angolan NGO employee whom he thought the new city was for, he shrugged and replied, "They are building a city for no one." Yet "they" or "them" (*eles*), the oft-used term to refer to an amorphous group on the top of the Angolan political and economic hierarchy, were clearly building a city for someone and for some reason. In the eyes of many of my interlocutors, who tied the aesthetics of the buildings to circulating beliefs about the foreign origins of national reconstruction and the Angolan elite, the elites were building a city for foreigners. As one former soldier in the People's Armed Forces for the Liberation of Angola (FAPLA) whose house was demolished to make way for the Nova Vida project commented, "They [the foreigners] get a house here, but me, a real Angolan, I get nothing" (data from observation, Kilamba Kiaxi, 1 December 2011).[8] Aesthetic and literal displacements were identified as the products of alliances between elites and foreigners, which underpinned new construction designs and the larger implementation of national reconstruction. In the political context of Angola, then, aesthetic dissent became a means of critiquing the government. The aesthetics of world-class city-making could be just as much the grounds for rejecting the process as for accepting it.

Despite their pretensions to annul the past and project the future, architecture and urban redevelopment are always haunted by history and politics. The Angolan government's idea that national reconstruction could escape from long-standing tensions about citizenship and autochthony was naive. If nothing else, it became the focus of these conflicts. As Luandans interacted with the city's new buildings, they were both physically and aesthetically unsettled. They worried that the foundations of their lives, like those of demolished buildings, might be undone not only by actual physical displacement but also by the materials and designs those new buildings introduced. Architectural design and materials provided the idioms for the expression of both political dissent and at times xenophobia, but they were also the very substances that generated these anxieties. They mobilized wartime discourses about the supposed foreign origins of the MPLA leadership. They pressed the case of the autochthonous citizen against a political elite who urban residents believed were selling them out to foreigners to make a profit off the urban landscape. Urban inhabitants' anger, then, reflected a political sensibility embedded in a notion of shared aesthetic judgments of "culture" and lifestyle. When the elite and foreigners were seen to be rejecting these through the design of the new Luanda, they were also seen to be rejecting the autochthonous Angolan citizen.

In the politically repressive context of contemporary Angola, critique does not always take the form of canonical protest practices, but this does not mean that it does not exist. This chapter has shown that Luandans mobilized the urban aesthetics that the MPLA-state promoted as indications of nation-building and prosperity to critique the political and economic pacts that they believed underpinned the buildings. This aesthetic dissent was ensconced in a longer political history of tensions over belonging in the country, which national reconstruction failed to resolve. What these dissenting views over Luanda's worlding project reveal is that urban aesthetics open a space for the discussion of politics. As the swing between praise and criticism of aesthetics revealed, it is one of the crucibles in which African perspectives on the stakes of worlding are being constituted. The horizons produced by the new city and infrastructure megaprojects sweeping across Africa can only be understood if their complex political connotations are substantively engaged. Tracking aesthetic dissent gives insight into residents' imaginations of what a desirable African urban might be, which departs from externally imposed notions of African cities being stuck between slums, breakdown, and megaprojects. Certain aspects of the design and implementation of the world city are rejected because they are entwined with repressive politics or seen to threaten emergent domestic categories of belonging. Others are admired for promising prosperity and comfort. The relationship to new urban worlds is not one of absolute embrace or rejection, just as politics is not defined by total collaboration or total resistance.

Beyond "Cut-and-Paste" Urbanism

The politics that emerged out of spectacle and Angolans' engagements with it ask for a reassessment, not just of the case of Luanda but also of practices of state spectacle, African cities, and megaproject developments. Spectacle did not just dazzle, it catalyzed. As state aesthetic promises and impositions began to conflict with historically rooted notions of design and materiality, local construction practices and urban redevelopment initiatives became sites of contestation. These struggles emerged from anger over civil and human rights violations. They also emerged, however, from diffuse notions of urban and political belonging that had accreted over time in the materials, designs, architectures, and construction practices of Luanda's musseques. In Luanda, belonging was an aesthetic and material condition. National reconstruction initiatives embodied this aesthetic politics in their appeals to comfort, but they had failed to account for other registers of aesthetic belonging that coexisted and often came into conflict with the desires for new city construction. In this conclusion I provide an overview of what happened in Luanda in the aftermath of the oil boom and the rise of a new political dispensation following President dos Santos's exit from politics after thirty-eight years in power. As the projects of the oil boom have become integrated into everyday life, a review of that period and its aftermath suggests the need to rethink the histories of planning and construction in African cities, and specifically to understand African urban worlding as not simply a "cut-and-paste" urbanism but rather as emerging through complex, if often undemocratic, transnational histories of planning and city making of which African cities are a part.

The End of Oil

The peak of the Angolan state's mobilization of oil spectacle coincided with the dramatic collapse of oil's capacity to sustain the aesthetic politics of national reconstruction. In December 2015, Urbinveste, a company headed by Isabel dos Santos, the oldest daughter of then-president José Eduardo dos

Santos, announced the official launch of the Luanda Metropolitan General Master Plan (PDGML). Colloquially referred to as "Plano Luanda," the PDGML sought to guide urban planning in the city until 2030. A simplified version of the plan was made publicly available on the internet. The eighty-page document reproduced the fundamentals of the state's aesthetic politics in its imagery and wording, once again repackaging violent removals as acts of care. In its discussion about the future of what it described as "nonstructured musseques," the plan argued that developers would engage in a "phased regeneration process . . . focused initially on the city's nonstructured musseque neighborhoods, which are frequently overcrowded, poorly served by essential infrastructure, and in areas that present serious risk to health. These will need to be displaced either into renewed accommodation nearby or to the new centralities which are being planned near to places of employment and with all the key amenities" (PlanoLuanda 2015, 59). In 2018, the plan was formally approved and gazetted, renamed the Luanda General Master Plan (PGML) ("Plano Director Geral de Luanda traz mudanças na capital do país" 2019). By 2022, however, little of the PGML had been implemented. Although some of the major new roads, especially on the previous edge of the city, had been built, the rest of the plan was languishing, threatening to become yet another iteration of the long history of abandoned urban master plans (Castro and Reschilian 2020).

The painfully obvious factor contributing to the collapse of the PGML was the dramatic fall in the international price of oil that had begun at the end of 2014. At first, it seemed as if it might be a temporary dip. Similar shocks had occurred in 2008 and oil had quickly recovered. State and private developers forged on with their projects. However, as the country crept into 2015, the price began to plunge. In February of that year, the government was forced to adjust the 2015 budget to account for the new assumption that oil would settle at forty dollars a barrel as opposed to the previously estimated eighty-one dollars a barrel. As foreign exchange reserves dried up, the government placed limits on foreign exchange transfers. Companies were unable to pay salaries and suppliers or to send profits out of the country. Angola's currency, the kwanza, plunged from an unofficial exchange rate of 100 kwanzas to the dollar to 500 kwanzas to the dollar by 2019 (Vollgraaff 2019). The official exchange rate was set at about 286 kwanzas to the dollar.[1] The emerging middle class was placed under severe strain as inflation and currency fluctuations collapsed the value of salaries, foreign currency bank accounts were converted into kwanzas, and debit cards were rendered useless overseas. School fees, medical bills, rent, and loan repayments threatened to bankrupt this now precarious group as prices that had been set in dollars now had to be paid in local currency. Unemployment spiraled and Angola found itself servicing $19 billion in oil-backed loans that China had extended during the boom. Angola's oil, however, was worth less than half of what it had been when the funds were originally granted, resulting in the mortgaging of the country's future oil production to service debt. When intersected with the deep corruption and mismanagement that permeates the state and private sector in Angola, the collapse of oil had devastating effects. After its garbage collection budget was cut to $10 million, the GPL found itself unable to pay service providers. After months of no waste collection, rubbish began to overwhelm the city, clogging roads, public spaces, and waterways (Gastrow 2017b). By the end of 2015, the city found itself caught up in a yellow fever outbreak. Public hospitals starved of funds struggled to treat patients. *A crise*—the crisis—as it was called, enveloped life.

The public knew that the collapse of oil-boom prosperity resulted not simply from the drop in international prices but also from the corruption, nepotism, and incompetence that had pervaded the management of oil revenues, procurement, and the execution of many projects (Schubert 2022, 178). It is for this reason that Ruy Blanes (2019, 45), writing about the austerity measures introduced in Angola in the wake of the oil crash, notes that for citizens, these measures were evidence not only of a financial crisis but also of the "moral crisis" of the country's leadership. Angolan leaders seemed aware of this. In an infamous 2017 interview with the *New York Times*, Lopo do Nascimento, a former Angolan prime minister and high-ranking member of the MPLA, described national reconstruction as "like opening a window and throwing out money" (Onishi 2017). Luandans began to look around and ask themselves what the outcomes of national reconstruction had actually been.

Stalled construction was one of the most obvious signs of the crisis. Although President dos Santos had already declared the end of national reconstruction in 2012, coupled with a move to "national development," key public and private investments in real estate and infrastructure development continued. Eventually, however, ambitions flagged, and construction slowed to a trickle. Empty luxury apartment towers dotted the city, wistfully waiting for the next surge in the price of oil. The state was quick to purchase a number of new buildings belonging to members of the presidential inner circle, essentially bailing them out of the crisis (Dias 2021, 318). The most shocking of these bailouts was the purchase of the entire Luanda Bay Project, undermining the long-repeated argument that this vanity project was justified because public funds had not been spent on it (Dias 2021, 318). It was not only the obvious excess of high-end real estate development that drew scorn, however. Chloé

Buire (2022) has shown how residents of Kilamba began to engage in acts of quotidian aesthetic dissent, complaining on social media and in television interviews about shoddy construction and maintenance inadequacies. State care, even when it had been delivered, was now portrayed as falling short.

As the promises of spectacle puttered out, aesthetic dissent transformed from oblique discussions of design and building quality to an explicit critique of the corruption and financial mismanagement of the oil boom. In July 2015, a Facebook campaign titled "SelfieLixo" (GarbageSelfie) emerged. Its organizers called on Luandans to pose in front of uncollected refuse to highlight the failure of the city authorities to perform their duties. These selfies mocked the typical tendency of social media to focus on desirable objects and experiences. People posed grimly in front of refuse piles, drawing the observer's eye to filth that overwhelmed the human subject. SelfieLixo reoriented the central symbol of the city away from oil-boom spectacle to the afterlives of the mismanagement that spectacle had produced (Gastrow 2017b). Three years later, another Facebook campaign gained equal notoriety. Titled "Acaba de me matar" (You just killed me), it was sparked by the music of Os Nanduko, an Angolan kuduro group. In February 2018, the band released a song titled "Vanessa," an ode to a victim of the rains of 2017, which had led to several deaths in Luanda, and to houses and roads being swept away. As part of the song's launch, the band shared images on social media that reenacted the deaths by portraying people with cement-blocks fallen on their chests (Tsandzana 2018). Suddenly, other people began producing similar images. As they proliferated across social media, Luanda's residents used these visuals of objects crushing people to critique the MPLA government for unemployment, poor education and health services, and high levels of corruption. Urban aesthetics again became the object of online politics in 2023 after President João Lourenço posted a message on Facebook encouraging Angolans to, among other things, "promote and create a good image of Angola overseas."[2] This post was accompanied by a photograph of the UN General Assembly building in New York. Angolans, frustrated with the collapse of opportunities in the wake of the pandemic and the ongoing post–oil boom crisis, took to Facebook and Instagram, posting photographs of magnificent buildings and cities from other countries claiming they were in Angola as a means of mocking the president's message and highlighting the obvious discrepancy between the promises of prosperity and comfort represented by the images versus their everyday reality. These social media campaigns highlighted the enduring centrality of urban aesthetics, materials, and objects to the negotiation of questions of belonging, inequality, and governance in Luanda. While the politics of spectacle and the accompanying challenges to violent acts of development that emerged from the musseques had faded from view, new ways of mobilizing urban materials and aesthetic judgments emerged. This suggested that while the nature of aesthetic politics had shifted, it remained present as a register that could be engaged.

Lourenço's Angola

If the crash of oil and financial mismanagement were the primary reasons for the transformation in the nature of aesthetic politics, it was the consequential shift in Angolan politics that overdetermined these changes. In March 2016, as pressure mounted in the wake of a botched 2015 show trial of Angolan activists and the economy continued to unravel, the MPLA announced that José Eduardo dos Santos would be stepping down as party leader in 2018. He would not head the party list in the 2017 election. His replacement was General João Lourenço, a longtime MPLA member who was minister of defense at the time.

At first, people were incredulous at the news. However, as the election drew closer and João Lourenço (popularly referred to as JLo), was indeed put forward as the MPLA's presidential candidate, hope swept through the electorate. Although Lourenço ran under the uninspiring slogan "Improve what is good and correct what is wrong" (*Melhorar o que está bem e corrigir o que está mal*), the promise of a change in leadership for the first time in thirty-eight years caused intense excitement. Indeed, during his initial years in the Presidency, it seemed that Lourenço really was striving to transform the country. He introduced a new visa regime, facilitating greater travel in and out of Angola. New regulations regarding investment made it easier, in theory, for small investors and foreigners to start up business ventures in the country. Human rights activists such as Luaty Beirão and Rafael Marques de Morais, who had been persecuted during dos Santos's reign, were invited to meet with the president. With a seeming new tolerance of political critique, Lourenço's rule at first saw a flourishing of new forms of community activism, what Ruy Blanes and Hitler Samussuku (2022, 477) have referred to as a "second wave of Angolan activism" following the first phase of the return of active protest politics between 2011 and 2015. Youth groups sprang up to represent the concerns of Luanda's various municipalities, actively engaging in protests about service delivery and living conditions. Environmental groups and feminist associations, although formed in the late dos Santos years, became more prominent under Lourenço

(Mouzinho and Cutaia 2017). Censorship of news was temporarily lifted. Most significant, Lourenço launched an extensive anticorruption campaign targeting longtime dos Santos allies as well as the former president's family.

Angolans enthusiastically welcomed and applauded these developments. Lourenço's popularity, however, swiftly declined. It became apparent to many that the anticorruption campaign did not involve a shift in governance practices but was an internal MPLA struggle aimed at removing dos Santos's circle and replacing it with Lourenço's. A parallel process took place in the security services, weakening morale while deepening the securitization of the country (Roque 2021). Independent media began to come under pressure again, and state media returned to their prior practices. While actions such as the return of the bodies of former UNITA generals to Angola and the inclusion of the traumatic 27 May events within the mandate of the Reconciliation Commission in Memory of the Victims of Political Conflicts (Comissão de Reconciliação em Memória das Vítimas dos Conflitos Políticos) seemed to be significant moves to heal deep wounds across Angolan society, they were marred by the intractability of the MPLA-dominated state and government on other issues. Although Savimbi's body was finally returned to his family, he was refused a state funeral and, in 2023, when the remains of the leaders of the 27 May uprising were finally returned to their families, independent tests revealed that the bones were not theirs (Henriques 2023). As political tensions rise, protesters continue to experience harassment and violent reprisals. In the most shocking incident of violence, in 2021, police massacred demonstrators calling for provincial autonomy in the small town of Cafunfo in the province of Lunda Norte.

As the economy continued to falter, Angolans grew angry at the lack of change and the failure to find solutions for their problems. The MPLA was too involved in internal battles to concern itself with the hardships of the majority. Instead, Lourenço introduced an IMF-backed austerity program, in which, as always, the already struggling suffered the collateral damage. Socioeconomic and political conditions intensified with the outbreak of the COVID-19 pandemic. Luandans were told to stay home. When the lockdown was lifted and a "state of calamity" introduced, strict regulations regarding circulation and sanitation remained in place. Selling in large informal markets was prohibited, curfews were established for restaurants, and official markets were only allowed to operate three days a week between 6:00 a.m. and 3:00 p.m. (*Crisis 24* 2020). The livelihoods of much of the population, who relied on the informal economy, floundered. Although people regularly broke regulations, this could subject them to violent reprisals from police, while those who obeyed orders found themselves unable to support themselves and their families (Roque 2021; Telo 2021; Human Rights Watch 2021). The effects were devastating. Lourenço's term has been marked by the advent of antipoor neoliberal austerity policies, spiraling unemployment, and internal party conflicts that have undermined attempts to implement coherent policies to assist the majority. In these kinds of circumstances, the kinds of spectacle that characterized the dos Santos regime were impossible. First, in the face of ever-growing poverty and unemployment, there was no public appetite for spectacle. When, in 2019, the minister of construction announced plans to build a Bairro dos Ministérios (Ministries District) in central Luanda, a mixed residential and government building development valued at $344 million, the public outrage led the state to quickly deny the project's existence (Dias 2021, 319). Second, Lourenço has not been able to control either the state apparatus or the MPLA to the extent that dos Santos did. Instead, he directs an increasingly securitized and economically unstable country, lacking clear policy objectives that could steer Angola back to stability.

Beyond "Cut-and-Paste" Urbanism

More than fifty years ago, Bernard Magubane (1971) warned scholars about the tendency to equate Africans' adoption of European consumption and sartorial practices with a desire for Europeanization. We would do well to heed Magubane's warning for contemporary analyses of new city and other kinds of megaproject constructions in Africa. Early analyses that tended to portray these projects as what Watson (2020) described as "cut-and-paste" failed to reckon with the complex desires, aesthetic norms, and histories with which these projects are entangled. Such approaches short-circuit attempts to reckon with the local desires, as well as various scales of political and economic interests and logics that drive their production (see also Cardoso 2016).

More recent work on megaprojects in Africa has increasingly focused on the domestic desires and practices from which these projects emerge. Scholars studying state institutions have found new city projects to be deeply embedded in domestic planning histories (Cardoso 2016; Croese 2017; Korah 2020; Fält 2019). In the case of Luanda, the origins of the new centrality initiative can be traced to planning tendencies and economic concerns that date back at least to the 1980s (see also Cardoso 2015). Urban development plans in Angola reflect decades of institutional discussions regarding how the urban environment should reflect aspirations to modernity, concerns about dedensification, and arguments about the best ways to manage urban expansion and demographic growth (Castro and Reschilian 2020). Megaprojects are commissioned by African governments, implemented by African bureaucracies, and speak to local desires and imaginations. The rise of new cities in Africa, as well as other substantial investments in infrastructure and real estate development, indicate notable shifts in transnational economic linkages, power relations, and political alliances. Recognizing the domestic origin of new city ideals is therefore necessary in order to understand the politics of contemporary city building in Africa. While the designs of new cities might take little account of the needs of the poor, they are deeply rooted in the elite and middle-class desires that determine local planning logics. This makes these plans powerful and for that reason particularly pernicious.

In recognizing the classed dimensions of new city buildings, however, we should not automatically dismiss them as distant from everyday aspirations. The new Luanda was desired and scorned by various socioeconomic groups; it was not simply an elite project. It drew from circulating imaginations of the "world-class city" while also being deeply embedded in local urban histories. It inspired ordinary people with promises of comfort while also generating profound antagonism to its very architectures, as its implementation challenged locally rooted notions of autochthony, nation, property, and class. Approaching spectacle as dazzling, megaprojects as imports, and new cities as limited to elite lifestyles does not help us understand the politics of contemporary African urbanism, or shed light on how African cities and citizens engage in worlding practices. While many Angolans felt alienated from designs conceived in architectural studios based outside the country, they also desired these very same aesthetics for their promises of international status and comfort through infrastructural provision.

The complex sentiments with which new city projects are received suggest a wide variety of sources for urban imaginations that scholarly literature has not sufficiently acknowledged. New scholarship on urbanism and planning in the Global South is pushing researchers to reassess their understandings of the formation of contemporary African cities. A growing literature on the role of socialist-aligned countries in construction and planning in Africa, Asia, and the Middle East disrupts any easy linear story of the movement from a colonial city to a postcolonial one whose futures and past are overdetermined by the previous metropole (Stanek 2020; Schwenkel 2013). In postindependence Angola, for instance, in the face of a skills vacuum, Cubans came to play a substantial role in urban planning and construction, building housing, and planning urban growth. North Koreans designed and built many of the significant public memorials. The Soviet Union is responsible for the city's best-known socialist-era landmark, the Agostinho Neto Mausoleum. Yugoslavians built two apartment blocks in central Luanda. Contemporary Luanda is a product of not just Portuguese colonialism and Indigenous confrontations with it but the complex politics of the Cold War. When they were first constructed, the "prédios cubanos" (Cuban buildings) were accused of being "foreign," and rumors circulated that the Cubans had built concrete tables and beds in them. Forty years later they have been absorbed into the city's identity. New research exploring Angola's contemporary economic and cultural relationships to Brazil is beginning to show the significant impact that Brazilian planners and architects had on twentieth- and twenty-first-century Angola (Cardoso 2022). A growing literature on policy mobilities (Croese 2017), political settlements (Goodfellow 2014), and urban interreferencing (Shatkin 2011), as well as master planning (Harrison and Croese 2023) and enclaving practices (Nielsen, Sumich, and Bertelson 2021; Ablo and Bertelson 2022; Ablo 2022), demands that we begin to think beyond the language of "African urban fantasies" that dominated early discussions of the building of new cities for the last decade, and instead study grounded ways African governments and urban residents have negotiated with, rejected, and embraced new plans, aesthetics, and imaginations of the urban. Contemporary urban redevelopment might rekindle modes of racialized unequal integration into global networks of finance, expertise, and governance. However, it is as African as any other kind of planning that has existed on the continent, even if the Africa it represents is largely an elitist exclusionary one. Urban redevelopment in Luanda acts as a site through which to study the political geographies that refract through worlding projects as residents draw on the aesthetic possibilities, material investments, and imaginations of belonging that exist in the musseques (and the rest of the city), places that oppose but also at times sit comfortably with world-city aspirations.

Concluding Notes

The case of Luanda during the oil boom offers an opportunity to better understand how material, affective, and aesthetic orientations wind through and link institutions and everyday action, shaping power struggles and contestations over the urban and with that, political belonging. It shows how the city itself acts as a political resource. Without doubt, elite political settlements shaped Luanda's geographies, as did the forms of provisional and improvisational everyday practices that have been celebrated in recent studies. But in the case of oil-boom Luanda, understanding how dissent emerged and in what forms it expressed itself requires a recognition that aesthetics provided a readily available resource through which to explore, explain, and contest Luanda's remaking. While the drying up of oil profits brought a sudden halt to much construction, it was not the international price of oil that suddenly pierced state spectacle—it had been unravelling at the same pace at which it was being made, as alternative emergent understandings of materials, design, and construction undermined its promises. Only by recognizing the critical potential of areas so often sidelined from analysis as constituting spaces of material worth can we track the dialogues that spectacle produced rather than view it as dazzling those who live in its presence.

Recognizing the critical potential of musseque materiality does not mean romanticizing these spaces. Life in musseques is hard. Residents must manage often severe water and electricity shortages. Their health suffers because of disintegrating or nonexistent sanitation and trash-collection systems. Arguing for the recognition of how histories of construction produce senses of political belonging should not be mistaken for saying that all is well. I in no way believe that people should be satisfied with the bare minimum of government services. In contrast, the government's success in appealing to comfort and care suggests that people desperately want life "with conditions." Nevertheless, in the same way as studies now recognize the critical role of provisional social relations in the making of urban life and space, they must do so for the informal material world. Prominent Angolan architect Ângela Mingas, one of the few voices to publicly defend the musseques as sites of architectural and historical significance, has emphasized that "the idea of the musseque is not to defend peoples' poor quality of life, but to defend the *origins* of the musseque. At this moment, we are still in the process of comprehending exactly what this centuries-old phenomenon emerging from Luanda is" ("2a parte da conversa com Ângela Mingas" 2015). Recognizing not just the musseques' but also other similar spaces' historical formation and contribution to the production of urban space, place, and meaning might shift how African cities are planned and conceived. Musseques emerged through histories of enslavement, structural marginalization, and racial capitalism. They are a sign of abandonment but also of lives made, futures imagined, and aspirations fulfilled. They have a material history, an aesthetic world, that could contribute to richer imaginations of urban futures and possibilities.

Felwine Sarr (2019, xiv) argues that utopian possibilities are not simply the stuff of dreams but exist in the everyday material world waiting to be recognized and nurtured. Utopia lies latent in seemingly nondescript places and objects, promising the possibility of transforming the prevailing order of things. In their obsession with the provisionality of the informal, contemporary studies have failed to recognize the political materiality of these areas, and with that, the utopian aspirations that inhere in them. Understanding provisionality and permanence as analytical frameworks and as always in coexistence enables us to bring musseques into conversation with other Indigenous and Black urbanisms across the globe as fugitive urban spaces, inheritors, perhaps, of the histories of marronage that shaped Luanda's hinterland throughout the period of the Atlantic slave trade (Ferreira 2013). As spaces that dwell both within and outside the normative visions of urbanism that have shaped Luanda's growth but have not been—and it seems to a certain degree cannot be—incorporated into them, musseques are both the site of the assertion of political claims as well as of the impossibility of such assertations in the face of systemized attempts to delegitimize and destroy these spaces. Even as the musseques bear the marks of racialized oppression that reaches back to the early years of the Atlantic slave trade, they also rewrite the geographies of domination in the city. Musseques constitute a countergeography of sentiment, history, and place-making only notable when assumptions about permanence and flight are reconsidered. Recognizing this does not automatically cast them in the position of heroic resistance; instead, it leads us to a different way of thinking the city, one that the elite desires underpinning the building of new cities have thus far refused to recognize. As Rahul Mehrotra (2008, 212) argues for the relation between informal and formal areas of Indian cities, the aim should not be to further "polarize" these different formations but to "reconcile these opposite conditions as being simultaneously valid. The existence of two worlds in the same space implies that one must accommodate and overlap varying uses, perceptions, and physical forms."

Musseques constitute an Indigenous Black urbanism that builds material communities of belonging to land and the city (see also McKittrick 2013). Oil spectacle failed not simply because reality caught up with phantasmagoria but because planners, state representatives, elites, and the burgeoning middle class failed to take note of these other material narratives and plots winding through the city. They failed to imagine Walter's delight (see chapter 2) at seeing his child sleep soundly in the house he had spent three years building, the care with which he had chosen the metal supports for his walls, his choice of higher-quality cement not only to ensure the safety of his family but to indicate that he was a person who deserved recognition. They did not see the thousands of Angolans who every year spend weekends and evenings sharing a drink and food while laying out plots. They ignored the mother who every weekend traveled from her rented house nearer the city center to the urban edge to see the progress being made by the pedreiro she had hired to build her home. They elided the construction markets in Kikolo and other parts of the city where Luandans flock to carefully select and assess the materials of home. They ignored the feeling of possibility that a newlywed couple felt as they watched a construction team begin to dig the foundations of their home.

David Harvey (2008, 23) reminds us that "aesthetic values" are central in realizing the right to the city. To return to the introduction, this is not only because the power to shape the aesthetic is also the power to shape the political and socioeconomic future of the city; it is also because, as Lewis Gordon (2018) argues, the recognition of one's aesthetic life is also a recognition of the value of that life. It is this recognition of the value of their lives and therefore of the material expression thereof that the majority of Luandans have not enjoyed. Their contributions to the making of the city have been glossed historically as provisional, poorly constructed, and undesirable rather than recognized as spaces of meaningful urbanism. The histories they represent have not been grappled with. This majority has never been invited to explain what they want from a future city. This exclusion of the majority has been and will continue to be Luanda's primary political problem, until such time as there is a means to not simply incorporate them into an overarching normative urbanism but to readjust conceptualizations of the urban to recognize their contributions. The problem of urban megaprojects, arguably, is not simply that they are implemented by elites but that they are undemocratic in their aesthetic imaginations because they tend to emerge out of undemocratic processes. Only by taking seriously the aesthetic challenge provided by spaces usually framed as "deviant," namely the musseque and its counterparts across the globe, can we begin to track alternative locally emergent aesthetic visions of cities and the histories of power that have shaped our urbanscapes. In doing this, sites of struggle, love, intimacy, and community usually ignored by elite-dominated distributions of the sensible come into focus.

ACKNOWLEDGMENTS

This book is a product of more than ten years of discussions. I am indebted to everyone who graciously provided care and support to me. My deepest appreciation is directed to the residents of Luanda who shared their stories, often painful ones. They are now scattered across the city and beyond. No doubt many of them will never read this book, but I hope that their concerns and their struggles are reflected in it and that the world it describes captures some of what it felt for them living through the oil-boom period. I would also like to thank Angolan state representatives who, contrary to what everyone told me would happen, took the time to meet with me and explain their vision for the city. I learned an immense amount from them about the challenges of urban planning in a context of notable political constraints.

Research is expensive and especially so in Luanda. I would like to acknowledge the generous support of the Wenner-Gren Foundation Dissertation Fieldwork Grant, the National Science Foundation Doctoral Dissertation Improvement Grant (Grant Number 1023797), and the Social Science Research Council International Dissertation Research Fellowship, with funds from the Andrew Mellon Foundation, for the initial funding for the project. Subsequent research was made possible by a Pozen Fellowship from the University of Chicago Human Rights Program, as well as financial support from the University of Chicago Center for the Study of Race, Politics, and Culture; the Urban Doctoral Fellows Initiative; and the University of Chicago Social Science Division. I received an American Council of Learned Society African Humanities Program Postdoctoral Fellowship that enabled me to undertake additional research needed to complete the book. An Urban Studies Foundation International Fellowship allowed for a fellowship at Harvard University in the fall of 2021, during which the bulk of this book was written.

Multiple organizations and individuals in Luanda provided institutional support, advice, and intellectual engagement in conceptualizing and carrying out my research. Rosa Melo assisted with my entry to Angola, and Manuel Alves da Rocha, Nelson Pestana, Dona Margarída, and Dona Lucia subsequently provided support for visas and an academic home at the Centro de Estudos e Investigação Científica at the Catholic University of Angola. Gilson Lázaro at Agostinho Neto University has been a colleague and friend since we were students, and I cannot thank him enough for his ongoing conversations.

Cesaltina Abreu, the late Samuel Aço, Miguel Dias, Paulo Faria, Catarina Gomes, Isabel Martins, Conceição Neto, and Cristina Pinto have been key interlocuters and friends. Development Workshop was central to my research and provided not only office space and research assistance but a collegial and supportive environment in which to learn about Luanda and Angola. I would like to extend a special thanks to Bernardo Alexandre, Helga Borges Silveira, Allan Cain, José Tiago Catito, Jeannette Dijkstra, João Domingos, Massomba Dominique, and the entire Parcil, Research, and GIS teams. My gratitude to the members of SOS Habitat is difficult to express. I thank all the communities that they work with for their willingness to let me into their lives. Your ongoing struggles for dignity are a source of inspiration. I would especially like to thank the core members of the SOS Habitat team: the late Luíz Araújo, André Augusto, Maria Candeia, Francisco Chikilson, Vítoria da Costa, Mateus Damião, Eva Pedro José Faria, Caetano Fernandes da Costa, Rafael Morais, Pimentel Luis Pacheco, the late Manuel Pinto, Pedro Narciso Rafael, and Alberto Sivi. OMUNGA welcomed me to Lobito and Benguela and explained the struggles faced by urban residents in those two cities. Special thanks go to the late José Patricínio and Jesse Lufendo for their conversations, humor, and political insights.

No research project is possible without friends. I would particularly like to thank Anabela Vidinhas, who was a source of care and exercised much patience with me. Ariana, Benjamin, Cabuenha, Carla G., Cédric, Christian G., Christian K., Cláudia R., Cláudio S., Hendrik, Indira, Ivan, Jenni, Jon, Kâmia M., Lena, Lioba, Luis Pedro, Machtheld, Martin H., Mary T., Miguel G., Murielle, Nadim, Rafael Marques, Solange, and Tobi provided friendship, laughter, and critical reflection in a city undergoing rapid change.

I moved through multiple institutional homes while researching and writing this book. The beginnings of this book were conceived while at the University of Chicago. Ralph Austen, Jean Comaroff, John Comaroff, Kesha Fikes, Susan Gal, Rachel Jean-Baptiste, Ana Lima, and William Mazzarella all provided guidance that shaped the final version of this research. Jennifer Cole read parts of the book for me and provided critical advice in its final stages. Anne Ch'ien took care of me and everyone else, and I am forever grateful for her assistance. Betsey Brada, Filipe Calvão, Kerry Chance, Lauren Coyle, Bernard Dubbeld, Falina Enriquez, Brain Horne, Sarah Kautz, Owen Kohl, George Paul Meiu, Erin Moore, Michal Ran-Rubin, Ender Ricart, Jonah Rubin, and Joshua Walker all contributed to my ideas. In Johannesburg, colleagues and friends at the University of the Witwatersrand and then the University of Johannesburg pushed me to refine my arguments. Particular thanks go to Keith Breckenridge,

Catherine Burns, Ruth Castel-Branco, Sharad Chari, Sarah Emily Duff, Joost Fontein, Casey Golomski, Pamila Gupta, Shireen Hassim, Achille Mbembe, Sarah Nutall, Ruth Sacks, Hannah Schultz, Nafisa Essop Sheik, Caio Simões de Araújo, Daria Trentini, Nolwazi Mkhwanazi, David Moore, Stephen Sparks, Jonathan Stadler, and Hylton White. At a crucial moment in the writing of this book, I was lucky to be awarded an Iso Lomso fellowship by the Stellenbosch Institute for Advanced Studies (STIAS). While the COVID pandemic prevented me from undertaking my planned project, it created the possibility of staying in place and writing. Edward Kirumira, Nel-Marie Loock, Noloyiso Mtembu, and Christoff Pauw were understanding about the very large number of divergences from my original plans. Especial thanks to Karin Brown and Leonard Katsokore, who took such good care of all the fellows. My fellowship at Harvard was hosted by Bruno Carvalho through the Harvard Mellon Urban Initiative. Without that fellowship the book would not have come into being. I especially thank him for agreeing to support me and organize my stay in a moment when international travel was particularly difficult. My participation in the 2022 African Urbanities Summer Institute at the invitation of Professor James Ogude provided me with feedback that led me to focus on Indigenous urbanism, and I deeply appreciate his encouragement in this regard. This book was completed during my first year at North Carolina State University, and I thank my colleagues for their warm encouragement.

Scholars working on Angola constitute an incredibly supportive community that I feel lucky to belong to. I am grateful to Stefanie Alisch, Jess Auerbach, Ruy Blanes, Chloé Buire, Ricardo Cardoso, Delinda Collier, Sylvia Croese, Mathias de Alencastro, Aharon DeGrassi (who also created the book's excellent maps), Rebecca Engebretson, Marta Lança, Vasco Martins, Cheryl Mei-ting Schmitz, Shana Melnysyn, Paulo Moreira, Justin Pearce, Didier Péclard, Rebecca Peters, Anne Pitcher, Paula Cristina Roque, Jon Schubert, Nadine Siegert, Ricardo Soares de Oliveira, Suzana Sousa, Antonio Tomás, and Sílvia Viegas for all the moments of laughter, intellectual exchange, and discussions in Luanda and beyond. Marissa Moorman has particularly encouraged me. From looking out for me in the field to reading multiple chapters from the book, she has provided me with a model of mentorship in the advice, care, and friendship she has provided. Finally, there are scholars and friends who I have come to know during this journey who listened and supported me. A particular thanks go to Bjørn Bertelson, Max Bolt, Mike Degani, Jatin Dua, Shakirah Hudani, Deborah James, Claire Mercer, Ghirmai Negash, Renugan Raidoo, and Drew Thompson, all of whom gave feedback either on specific chapters or discussed with me more general ideas that run through this book.

It is a rare thing to find an editor who understands the broader project that one is invested in, but I was lucky to have such an editor in María Garcia, who stewarded the project through its various stages at the University of North Carolina Press. Many people at the press read, edited, and provided other supports for this book, and my thanks goes to the entire team for their work. Four anonymous reviewers provided advice that much improved the manuscript. Parts of chapters 3 and 5 were published in *Politique Africaine* (Gastrow 2013–14), the *Avery Review* (Gastrow 2015), and *Antipode* (Gastrow 2017c). I would like to thank these journals for their permission to reuse the work in this book. MakaAngola generously granted permission to reprint two of the organization's photographs in chapter 1.

Anyone who has engaged in long-term research knows that it involves substantial sacrifices of time, labor, and love, generally born by those who are closest to you. My love and appreciation go to my parents, Peter and Shelagh Gastrow, who from early on insisted that all their children be aware of a world taking place beyond their immediate experiences. Vanya Gastrow, Michael Gastrow, Camaren Peter, and my nephews and nieces, David, Myer, Benjamin, Thomas, and Freya, thank you for putting up with an errant aunt and sister who missed birthdays, weddings, and other important days. To the family I choose, Khwezi Mkhize, my thanks for your care for Chris, Nava, and me is beyond measure. Lewis and Jane Gordon have always provided a warm home in moments when it was needed. This book is dedicated to Christopher Ouma. The manuscript was written in spurts during a pandemic in which we lost loved ones and struggled to find support. His love and everyday acts of care and optimism in the face of many obstacles guided me through a difficult period. To our beautiful Nava, you have provided a constant source of joy and love which raises my spirits every day.

GLOSSARY

anexo: Annex. Used to refer to rooms built in the yards of homes.

autoconstrução: Self-building.

bairro: Neighborhood. A contemporary word for musseque.

bloco: Concrete block.

camponês: Literally translated as "peasant" but typically used for any agriculturalist seen to be small scale and living according to any version of an imagined "traditional" life.

cantina: Small shop.

casa: House.

casa de bloco: House built of concrete blocks.

casa de chapa: House built of corrugated iron.

casa evolutiva: Houses in rehousing zones in which only a basic construction is provided. Residents are expected to finish off the house and add additional rooms themselves.

chapa: Corrugated iron.

cidade: Literally translated as "city" but also used to refer to Luanda's historical colonial urban core, or any area of formal urban settlement.

construção definitíva: Permanent construction. In the context of musseques, also used to refer to houses made of concrete blocks.

construção provisória: Provisional construction. Used to refer to any construction of materials that are not concrete blocks or brick.

cubata: Hut.

indígena: Native.

kwanza: Angolan currency.

mato: Bush.

pedreiro: Mason or bricklayer. Used to refer to professionals who design homes and oversee housing construction in musseques.

povo: People. But used in Portuguese to refer to something akin to "the masses" or "the people" as revolutionary masses.

quintal: Generally translated as "yard" (area outside a house), but also used to refer to Luanda's barracoons during the period of the Atlantic slave trade.

senzala: Kimbundu word for "village." Also used in Luanda from the seventeenth to the end of the nineteenth century to describe areas of African settlement.

sobrado: Two-story home typical of Luanda between the seventeenth and nineteenth centuries.

NOTES

Introduction

1. I have used local spellings for the names of these and other areas, which sometimes deviate from English spellings.

2. Although Angola's civil war lasted twenty-seven years (1975–2002), the country had been in the grips of armed conflict since the early 1960s. Between January and March 1961, the first instances of armed nationalist anticolonial struggle took place in various locations across Angola. The Portuguese responded with a brutal counterinsurgency campaign that plunged the country into conflict until its independence. Strictly speaking, then, Angolans experienced various degrees of armed conflict from 1961 until 2002.

3. In 2018, for instance, rumors spread in Kenya that Mombasa Port was being used as collateral to fund the construction of the new Chinese-financed Standard Gauge Railway (Brautigam 2022). In the same year, *Africa Confidential* reported that the Zambian government was considering handing over the national electricity company, ZESCO, to China in order to service its debt, a claim that the government denied (Servant 2019).

4. One of the few scholars to present careful comparative calculations of external debt in comparison to revenues, Aharon de Grassi (2015, 14), shows that while external debt grew from $9.1 billion in 2002 to $24 billion in 2013, the Angolan state's capacity to service it was eased as revenues grew from $4.1 billion to $47 billion over the same time period.

5. World Bank, "GDP (Current US$)—Angola," n.d., https://data.worldbank.org /indicator/NY.GDP.MKTP.CD?locations=AO.

6. Pearce (2015) has highlighted that these divisions were not particularly salient before the war but emerged as flashpoints as the territorial logic of the war split the coast from the interior. Rhetoric mobilized by warring parties to describe each other also encouraged shifts in identification and politics among Angolans.

7. World Bank, "Mortality Rate, Under-5 (per 1,000 Live Births)—Angola," n.d., https://data.worldbank.org/indicator/SH.DYN.MORT?locations=AO; World Bank, "Life Expectancy at Birth, Total (Years)—Angola," n.d., https://data.worldbank.org /indicator/SP.DYN.LE00.IN?locations=AO.

8. These included the 2003–4 Government Program, the 2005 Strategy for Combatting Poverty, and the 2007 "Angola 2025" Plan (GURN 2002; Ministério do Planeamento 2005, 2007).

9. Since the early 1980s, the MPLA had used oil-backed lending to ensure smooth access to funds. This system was opaque, and spending was often unaccountable (Soares de Oliveira 2015).

10. Presidential Decree 217/11 of 8 August, *Diário da República*, 1st ser., no. 150; Presidential Decree 218/11 of 8 August, *Diário da República*, 1st ser., no. 150.

11. Dias 2021 provides a comprehensive review of MPLA associates' links to leading private real estate developments in Luanda.

12. While the 2010 Constitution provides for municipal-level elections known as *autarquias*, as of early 2024, they have never been held.

13. Resolution 20/09 of 11 March, *Diário da* República, 1st ser., no. 45, formalized the PNUH, but the legislative basis for the program was laid in 2006 and 2007 with the passing of Resolution 60/06 of 4 September, *Diário da República*, 1st ser., no. 107, and the Framework Housing Law (Law 03/07 of 3 September, *Diário da República*, 1st ser., no. 106).

14. The municipal divisions of the city changed dramatically after 2012 and then again in 2017. Luanda now has nine municipalities, of which Cazenga remains one.

15. The ANC was the largest antiapartheid liberation organization in South Africa. After the official end of apartheid with the democratic elections of 1994, the ANC became the ruling party of South Africa, to this day holding a majority of seats in Parliament.

Chapter One

1. See, for instance, the story of Dona Lili in Gastrow 2020b.

2. Law 3/76 of 3 March, *Diário da República*, 1st ser., no. 52; Law 43/76 of 19 June, *Diário da República*, 1st ser., no. 144.

3. Abandonment was defined as an unjustified absence from the national territory for more than forty-five days. A persona non grata was any person who had collaborated with the Portuguese fascist state or any member of "antinational organizations."

4. Exceptions were granted for people absent from the country to carry out a mission on behalf of the state, or for medical or educational reasons.

5. The INH was disbanded with the establishment of the State Secretariat for Housing, and then reestablished after the end of the civil war.

6. Despite independent Angola's socialist pretensions, private property was allowed. In theory, families who had owned houses prior to independence and did not leave Angola were allowed to remain in and continue to officially own their properties.

7. On *autoconstrução dirigida*, see Joint Executive Decree no. 91/80 of 13 December, *Diário da República*, 1st ser., no. 293; Decree 188/80 of 17 November, *Diário da República*, 1st ser., no. 271. On GARM, see Dispatch no. 57/86 of 29 September, *Diário da República*, 1st ser., no. 78. Also see Kasack 1992.

8. *Cooperantes* were international collaborators who came to assist socialist Angola in building state institutions and delivering public services.

9. The Ilha, a small spit of land that juts off Luanda, is one of the city's primary leisure areas.

10. Dispatch No. 13/90 of 11 August, *Diário da República*, 1st ser., no. 36; also see

"Aprovado programa de emergência para o sector da habitação" 1991. The commission charged with managing it, the Comissão Nacional AD-HOC para a Habitação, served by the Grupo Técnico da Comissão Nacional AD-HOC para a Habitação, was created in August 1990 and reported to the State Secretariat for Urbanism, Housing, and Water (SEUHA). After SEUHA was broken up, the program was transferred to the newly established State Housing Secretariat (SEH). For more details, see also "Edifícios: À espera de acabamento" 1993; and "Habitação: Cem milhões de doláres" 1992.

11. Law 19/91 of 25 May, *Diário da República*, 1st ser., no. 22. Referred to as the Lei sobre a venda do patrimônio do estado (Law regarding the sale of state property).

12. The initiation of urban demolitions to enable road construction had been one of the initial flashpoints between the central government and the GPL under the Vamos Salvar Luanda initiative, with the former stepping in to prevent them.

13. During the next few weeks, the publicly announced numbers of people to be transferred fluctuated wildly, with one report stating that 13,000 families were to be removed. See "Desordeiros provocam tumultos na Boavista" 2001; and "Governo prepara tumultos para sinistrados" 2001.

14. Dar Al-Handasah is widely referred to in Angola as Grupo Dar.

15. The notion of the "Dubaization" of cities across the world is not a new one. Yasser Elseshtawy formally introduced the concept into urban studies in the early 2000s. He now runs a blog titled Dubaization, where he describes the phenomenon as "the act of building a city which relies on spectacular non-contextual architecture." See https://dubaization.com/dubaization.

16. Promotional pamphlet for the Projecto de Baía, 2008. Author's personal collection.

17. President Marien Ngouabi Road is commonly referred to as Rua António Barroso, its colonial toponym.

18. Jaime had previously held positions as the governor of the Angolan National Bank and deputy prime minister. He was eventually dismissed from his position in ANIP after reports of abuse of funds during his time at the BNA began to threaten US-Angolan relations.

19. Presidential Decree no. 59/11 of 1 April, *Diário da República*, 1st ser., no. 62.

20. Decree 87/08 of 26 September 2008, *Diário da República*, 1st ser., no. 181.

Chapter Two

1. All political parties are assigned a number (1, 2, 3, etc.) on the ballot and use that number during their campaigns to inform voters how to identify them.

2. MPLA 2012 election video, author's personal collection.

3. On "disappeared life," see the beautiful and powerful collaboration between Paulo Moreira and Lino Damião (2022) celebrating the history of Luanda's Chicala neighborhood.

4. One exception has been the advocacy of Ângela Mingas, head of the architecture department at Lusíada University in Luanda. In interviews and presentations, she has advocated for recognizing the historical, geographic, and architectural

contributions of the musseques. She runs the Musseke project, which works with students to study and conduct interviews in the city's musseques.

5. "Senzala," a Portuguese term derived from Kimbundu, refers to "an African village or African neighborhood near colonial settlements" (Neto 2012, 262).

6. Some scholars argue that practices of enslavement continued until the early twentieth century (Clarence-Smith 1979). The abolition of slavery was immediately followed by the institution of a forced labor system that remained in place until 1961 (Bender 2004).

7. The term "detribalized" emerged within colonial policy concerns as well as anthropological literature to refer to Africans who colonial authorities believed were no longer bound by the strictures of customary authority and practices.

8. There are burgeoning critiques of such imaginations of African urbanism. See, for instance, Smith 2019.

9. "Camponês" is a complex term to translate. While its literal translation is "peasant," it is commonly used to refer to any small-scale farmer. See later in this chapter for a comprehensive account of the word's meanings.

10. This was not always possible. As Cain (2007) notes, the shortage of available land has forced many Luandans to move to areas distant from their immediate kinship networks, resulting in an increasingly plural ethnic and religious composition in Luanda's musseques.

11. "Bairro 3" is a pseudonym for a neighborhood discussed in greater detail in chapter 3.

12. "Bairro 1" is a pseudonym.

13. Dos Santos passed away in 2022.

14. The MPLA refers to the May 1977 events as an attempted coup, but it remains uncertain to what extent this depiction is accurate. What is true is that on 27 May 1977, civilians and troops inspired by the former minister of interior Nito Alves attempted to take over key state institutions in the city. Their attempts were brutally quashed by Cuban troops loyal to the government; extensive purges characterized by torture and disappearances followed. This event is viewed as being responsible for the transformation of the MPLA into a vanguard rather than a popular movement. It also marks the beginning of what has been referred to as a "culture of fear" that pervades many discussions of politics in Angola (although this has slowly begun to shift since the end of the civil war in 2002).

15. Angola is officially politically divided into provinces, which are then further differentiated into municipalities and then communes. Communes are further split into bairros in urban areas and *povoações* in rural areas. Unofficially bairros are divided into sectors, which are then subdivided into quarters (*quarterões*), then blocks (*blocos*) and occasionally buildings (*prédios*) if there are mid- or high-rises in the relevant areas. It is these unofficial subdivisions that residents' committees manage. Many also manage bairros given that there is not yet any elected local government in Angola. It is important to note that, given that the divisions of sectors, quarters, and blocks reaches back into the 1970s, their borders do not always perfectly align with official neighborhood boundaries.

16. The 2010 Constitution provides for local elections known as *autarquias*, designed to usher in official bottom-up local political representation. However, these have not yet taken place. As a result, there is no system of officially elected local governance in Angola. Instead residents' committees exist as a voluntary form of organization to feed neighborhood concerns to municipal authorities.

17. Residents' committees were formalized through the passing of Law No. 7/16 of 1 June 2016, *Diário da República*, 1st ser., no. 87. They were defined as nonpartisan voluntary organizations that assisted in bettering the lives of people in the neighborhoods. The legislation empowers them to cooperate with the local administration and local government (when it one day exists), on the following issues, among others: identifying citizens and foreigners in the neighborhood; reporting illegal construction and land occupations; informing the administration about the presence of illegal immigrants, illegal commerce, and illegal churches; managing violations of the law including laws pertaining to sanitation and hygiene; and keeping the neighborhood clean.

18. "Amigos da Cazenga" is a pseudonym.

Chapter Three

1. Pseudonyms have been used for the names of the neighborhoods around Nova Vida.

2. I refer to the "Luanda region" because the boundaries of Luanda province were redrawn in 2012 during my fieldwork. Panguila initially fell within Luanda's borders but after the redrawing of the borders fell outside of it.

3. The principal pieces of legislation governing tenure and property rights as regards land and housing are the 2010 Constitution, the 2004 Territorial Planning Law (Law 3/04 of 25 June, *Diário da República*, 1st ser., no. 51), the 2004 Land Law (Law 9/04 of 9 November, *Diário da República*, 1st ser., no. 90), the 2007 Land Law regulations (Decree 58/07 of July 13, *Diário da República*, 1st ser., no. 84), the 1988 Family Law (Law 1/88 of 20 February, *Diário da República*, 1st ser., no. 8), and Angola's Civil Code. There are, furthermore, several province-specific decrees and resolutions that regulate projects and policies in those areas.

4. "Acquisitive prescription" refers to a method of acquiring property through its occupation or possession over a legally specified time period.

5. Angolan Civil Code, Articles 1293 through 1297.

6. In April 2023 opposition parties complained about this confusion of state and party, arguing that people "lost their fear" of building in an area once a CAP was present. See DF 2023.

7. In contemporary Luanda, Maculusso is considered a central and desirable neighborhood. The "sanitation syndrome," that is, the use of the threat of disease as justification for the segregation of Africans from Europeans in colonial cities, was a trope found across the African continent. See Swanson 1977.

8. Dispatch 8/07 of 13 April, *Diário da República*, 1st ser., no. 45.

9. Although there were different models of housing, with the exception of the

casa evolutiva discussed in chapters 3 and 4, there were no significant differences between the models. If a particular tranche of houses had been commissioned by the same client, they generally followed the same model.

10. "Proposta preliminar: Plano director de Nova Vida," slide presentation by Aurecon, author's personal collection.

11. Known as *autoconstrução dirigida* (literally, "directed self-building"), this form of building was akin to site-and-service programs. In theory, recipients were meant to receive plots that had infrastructure connections and assistance with purchasing materials and construction. I never witnessed a successful example of these initiatives during my research.

Chapter Four

1. Vamos Andar is a pseudonym.

2. In Luanda, people purchasing water from public water stands and private suppliers pay considerably more per liter than those who access it through the grid. Ironically, the wealthy therefore tend to pay less for water than the poor do (Cain and Baptista 2020).

3. Angola's 2014 census statistics do not break down how many households have access to water from the grid in their homes. Rather, it calculates how many people have access to what it calls "water suitable for drinking." I do not know anyone who drinks water directly from the tap in Angola without treating it, and so what exactly this measure represents is unclear. The statistics provided for the access to "water suitable for drinking" at the national level perhaps better represent what the primary sources of general-purpose water are for households, while those for Luanda seem to largely indicate what proportion of the population is able to access water through largely formal means (i.e., not buying it from tankers or from stores). The 2014 census included "tap connected to the public network, public fountain, borehole with pump, waterhole or protected springs" in its definition of "water suitable for drinking" (INE 2016, 70). These definitions still seem lacking, however, as even people with access to indoor plumbing have water tanks and often purchase water from private sources.

4. People in Luanda tended to refer to partners with whom they lived and raised children as wives or husbands even if they were not formally married. I have chosen to use people's terminologies for their various relationships rather than judge them against state-sanctioned categories.

5. The Escom group has been linked to multiple financial scandals in Angola. See Marques de Morais 2018.

6. At the time of this writing, people who had been rehoused were not yet required to do so.

7. Publicity booklet released at the launch of Kilamba, July 2011. Author's personal collection.

8. By 2011, the initial aims of the project had been overcome by property speculation. Houses were now beyond the reach of the average civil servant, and the

project's second and third phases were subsidized by a consortium of banks and had to be paid off with credit and loans.

9. Diogo used the English word "skills."

10. This is a private real estate project aimed at the middle class and elites.

11. A newspaper later reported that the casa evolutivas did not comply with the government's regulations regarding adequate housing. See "Residências do Zango 3 e 4 a margem da lei" 2013.

Chapter Five

1. Rialto was destroyed for the construction of the plaza dedicated to the "Unknown Soldier," a memorial to all those who had died fighting during the country's civil war.

2. Civil society letter to the Minister of Culture, 28 January 2009. Author's personal collection.

3. "In defense of what remains of Luanda" (title of civil society petition), 2 March 2009. Author's personal collection.

4. Cheryl Mei-ting Schmitz (2014) found similar relations of suspicion and antagonism in her study of quotidian Chinese-Angolan relations.

5. *Capim* translates as "grass," but in the context of the conversation it made more sense to translate it as "bush." People often described an area as being full of capim when they arrived there; removing it was one of the signs of creating a neighborhood. The word therefore did not simply connote "grass" but was associated with a wildness, or "bush."

6. "Chave na mão" ("turnkey") is when a contractor is responsible for all aspects of project design and construction. They deliver a ready-to-use product to the client.

7. When using terms such as "the Angolan" or "Angolaness," I am not suggesting that a single or stable vision exists of them. Rather, I am voicing my interlocutors' words. Their statements often expressed deeply problematic notions of citizenship and nation that reinforced discriminatory understandings of musseque residents as ill-equipped to cope with the demands of the world city. These accounts would, no doubt, be challenged by other Angolans but were nevertheless ubiquitous in the interviews I conducted.

8. The FAPLA were the MPLA-government armed forces during the civil war.

Conclusion

1. "Angolan Kwanza," *Trading Economics*, n.d., accessed 29 November 2023, https://tradingeconomics.com/angola/currency.

2. J. Lourenço, "Promover e criar uma boa imagem de Angola no estrangeiro," Facebook, 18 April 2023, https://www.facebook.com/photo/?fbid=785255429622663.

REFERENCES

Ablo, A. D. 2022. "Private Urbanism and the Spatial Rationalities of Urban Governance." *Urban Studies* 60, no. 3: 442–60.

Ablo, A. D., and B. E. Bertelsen. 2022. "A Shadowy 'City of Light': Private Urbanism, Large-Scale Land Acquisition and Dispossession in Ghana." *International Journal of Urban and Regional Research* 46, no. 3: 370–86.

Africa Confidential. 2002. "An Edited Peace: Quick Moves to a Ceasefire; Much Slower Ones on Political and Economic Reform." 19 April.

Agha, Menna, and Léopold Lambert. 2020. "Outrage: Informality Is a Fallacy." *Architectural Review*, 16 December. https://www.architectural-review.com/essays /outrage/outrage-informality-is-a-fallacy.

Aguilar, Renato. 2001. "Angola's Incomplete Transition." Discussion Paper no. 2001/47. United Nations University.

Amado, F. R., F. Cruz, and Ralph Hakkert. 1992. "Urbanização e desurbanização em Angola." *Cadernos de População e Desenvolvimento* 1, no. 1: 57–92.

Amnesty International. 2003. *Angola: Mass Forced Evictions in Luanda—A Call for a Human Rights–Based Housing Policy.* London: AI Index.

———. 2007. *Angola. Lives in Ruins: Forced Evictions Continue.* London: AI Index.

———. 2008. Letter to Ms. Anna Tibaijuka, 6 October. REF: TIGO IOR. 40/021/2008. Also signed by Human Rights Watch, Centre on Housing Rights and Eviction, and Habitat International Coalition. Author's personal collection.

———. 2009. *Angola: Forced Evictions on a Mass Scale.* London: AI Index.

Anand, N. 2011. "Pressure: The Politechnics of Water Supply in Mumbai." *Cultural Anthropology* 26, no. 4: 487–509.

Anand, N., A. Gupta, and H. Appel. 2018. *The Promise of Infrastructure.* Durham, NC: Duke University Press.

Anderson, D., and R. Rathbone. 2000. *Africa's Urban Past.* London: Heinemann.

Appel, H. 2012. "Walls and White Elephants: Oil Extraction, Responsibility, and Infrastructural Violence in Equatorial Guinea." *Ethnography* 13: 439–65.

"Aprovado programa de emergência para o sector da Habitação." 1991. *Jornal de Angola*, 31 May, 1.

Apter, Andrew. 2005. *The Pan-African Nation: Oil and the Spectacle of Culture in Nigeria.* Chicago: University of Chicago Press.

Araújo, L. 2010. "Um lágrima pelo povo e pelo e pelo Estado de Angola." *Pambazuka News*, 4 April. https://www.pambazuka.org/pt/governance/uma-l%C3 %A1grima-pelo-povo-e-pelo-estado-de-angola.

Auerbach, J. 2020. *From Water to Wine: Becoming Middle Class in Angola.* Toronto: University of Toronto Press.

Baptista, J. 1993. "Ainda sobre o 'despejo arbitrário.'" *Jornal de Angola*, 2 February, 2.

Barber, K. 1982. "Popular Reactions to Petro-Naira." *Journal of Modern African Studies* 20, no. 3: 431–50.

Bender, G. J. 2004. *Angola under the Portuguese: The Myth and the Reality*. Trenton, NJ: Africa World.

Benjamin, Walter. 1968. "The Work of Art in the Age of Mechanical Reproduction." In *Illuminations*, edited by Hannah Arendt, 217–51. New York: Schocken.

———. 2002 [1935]. *The Arcades Project*. Translated by Howard Eiland and Kevin McLaughlin. Cambridge, MA: Belknap and Harvard University Press.

Berry, Sara. 1993. *No Condition Is Permanent: The Social Dynamics of Agrarian Change in Sub-Saharan Africa*. Madison: University of Wisconsin Press.

Birmingham, David. 2006. "Race and Class in a 'Fascist' Colony." In *Empire in Africa: Angola and Its Neighbors*, 80–95. Athens: Ohio University Press.

———. 2016. *A Short History of Modern Angola*. Oxford: Oxford University Press.

Bissell, W. C. 2010. *Urban Design, Chaos and Colonial Planning in Zanzibar*. Bloomington: Indiana University Press.

Blanes, R. 2019. "Austerity en Route, from Lisbon to Luanda." *Focaal—Journal of Global and Historical Anthropology* 83: 37–50.

Blanes, R. L., and H. Samussuku. 2022. "Afro-Autarky: *Onjangos* and Utopias of Contemporary Angolan Activism." *Critical Times* 5, no. 2: 475–93.

Blomley, N. 1998. "Landscapes of Property." *Law & Society Review* 32, no. 3: 567–612.

Bolt, M. 2021. "Fluctuating Formality: Home Ownership, Inheritance and the Official Economy in Urban South Africa." *Journal of the Royal Anthropological Institute* 27, no. 4: 976–94.

Bourdieu, P. 1984. *Distinction: A Social Critique of the Judgement of Taste*. Cambridge, MA: Harvard University Press.

Brautigam, D. 2022. "Mombasa Port: How Kenya's Auditor-General Misread China's Standard Gauge Railway Contracts." *The Conversation*, 16 May. https://theconversation.com/mombasa-port-how-kenyas-auditor-general-misread-chinas-standard-gauge-railway-contracts-182610.

Brautigam, D., and Jyhjong Hwang. 2016. "Eastern Promises: New Data on Chinese Loans in Africa, 2000–2014." Working Paper no. 2016/4. China-Africa Research Initiative, School of Advanced International Studies, Johns Hopkins University, Washington, DC. http://www.sais-cari.org/publications.

Brinkman, I. 2003. "War and Identity in Angola: Two Case Studies." *Lusotopie* 10: 195–221.

Buire, C. 2014. "The Dream and the Ordinary: An Ethnographic Investigation of Suburbanisation in Luanda." *African Studies* 73, no. 2: 290–312.

———. 2017. "New City, New Citizens? A Lefebvrian Exploration of State-Led Housing and Political Identities in Luanda, Angola." *Transformation: Critical Perspectives on Southern Africa* 93: 13–40.

———. 2018. "Intimate Encounters with the State in Post-war Luanda, Angola." *Journal of Development Studies* 54, no. 12: 2210–26.

————. 2022. "Crumbling Modernisms: Luanda Architectonic Utopias after the Boom." *Critical African Studies* 14, no. 3: 274–92.

Cain, A. 2007. "Housing Micro-finance in Angola: Overcoming Socioeconomic Exclusion through Land Tenure and Access to Credit." *Environment and Urbanization* 19, no. 2: 361–90.

————. 2010. "Research and Practice as Advocacy Tools to Influence Angola's Land Policy." *Environment & Urbanization* 22, no. 2: 505–22.

————. 2013. "Angola: Land Resources and Conflict." In *Land in Postwar Peacebuilding*, edited by Jon Unruh and Rhodri C. Williams, 177–204. New York: Earthscan.

————. 2017a. "The Cooperative Housing Sector in Angola." Luanda: Development Workshop; and Johannesburg: Centre for Affordable Housing in Africa. http://housingfinanceafrica.org/documents/cooperative-housing-sector-angola/.

————. 2017b. "The Private Housing Sector in Angola: Angola's Tentative Development of a Private Real-Estate Market." Centre for Affordable Finance in Africa and Development Workshop. https://housingfinanceafrica.org/app/uploads/DWA_CAHF_Private-Sector-Housing-in-Angola_February-2017.pdf.

Cain, A., and A. C. Baptista. 2020. "Community Management and the Demand for 'Water for All' in Angola's *Musseques*." *Water* 12, no. 6: 1592. https://doi.org/10.3390/w12061592.

Caldeira, A. M. 2013. "Luanda in the 17th Century: Diversity and Interaction in the Process of Forming an Afro-Atlantic City." *Nordic Journal of African Studies* 22, nos. 1 and 2: 72–104.

Caldeira, T. P. 2017. "Peripheral Urbanization: Autoconstruction, Transversal Logics, and Politics in Cities of the Global South." *Environment and Planning D: Society and Space* 35, no. 1: 3–20.

Callaci, E. 2017. *Street Archives and City Life: Popular Intellectuals in Postcolonial Tanzania*. Durham, NC: Duke University Press.

Candeias, Pedro, Jorge Malheiros, José Carlos Marques, and Ermelinda Liberato. 2019. "Portuguese Emigration to Angola (2000–2015): Strengthening a Specific Postcolonial Relationship in a New Global Framework?" In *New and Old Routes of Portuguese Emigration*, edited by Cláudia Pereira and Joana Azevedo, 209–35. IMISCOE Research Series. Cham, Switzerland: Springer.

Canham, Hugo ka. 2023. *Riotous Deathscapes*. Durham, NC: Duke University Press.

Cardoso, R. 2015. "The Crude Urban Revolution: Land Markets, Planning Forms, and the Making of the New Luanda." PhD diss., University of California, Berkeley.

————. 2016. "The Circuitries of Spectral Urbanism: Looking Underneath Fantasies in Luanda's New Centralities." *Urbanisation* 1, no. 2: 95–113.

————. 2022. "Seeing Luanda from Salvador: Lineaments of a Southern Atlantic Urbanism." *Antipode* 54, no. 3: 729–51.

Carima, A. 1994. "Dois inquilínos legais para uma casa apenas." *Jornal de Angola*, 5 February, 7.

Castel-Branco, R. 2021. "A Radical Politics of Distribution? Work, Welfare and Public Works Programs in Rural Mozambique." PhD diss., University of the Witwatersrand.

Castro, J. C., and P. R. Reschilian. 2020. "Metropolozação e planejamento territorial como perspectiva de desenvolvimento em Angola." *Cadernos Metrópole* 22, no. 49: 841–68.

"Cento e vinte famílias habitam sem condições de alojamento." 1979. *Jornal de Angola*, 28 July, 3.

Chatterjee, Partha. 2004. *The Politics of the Governed: Reflections on Popular Politics in Most of the World*. New York: Columbia University Press.

Choplin, A., and A. Frank. 2010. "A Glimpse of Dubai in Khartoum and Nouakchott: Prestige Urban Projects on the Margins of the Arab World." *Built Environment* 36, no. 2: 192–205.

Clarence-Smith, W. G. 1979. *Slaves, Peasants and Capitalists in Southern Angola, 1840–1926*. Cambridge: Cambridge University Press.

"CM aprova programa de apoio aos sinistrados." 2001. *Jornal de Angola*, 26 April, 4.

"Comissariado de Luanda: Comunicação sobre a construção clandestina." 1977. *Jornal de Angola*, 14 July, 3.

"Construção clandestina: Chegou a hora de resolver a problema." 1977. *Jornal de Angola*, 5 March, 3.

Coquery-Vidrovitch, C. 2009. *The History of African Cities South of the Sahara: From the Origins to Colonization*. Princeton, NJ: Markus Wiener.

Corkin, Lucy. 2011. "Uneasy Allies: China's Evolving Relations with Angola." *Journal of Contemporary African Studies* 29, no. 2: 169–80.

———. 2012. "Angolan Political Elites' Management of Oil Credit Lines." In *China and Angola: A Marriage of Convenience?*, edited by Marcus Power and Ana Cristina Alves, 45–67. Cape Town: Pambazuka.

Coronil, F. 1997. *The Magical State: Nature, Money and Modernity in Venezuela*. Chicago: University of Chicago Press.

Cortez, J. 1960. "A habitação dos AxiLuanda." *Memórias e Trabalhos do Instituto de Investigação Científica de Angola* 2: 145–75.

Côté-Roy, L., and S. Moser. 2019. "'Does Africa Not Deserve Shiny New Cities?' The Power of Seductive Rhetoric around New Cities in Africa." *Urban Studies* 56, no. 12: 2391–407.

Coulthard, G. S. 2014. *Red Skin, White Masks: Rejecting the Colonial Politics of Recognition*. Minneapolis: University of Minnesota Press.

Cowcher, Kate E. 2014. "Luanda Onde Está? Contemporary African Art and the Rentier State." *Critical Interventions* 8, no. 2: 140–59.

Crisis 24. 2020. "Angola: Authorities Extend State of Calamity Measures through September 8." 24 April. https://crisis24.garda.com/alerts/2020/08/angola-authorities-extend-state-of-calamity-measures-through-september-8-update-10.

Croese, Sylvia. 2011. "One Million Houses? Angola's National Reconstruction and

Chinese and Brazilian Engagement." In *Strengthening the Civil Society Perspective*, series 2, *China and Other Emerging Powers in Africa*, 7–29. Cape Town: Fahamu.

———. 2013. "Post-war State-Led Development at Work in Angola: The Zango Housing Project in Luanda as a Case Study." PhD diss., Stellenbosch University.

———. 2015. "Inside the Government, but Outside the Law: Residents' Committees, Public Authority and Twilight Governance in Post-war Angola." *Journal of Southern African Studies* 41, no. 2: 405–17.

———. 2017. "Global Urban Policymaking in Africa: A View from Angola through the Redevelopment of the Bay of Luanda." *International Journal of Urban and Regional Research* 42, no. 2: 198–209.

Croese, Sylvia, and M. A. Pitcher. 2019. "Ordering Power? The Politics of State-led Housing Delivery under Authoritarianism—The Case of Luanda, Angola." *Urban Studies* 56, no. 2, 401–18.

Dar al-Handasah. 1996a. "Institutional and Financial Aspects." Urban Land Use and Growth Management Plan and Road and Storm Water Drainage for a Pilot Musseque, City of Luanda. Technical Paper 4. Luanda: Governo Provincial de Luanda.

———. 1996b. "Urban Land Use and Environmental Assessment." Urban Land Use and Growth Management Plan and Road and Storm Water Drainage for a Pilot Musseque, City of Luanda. Technical Paper 6. Luanda: Governo Provincial de Luanda.

Datta, Ayona. 2016. "Introduction: Fast Cities in an Urban Age." In *Mega-urbanization in the Global South: Fast Cities and New Urban Utopias of the Post-colonial State*, edited by Ayona Datta and Abdul Shaban, 1–27. London: Routledge.

de Boeck, Filip. 2011. "Inhabiting Ocular Ground: Kinshasa's Future in Light of Congo's Spectral Urban Politics." *Cultural Anthropology* 26, no. 2: 263–86.

de Boeck, Filip, and Sammy Baloji. 2016. *Suturing the City: Living Together in Congo's Urban Worlds*. London: Autograph ABP.

de Boeck, Filip, and Marie-Françoise Plissart. 2004. *Kinshasa: Tales of an Invisible City*. Ghent-Amsterdam: Ludion.

Degani, M. 2022. *The City Electric: Infrastructure and Ingenuity in Postsocialist Tanzania*. Durham, NC: Duke University Press.

de Grassi, A. 2015. "Provisional Reconstructions: Geo-histories of Infrastructure and Agrarian Configuration in Malanje, Angola." PhD diss., University of California, Berkeley.

de Grazia, V. 2005. *Irresistible Empire: America's Advance through the Twentieth Century*. Cambridge, MA: Belknap and Harvard University Press.

de Melo, A. 2001. "Moradores da Boavista serão transferidos para Viana." *Jornal de Angola*, 27 April, 9.

Desai, R., C. McFarlane, and S. Graham. 2015. "The Politics of Open Defecation: Informality, Body and Infrastructure in Mumbai." *Antipode* 47, no. 1: 98–120.

"Desestimular a ocupacão illegal de terrenos." 1999. *Jornal de Angola*, 7 October, 8.

"Desordeiros provocam tumultos na Boavista." 2001. *Jornal de Angola*, 2 July, 1.

Development Workshop. 2005. *Terra: Urban Land Reform in Post-war Angola—Research, Advocacy and Policy Development*. Luanda: Development Workshop.

———. 2010. *Perfil do Município do Cazenga*. Luanda: Development Workshop.

DF. 2023. "'Comités de Acção do MPLA em áreas proibidas estimulam construções anárquicas em Luanda,' acusam FNLA e PRS." *NovoJornal*, 21 April. https://www.novojornal.co.ao/politica/interior/comites-de-accao-do-mpla-em-areas-proibidas-estimulam-construcoes-anarquicas-em-luanda-acusam-fnla-e-prs-112857.html.

Dias, J. 1986. "Changing Patterns of Power in the Luanda Hinterland: The Impact of Trade and Colonisation on the Mbundu, ca. 1845–1920." *Paideuma: Mitteilungen zur Kulturkunde* 32: 285–318.

Dias, M. 2020. "Fantasias globais e realidades locais: O projecto de reconversão urbana do Cazenga e Sambizanga, Luanda." MA thesis, University of Porto.

———. 2021. "Centralised Clientalism, Real Estate Development and Economic Crisis: The Case of Postwar Luanda." *African Geographical Review* 40, no. 3. doi:10.1080/19376812.2021.1933555.

"Distribuidas chaves de 100 novas residências no acto central do Dia do Construtor." 1979. *Jornal de Angola*, 4 December, 1.

do Amaral, I. 1983. "Luanda e os seus 'muceques': Problemas de geografia urbana." *Finisterra* 18, no. 36: 293–325.

Doherty, J. 2017. "Life (and Limb) in the Fast Lane: Disposable People as Infrastructure in Kampala's Boda Boda Industry." *Critical African Studies* 9, no. 2: 192–209.

———. 2019. "Maintenance Space: The Political Authority of Garbage in Kampala, Uganda." *Current Anthropology* 60, no. 1: 24–46.

Dorries, Heather. 2022. "Indigenous Urbanism as an Analytic: Towards Indigenous Urban Theory." *International Journal of Urban and Regional Research*. doi:10.1111/1468-2427.13129.

dos Santos, D. 1990a. "The Second Economy in Angola: *Esquema* and *Candonga*." In *The Second Economy in Marxist States*, edited by Maria Łoś, 157–74. London: Macmillan.

———. 1990b. "Soares da Costa e Transnáutico garantem para os próximos tempos investimentos de valto da economia angolana." *Jornal de Angola*, 18 February, 1.

Duarte de Carvalho, R. 2008. *A Câmera, a escrita e a coisa dita . . . fitas, textos, e palestras*. Lisboa: Cotovia.

"Edifícios: À espera de acabamento." 1993. *Jornal de Angola: Segundo Caderno*, 1 September, 3.

Eduardo, D. 1982. "Prédio Oliva com os dias contados." *Jornal de Angola*, 3 November, 3.

———. 1983. "O trabalho da Emproci face ao estado de alguns imóveis." *Jornal de Angola*. 22 December, 2.

———. 1984. "Quais são as persepctivas de habitação no novo ano que começa?" *Jornal de Angola*, 1 January, 1.

EIA (U.S. Energy Information Administration). 2024. "US FOB Costs of Angola Crude Oil." https://www.eia.gov/dnav/pet/hist/LeafHandler.ashx?n=PET &s=IAO0000004&f=A.

Elias, N. 2000. *The Civilising Process: Sociogenetic and Psychogenetic Investigations.* Oxford, UK: Blackwell.

Elinoff, E. 2016. "A House Is More Than a House: Aesthetic Politics in a Northeastern Thai Railway Settlement." *Journal of the Royal Anthropological Institute* 22: 610–32.

Enwezor, O. 2003. "Terminal Modernity: Rem Koolhaas's Discourse on Entropy." In *What Is OMA: Considering Rem Koolhaas and the Office for Metropolitan Architecture*, edited by Véronique Patteeuw, 103–19. Rotterdam: NAi Publishers.

Fabian, J. 2002. *Time and the Other: How Anthropology Makes Its Object.* New York: Columbia University Press.

Fält, L. 2019. "New Cities and the Emergence of 'Privatized Urbanism' in Ghana." *Built Environment* 44, no. 4: 438–60.

Faria, Paulo C. J. 2013. *The Post-war Angola: Public Sphere, Political Regime, and Democracy.* Newcastle upon Tyne, UK: Cambridge Scholars.

Fassin, D. 2009. "Les économies morales revisitées." *Annales: Histoire, Sciences Sociales* 64: 1237–66. https://www.cairn.info/revue—2009-6-page-1237.htm.

Ferguson, James. 1999. *Expectations of Modernity: Myths and Meanings on the Zambian Copperbelt.* Berkeley: University of California Press.

Ferreira, R. 2013. "Slavery and the Social and Cultural Landscapes of Luanda." In *The Black Urban Atlantic in the Age of the Slave Trade*, edited by Jorge Cañizares-Esguerra, Matt D. Childs, and James Sidsbury, 185–206. Philadelphia: University of Pennsylvania Press.

Francisco, A., and M. Viera. 2015. "Novo 'burrismo' ou preparação para um colonização chinesa?" *Central Angola 7311*, 6 March. Author's personal collection.

Frias, S., and C. U. Rodrigues. 2018. "Private Condominiums in Luanda: More Than Just the Safety of Walls, a New Way of Living." *Social Dynamics* 44, no. 2: 341–58.

"Fui espancado por 20 homens." 1993. *Jornal de Angola*, 18 August, 5.

Gal, S. 2002. "A Semiotics of the Public/Private Distinction." *Differences* 13, no. 1: 77–95.

Gandy, M. 2005a. "Cyborg Urbanization: Complexity and Monstrosity in the Contemporary City." *International Journal of Urban and Regional Research* 29, no. 1: 26–49.

———. 2005b. "Learning from Lagos." *New Left Review* 33: 36–52.

———. 2006. "Planning, Anti-planning and the Infrastructure Crisis Facing Metropolitan Lagos." *Urban Studies* 43, no. 2: 371–96.

"Garantido apoio às vítimas das chuvas." 2001. *Jornal de Angola*, 18 April, 1.

Gastrow, C. 2013–14. "'Vamos Construir!': Revendications foncières et géographie du pouvoir à Luanda, Angola." *Politique Africaine* 132: 49–72.

———. 2015. "Thinking Futures through the Slum." *Avery Review*, no. 9. https://averyreview.com/issues/9/thinking-futures.

———. 2017a. "Cement Citizens: Housing, Demolition and Political Belonging in Luanda, Angola." *Citizenship Studies* 21, no. 2: 224–39.

———. 2017b. "Urban." *Somatosphere.* http://somatosphere.net/2017/urban
.html/.

———. 2017c. "Aesthetic Dissent: Urban Redevelopment and Political Belonging
in Luanda, Angola." *Antipode* 49, no. 2: 377–96.

———. 2020a. "Urban States: The Presidency and Planning in Luanda, Angola."
International Journal of Urban and Regional Research 44, no. 2: 366–83.

———. 2020b. "DIY Verticality: The Politics of Materiality in Luanda." *City & Society* 32, no. 1: 93–117.

———. 2021. "Capturing *Poder Popular*: Governance and Control in Early Socialist
Angola." In *African Socialisms*, edited by Françoise Blum, 433–53. Paris: Maison
des Sciences de l'Homme.

Geschiere, P. 2009. *The Perils of Belonging: Autochthony, Citizenship, and Exclusion in
Africa and Europe.* Chicago: University of Chicago Press.

Geschiere, P., and F. Nyamnjoh. 2000. "Capitalism and Autochthony." *Public Culture* 12, no. 2: 423–52.

Ghertner, D. Asher. 2015. *Rule by Aesthetics: World-Class City Making in Delhi.*
Oxford: Oxford University Press.

Gilroy, P. 1993. *The Black Atlantic: Modernity and Double Consciousness.* London:
Verso.

Gluckman, M. 1960. "Tribalism in Modern British Central Africa." *Cahiers d'Études
Africaines* 1, no. 1: 55–70.

Goodfellow, T. 2014. "Rwanda's Political Settlement and Urban Transition: Expropriation, Construction, and Taxation in Kigali." *Journal of East African Studies* 8,
no. 2: 311–29.

Gordon, L. R. 2013. "On the Temporality of Indigenous Identity." In *The Politics of
Identity: Emerging Indigeneity*, edited by Michelle Harris, Martin Nakata, and
Bronwyn Carlson, 60–77. Sydney: University of Technology.

———. 2018. "Black Aesthetics, Black Value." *Public Culture* 30, no. 1: 19–34.

"Governo constrói 7,500 casas em Luanda." 2001. *Jornal de Angola*, 8 November, 1.

"Governo prepara tumultos para sinistrados." 2001. *Jornal de Angola*, 30 April, 9.

"GPL atira cidadãos a rua." 1999. *Jornal de Angola*, 27 January, 9.

"GPL concede terreno a Sonangol." 1994. *Jornal de Angola*, 1 December, 5.

"GPL continua a desalojar." 1999. *Jornal de Angola*, 29 January, 8.

"GPL descarta culpa." 2009. *O País*, 31 July, 23.

Graham, S., and S. Marvin. 2001. *Splintering Urbanism: Networked Infrastructures,
Technological Mobilities and the Urban Condition.* London: Routledge.

Greger, Otto. 1990. "Angola." In *Housing Policies in the Socialist Third World*, edited
by Kosta Mathéy, 129–45. London: Mansell.

Griffiths, Aaron. 2004. "The End of the War: The Luena Memorandum of Understanding." In *From Military Peace to Social Justice: The Angolan Peace Process*,
edited by Guus Meijer, 24–27. London: Accord.

Guardiola, N. 2003. "Assalto à baía." *Expresso*, 22 November, 62–70.

GURN (Governo de Unidade e Reconciliação Nacional). 2002. *Programa do Governo para o périodo 2003–2004.* Luanda: GURN.

"Habitação: Cem milhões de doláres." 1992. *Jornal de Angola*, 23 May, 6.

Harms, Eric. 2012. "Beauty as Control in the New Saigon: Eviction, New Urban Zones, and Atomized Dissent in a Southeast Asian City." *American Ethnologist* 39, no. 4: 735–50.

Harrison, P., and S. Croese. 2023. "The Persistence and Rise of Masterplanning in Urban Africa: Transnational Circuits and Local Ambitions." *Planning Perspectives* 38, no. 1: 25–47.

Harvey, D. 2008. "The Right to the City." *New Left Review* 53: 23–40.

Henriques, L. 2023. "Angola: Corpos de vítimas do 27 de maio não correspondem ao seu ADN—familiares." *RFI* (Radio France Internationale), 23 March. https://www.rfi.fr/pt/angola/20230323-angola-corpos-de-v%C3%ADtimas-do-27-de-maio-n%C3%A3o-correspondem-ao-seu-adn-familiares.

Hickel, Jason. 2014. "'Xenophobia' in South Africa: Order, Chaos, and the Moral Economy of Witchcraft." *Cultural Anthropology* 29, no. 1: 103–27.

"Hitler: Os apartamentos do Kilamba." n.d. YouTube video. https://www.youtube.com/watch?v=le_P37SDLW0.

Hodges, T. 2004. *Angola: Anatomy of an Oil State*. Oxford: James Currey; Bloomington: Indiana University Press.

Hodgson, D. L. 2009. "Becoming Indigenous in Africa." *African Studies Review* 52, no. 3: 1–32.

Hoffman, D. 2017. *Monrovia Modern: Urban Form and Political Imagination in Liberia*. Durham, NC: Duke University Press.

Holston, James. 1991a. "Autoconstruction in Working-Class Brazil." *Cultural Anthropology* 6, no. 4: 447–65.

———. 1991b. "The Misrule of Law: Land and Usurpation in Brazil." *Comparative Studies in Society and History* 33, no. 4: 695–725.

———. 2009. "Insurgent Citizenship in an Era of Global Peripheries." *City & Society* 21, no. 2: 245–67.

Human Rights Watch. 2003. *Struggling through Peace: Return and Resettlement in Angola*. 15 August. https://www.hrw.org/report/2003/08/15/struggling-through-peace/return-and-resettlement-angola.

———. 2007. *They Pushed Down the Houses* 19, no. 7 (A). https://www.hrw.org/reports/2007/angola0507/angola0507.htm.

———. 2021. "Angola: Events of 2020." *World Report*. https://www.hrw.org/world-report/2021/country-chapters/angola.

Hutchison, Y. 2020. "African Indigeneity: The Southern African Challenge." In *Indigeneity and Nation*, edited by G. N. Devy and Geoffrey V. Davis, 102–16. London: Routledge.

INE (Instituto Nacional de Estatística). 2016. *Resultados definitivos do recenseamento geral da população e da habitação de Angola 2014*. Luanda: INE.

Jackson, S. 2006. "Sons of Which Soil? The Language and Politics of Autochthony in Eastern DR Congo." *African Studies Review* 49, no. 2: 95–123.

James, C. L. R. 1989 [1938]. *The Black Jacobins: Toussaint L'Ouverture and the San Domingo Revolution*. 2nd ed. London: Vintage.

Johnson, C. E. 2018. "The Moral Economy of Comfortable Living: Negotiating Individualism and Collectivism through Housing in Belgrade." *Critique of Anthropology* 38, no. 2: 156–71.

José, H. 2011. "The Regularization of Illegal Occupants: An Exercise of Citizenship." *Revista IPGUL*, special edition, 4–9.

José, M. 2023. "Angola: Milhares de desalojados por demolições aguardam há anos por promessas do governo." *Voz de America*, 4 October. https://www.voaportugues.com/a/angola-milhares-de-desalojados-por-demolições-aguardam-há-anos-por-promessas-do-governo/7296899.html.

Kaika, M., and E. Swyndegouw. 2000. "Fetishizing the Modern City: Phantasmagoria of Urban Technological Networks." *International Journal of Urban and Regional Research* 24, no. 1: 120–38.

Kasack, S. 1992. "Perspektiven für partizipatives Squatterupgrading in Luanda/Angola—eine Feasibility-Studie im QuartierLixeira, Bairro Sambizanga." PhD diss., Rheinischen Friedrich-Wihelms-Universität.

Keniston, B. 2022. "No Asylum for Her Majesty: The British FCO and Complicity with Apartheid." *South African Historical Journal* 73, no. 4: 859–77.

Kimari, W., and H. Ernstson. 2020. "Imperial Remains and Imperial Invitations: Centering Race within the Contemporary Large-Scale Infrastructures of East Africa." *Antipode* 52: 825–46.

King, Tiffany Lethabo. 2016. "New World Grammars: The 'Unthought' Black Discourses of Conquest." *Theory and Event* 19, no. 4. https://muse.jhu.edu/article/633275.

Klieman, K. 2003. *The Pygmies Were Our Compass: Bantu and Batwa in the History of West Central Africa, Early Times to C. 1900 C.E.* Portsmouth, NH: Heinemann.

Koolhaas, R., S. Boeri, S. Kwinter, N. Tazi, and H. U. Obrist. 2000. *Mutations.* New York: Actar.

Korah, P. I. 2020. "Exploring the Emergence and Governance of New Cities in Accra, Ghana." *Cities* 99. https://doi.org/10.1016/j.cities.2020.102639.

Kuper, A. 2003. "The Return of the Native." *Current Anthropology* 44, no. 3: 389–402.

Larkin, B. 2018. "Promising Forms: The Political Aesthetics of Infrastructure." In *The Promise of Infrastructure*, edited by Nikhil Anand, Akhil Gupta, and Hannah Appel, 175–202. Durham, NC: Duke University Press.

Latour, Bruno. 2007. *Reassembling the Social: An Introduction to Actor-Network-Theory.* Oxford: Oxford University Press.

Lázaro, G. J. S. 2010. "Angola: Discursos e práticas dominantes de reconciliação e construção da nação." MA thesis, Instituto Universitário de Lisboa.

Lopes, A. M. 1994. "Violação da propriedade privada." *Jornal de Angola*, 8 February, 2.

Louçã, F., J. Costa, and J. Texeira Lopes. 2014. *Os donos angolanos de Portugal.* Lisbon: Betrand.

"Luanda continua em debate." 1993. *Jornal de Angola*, 13 May, 1.

"Luanda cuide-se." 1993. *Jornal de Angola*, 9 May, 1.

Mabeko-Tali, J.-M. 2001. *Dissedências e poder de estado (1962—1977): Ensaio de história política*, vol. 2, *1974–1977*. Luanda: Nzila.

Magubane, B. 1971. "A Critical Look at Indices Used in the Study of Social Change in Colonial Africa." *Current Anthropology* 12, no. 4-5: 419–45.

Mains, D. 2019. *Under Construction: Technologies of Development in Urban Ethiopia*. Durham, NC: Duke University Press.

Makana, S. 2018. "Contested Encounters: Toward a Twenty-First-Century African Feminist Ethnography." *Meridians: Feminism, Race, Transnationalism* 17, no. 2: 361–75.

Makhulu, A.-M. 2015. *Making Freedom: Apartheid, Squatter Politics and the Struggle for Home*. Durham, NC: Duke University Press.

Malaquis, A. 2012. "China Is Angola's New Best Friend—For Now." In *China and Angola: A Marriage of Convenience?*, edited by Marcus Power and Ana Cristina Alves, 26–44. Cape Town: Pambazuka.

Malkki, L. 1995. *Purity and Exile: Violence, Memory, and National Cosmology among Hutu Refugees in Tanzania*. Chicago: University of Chicago Press.

Mamdani, M. 1996. *Citizen and Subject: Contemporary Africa and the Legacy of Late Colonialism*. Princeton, NJ: Princeton University Press.

Marcum, J. 1969. *The Angolan Revolution*, vol. 1, *The Anatomy of an Explosion (1950—1962)*. Cambridge, MA: MIT Press.

Marcus, G. E. 1995. "Ethnography in/of the World System: The Emergence of Multi-sited Ethnography." *Annual Review of Anthropology* 24, no. 1: 95–117.

Marques de Morais, R. 2009. "The Influence Peddling of Grupo Gema." *MakaAngola*, December. http://www.makaangola.org/wp-content/uploads /2012/04/TraficoInfluenciasGrupoGema_EN.pdf.

———. 2012. "Water for Chevron and Lessons for the Government." *MakaAngola*, 18 December. https://www.makaangola.org/2012/12/water-for-chevron-and-a -lesson-for-the-government/.

———. 2018. "Half-a-Billion-Dollar Scam of Espírito Santo Bank in Angola." *Maka Angola*, 5 March. https://www.makaangola.org/2018/03/the-half-a-billion-dollar -scam-of-espirito-santo-bank-in-angola/.

Martins, I. 2000. "Luanda: A cidade e a arquitectura." PhD diss., University of Porto.

Martins, V. 2017. "Politics of Power and Hierarchies of Citizenship in Angola." *Citizenship Studies* 21, no. 1: 100–115.

Mateus, E. 2009. "'Cavalaria de Aço' devasta Iraque e sua 'capital' Bagdad." *O Pais*, 31 July, 20.

Matlon, J. 2022. *A Man among Other Men: The Crisis of Black Masculinity in Racial Capitalism*. Ithaca, NY: Cornell University Press.

Mazzarella, William. 2006. *Shovelling Smoke: Advertising and Globalisation in Contemporary India*. Durham, NC: Duke University Press.

Mbembe, A. 2001. *On the Postcolony*. Berkeley: University of California Press.

———. 2002. "African Modes of Self-Writing." *Public Culture* 14, no. 1: 239–73.

McFarlane, C. 2010. "Infrastructure, Interruption, and Inequality: Urban Life in the Global South." In *Disrupted Cities: When Infrastructure Fails*, edited by Stephen Graham, 131–44. New York: Routledge.

McGovern, Mike. 2011. *Making War in Côte d'Ivoire*. Chicago: University of Chicago Press.

McKay, R. 2017. *Medicine in the Meantime: The Work of Care in Mozambique*. Durham, NC: Duke University Press.

McKittrick, K. 2006. *Demonic Grounds: Black Women and Cartographies of Struggle*. Minneapolis: University of Minnesota Press.

———. 2011. "On Plantations, Prisons, and a Black Sense of Place." *Social & Cultural Geography* 12, no. 8: 947–63.

———. 2013. "Plantation Futures." *Small Axe*, no. 42 (November): 1–15.

Mehrotra, R. 2008. "Negotiating the Static and Kinetic City: The Emergent Urbanism of Mumbai." In *Other Cities, Other Worlds: Urban Imaginaries in a Globalizing Age*, edited by A. Huyssen, 205–18. Durham, NC: Duke University Press.

Melly, C. 2017. *Bottleneck: Moving, Building, and Belonging in an African City*. Chicago: University of Chicago Press.

Mendelsohn, B. 2018. "Making the Urban Coast: A Geosocial Reading of Land, Sand and Water in Lagos, Nigeria." *Comparative Studies of South Asia, Africa and the Middle East* 38, no. 3: 455–72.

Mendes, A. C. 1988. "Slum Housing in Luanda, Angola: Problems and Possibilities." In *Slum and Squatter Settlements in Sub-Saharan Africa*, edited by R. A. Obudho and Constance C. Mhlanga, 231–43. New York: Praeger.

Mercer, C. 2014. "Middle Class Construction: Domestic Architecture, Aesthetics, and Anxieties in Tanzania." *Journal of Modern African Studies* 52, no. 2: 227–50.

Messiant, Christine. 1992. "Social and Political Background to the 'Democratization' and Peace Process in Angola." In *Democratization in Angola*, 13–42. Amsterdam: Eduardo Mondlane Foundation.

———. 2001. "The Eduardo dos Santos Foundation: Or, How Angola's Regime Is Taking Over Civil Society." *African Affairs* 100: 287–309.

———. 2008. "The Mutation of Hegemonic Domination: Multiparty Politics without Democracy." In *Angola: The Weight of History*, edited by Patrick Chabal and Nuno Vidal, 93–123. London: Hurst.

Miller, J. 1988. *Way of Death: Merchant Capitalism and the Angolan Slave Trade, 1730–1830*. Madison: University of Wisconsin Press.

Mingas, Â. C. B. L. 2011. "Centro histórico da cidade de Luanda: História, caracterização e estratégias de intervenção para a salvaguarda." MA thesis, University Lusíada do Porto.

Ministério do Planeamento. 2005. *Estratégia de combate de pobreza: Reinserção social, reabilitação e reconstrução, e estabilização económica*. Luanda: Governo de Reconciliação Nacional.

———. 2007. *Angola 2025: Angola, um país com futuro*. Luanda: República de Angola.

Mitchell, Clyde. 1956. *The Kalela Dance*. Manchester, UK: Rhodes-Livingstone Institute.

Monteiro, R. L. 1973. *A família nos musseques de Luanda: Subsídios para o seu estudo.* Luanda: Fundação de Acção Social no Trabalho em Angola.

Monteith, W. 2019. "Markets and Monarchs: Indigenous Urbanism in Postcolonial Uganda." *Settler Colonial Studies* 9, no. 2: 247–65.

Moorman, M. 2008. *Intonations: A Social History of Music and Nation in Luanda, Angola, from 1945 to Recent Times.* Athens: Ohio University Press.

Moreira, P., and L. Damião. 2022. "Chicala." In *Critical Neighbourhoods: The Architecture of Contested Communities*, edited by Paulo Moreira, 33–63. Zürich: Park.

Morton, D. 2013. "From Racial Discrimination to Class Segregation in Postcolonial Urban Mozambique." In *Geographies of Privilege*, edited by F. W. Twine and B. Gardner, 260–92. New York: Routledge.

———. 2019. *Age of Concrete: Housing and the Shape of Aspiration in the Capital of Mozambique.* Athens: Ohio University Press.

Moser, S. 2015. "New Cities: Old Wine in New Bottles?" *Dialogues in Human Geography* 5, no. 1: 31–35.

Moser, S., and L. Côté-Roy. 2021. "New Cities: Power, Profit and Prestige." *Geography Compass* 15, no. 1: e12549.

Mourão, F. A. A. 2006. *Continuidades e descontinuidades: De um processo colonial através uma leitura de Luanda—Uma interpretação do desenho urbano.* Luanda: FESA; São Paulo: CEA/USP.

Mouzinho, A., and S. Cutaia. 2017. "Reflections on Feminist Organizing in Angola." *Feminist Africa* 22: 33–51.

Mukuna, P. 2003. "Luandenses prestigiados querem travar mega-projecto da Baía de Luanda." *Agora*, 1 November, 11.

Murray, M. J. 2015. "City-Doubles: Re-urbanism in Africa." In *Cities and Inequalities in a Global and Neoliberal World*, edited by Faranak Miraftab, David Wilson, and Kenneth Salo, 92–109. New York: Routledge.

Muvuma, A. 2013. "Nobel da Paz para JES . . . pela independência da África do Sul!" *MakaAngola*, 17 January. https://www.makaangola.org/2013/01/nobel-da-paz-para-jes-pela-independencia-da-africa-do-sul/.

Myers, G. 2015. "A World-Class City-Region? Envisioning the Nairobi of 2030." *American Behavioral Scientist* 59, no. 3: 328–46.

"Nacionalizar a construção civil." 1975. *Jornal de Angola*, 27 December, 2.

Naqvi, I. 2018. "Contesting Access to Power in Urban Pakistan." *Urban Studies* 55, no. 6: 1242–56.

Ndjio, B. 2005. "Carrefour de la Joie: Popular Deconstruction of the African Postcolonial Public Sphere." *Africa* 75: 265–94.

Neto, C. 2012. "In Town and Out of Town: A Social History of Huambo (Angola), 1902–1961." PhD diss., School of Oriental and African Studies, University of London.

Nielsen, M. 2011. "Inverse Governmentality: The Paradoxical Production of Peri-urban Planning in Maputo, Mozambique." *Critique of Anthropology* 31, no. 4: 329–58.

Nielsen, M., J. Sumich, and B. E. Bertelsen. 2021. "Enclaving: Spatial Detachment as an Aesthetics of Imagination in an Urban Sub-Saharan African Context." *Urban Studies* 58, no. 5: 881–902.

"No Place for the Poor, Angola." 2001. *Economist*, 4 August, 42.

Nyamnjoh, Francis B. 2007. "'Ever-Diminishing Circles': The Paradoxes of Belonging in Botswana." In *Indigenous Experience Today*, edited by Marisol de la Cadena and Orin Starn, 305–32. London: Routledge.

———. 2012. "Blinded by Sight: Divining the Future of Anthropology in Africa." *Africa Spectrum* 47, no. 2/3: 63–92.

Oliveira, V. S. 2022. *Slavery and Abolition: Gender, Commerce and Economic Transition in Luanda*. Madison: University of Wisconsin Press.

Ong, Aihwa. 2006. *Neoliberalism as Exception: Mutations in Citizenship and Sovereignty*. Durham, NC: Duke University Press.

———. 2011. "Introduction: Worlding Cities or the Art of Being Global." In *Worlding Cities: Asian Experiments and the Art of Being Global*, edited by Ananya Roy and Aihwa Ong, 1–26. Oxford, UK: Blackwell.

Onishi, N. 2017. "Angola's Corrupt Building Boom: 'Like Opening Up a Window and Throwing Money Out.'" *New York Times*, 24 June. https://www.nytimes.com/2017/06/24/world/africa/angola-luanda-jose-eduardo-dos-santos.html.

Pearce, Justin. 2001. "Poor Angolans Lose Bay View to the Rich." *The Guardian*, 17 August. https://www.theguardian.com/world/2001/aug/18/3.

———. 2005. *An Outbreak of Peace: Angola's Situation of Confusion*. Cape Town: David Philip.

———. 2015. *Political Identity and Conflict in Central Angola, 1975–2002*. New York: Cambridge University Press.

Péclard, D. 2012. "UNITA and the Moral Economy of Exclusion in Angola, 1966–1977." In *Sure Road? Nationalisms in Angola, Guinea-Bissau and Mozambique*, edited by Eric Morier-Genoud, 149–74. Leiden, the Netherlands: Brill.

Pelican, M. 2009. "Complexities of Indigeneity and Autochthony: An African Example." *American Ethnologist* 36, no. 1: 52–65.

Pepetela. 1990. *Luandando*. Luanda: Elf-Aquataine, Angola.

Perdiz, R. 1985. "Emproci quer por cobro a degradação dos imóveis de Luanda." *Jornal de Angola*, 27 February, 10.

"Plano Director Geral de Luanda traz mudanças na capital do país." 2019. *Jornal de Angola*, 2 February. https://www.jornaldeangola.ao/ao/noticias/plano-director-geral-de-luanda-traz-mudancas-na-capital-do-pais/.

PlanoLuanda. 2015. *PlanoLuanda: Construção de uma cidade para o futuro*. Author's personal collection.

Power, Marcus. 2012. "Angola 2025: The Future of the 'World's Richest Poor Country' as Seen through a Chinese Rear-View Mirror." *Antipode* 44, no. 3: 993–1014.

"PR aponta soluções para acudir sinistrados." 2001. *Jornal de Angola*, 17 April, 3.

"PR convoca reunião de emergência." 2001. *Jornal de Angola*, 17 April, 1.

Pratt, M. L. 1985. "'Scratches on the Face of the Country'; Or, What Mr. Barrow Saw in the Land of the Bushmen." *Critical Inquiry* 12, no. 1: 119–43.

"Preços elevados sem justificação." 2011. *Jornal de Angola*, 27 February.

"Projectos de realojamento serão estendidos a todo o país." 2001. *Jornal de Angola*, 8 July, 1.

"Proteger os cidadãos." 2001. *Jornal de Angola*, 2 July, 2.

Quayson, Ato. 2014. *Oxford Street, Accra: City Life and the Itineraries of Transnationalism*. Durham, NC: Duke University Press.

Rakodi, C. 1986. "Colonial Urban Policy and Planning in Northern Rhodesia and Its Legacy." *Third World Planning Review* 8 no. 3: 193–217.

Ramiro, A. 1980. "Um quebra-cabeças que merece solução começando pelos próprios moradores." *Jornal de Angola*, 10 May, 1.

———. 1986. "Carência da habitação: A crise é cada vez mais séria." *Jornal de Angola*, 3 December, 10.

Rancière, J. 2010. *Dissensus: On Politics and Aesthetics*. London: Continuum.

Redinha, J. 1964. *A habitação tradicional angolana, aspectos da sua evolução*. Luanda: Centro Informação e Turismo de Angola.

"Residências do Zango 3 e 4 a margem da lei." 2013. *Novo Jornal*, 5 August. https://novojornal.co.ao/reportagem/interior/residencias-do-zango-3-e-4-a-margem-da-lei-8985.html.

Rijke-Epstein, Tasha. 2023. *Children of the Soil: The Power of Built Form in Urban Madagascar*. Durham, NC: Duke University Press.

Rita, G. 2010. "Requalificação urbana de Luanda." *Revista IPGUL* 3: 4.

Robson, Paul, and Sandra Roque. 2001. *Aqui na cidade nada sobre para ajudar: Buscando solidariedade e acção collectiva em bairros peri-urbanos de Angola*. Luanda: Development Workshop.

Rocha, A. 2015. "Angola dirige-se para um disastre político e social." *Deutsche Welle*, 29 January. http://www.dw.de/angola-dirige-se-para-um-desastre-pol%C3%ADtico-e-social/a-18235304.

"Rocha leva embaixadores à Boavista e Zango." 2001. *Jornal de Angola*, 11 October, 15.

Rodgers, D., and B. O'Neill. 2012. "Infrastructural Violence: Introduction to the Special Issue." *Ethnography* 13, no. 4: 401–12.

Rodrigues, C. U. 2012. "Angolan Cities: Urban (Re)segregation." In *African Cities: Competing Claims on Urban Spaces*, edited by Paul Nugent and Francesca Locatelli, 37–53. Leiden, the Netherlands: Brill.

Roque, Paula Cristina. 2021. *Governing in the Shadows: Angola's Securatized State*. Oxford: Oxford University Press.

Roque, Sandra. 2009. "Ambitions of Cidade: War-Displacement and Concepts of the Urban among Bairro Residents in Benguela, Angola." PhD diss., University of Cape Town.

———. 2011. "Cidade and Bairro: Classification, Constitution and Experience of Urban Space in Angola." *Social Dynamics* 37, no. 3: 332–48.

Roy, A. 2017. "Dis/possessive Collectivism: Property and Personhood at City's End." *Geoforum* 80: A1–11.

Santana, P. 1997. "Processo de venda de casas estagnado." *Jornal de Angola*, 30 June, 2.

Sarr, F. 2019. *Afrotopia*. Minneapolis: University of Minnesota Press.

Sawyer, L. 2019. "Natures Remade and Imagined: 'World-City' Beautification and Real Estate Reclamation in Lagos." In *Grounding Urban Natures: Histories and Futures of Urban Ecologies*, edited by H. Ernston and S. Sörlin, 83–107. Cambridge, MA: MIT Press.

Schmitz, C. M. 2014. "Significant Others: Security and Suspicion in Chinese-Angolan Encounters." *Journal of Current Chinese Affairs* 43, no. 1: 41–69.

Schubert, J. 2015. "2002, Year Zero: History as Anti-politics in the 'New Angola.'" *Journal of Southern African Studies* 41, no. 4: 835–52.

———. 2017. *Working the System: A Political Ethnography of the New Angola*. Ithaca, NY: Cornell University Press.

———. 2022. "Disrupted Dreams of Development: Neoliberal Efficiency and Crisis in Angola." *Africa* 92: 171–90.

Schwenkel, C. 2013. "Post/socialist Affect: Ruination and Reconstruction of the Nation in Urban Vietnam." *Cultural Anthropology* 28, no. 2: 252–57.

"Se bem canta em Viana." 2001. *Jornal de Angola*, 17 July, 17.

"2a parte da conversa com Ângela Mingas." 2015. *Acrimar: Arquitectura e urbanismo*, 2 March. http://acrimararquitectura.blogspot.com/2015/03/2-parte-da-conversa -com-angela-mingas.html.

Servant, J.-C. 2019. "China Steps In as Zambia Runs Out of Loan Options." *The Guardian*, 11 December. https://www.theguardian.com/global-development/2019 /dec/11/china-steps-in-as-zambia-runs-out-of-loan-options.

Shatkin, G. 2011. "Planning Privatopolis: Representation and Contestation in the Deveopment of Urban Integrated Mega-Projects." In *Worlding Cities: Asian Experiments and the Art of Being Global*, edited by Ananya Roy and Aihwa Ong, 77–97. Oxford, UK: Blackwell.

Shoko, R. 2002. "Angola Faces Deepening Health Crisis." *Reliefweb*, 14 June. https:// reliefweb.int/report/angola/angola-faces-deepening-health-crisis.

Sikiti da Silva, I. 2009. "Angola: Slow Recovery." Open Society Foundation. *Voices*, 18 May. https://www.opensocietyfoundations.org/voices/angola-slow -recovery.

Silva, V. 2011. "Luanda privatizado." *Novo Jornal*, 12 August, 10–13.

Silver, J. 2023. *The Infrastructure South: Techno-environments of the Third Wave of Urbanization*. Cambridge, MA: MIT Press.

Simone, A. 2004. "People as Infrastructure: Intersecting Fragments in Johannesburg." *Public Culture* 16, no. 3: 407–29.

———. 2010. *City Life from Jakarta to Dakar: Movements at the Crossroads*. New York: Routledge.

Smith, C. 2019. *Nairobi in the Making: Landscapes of Time and Urban Belonging*. Suffolk, UK: James Currey.

Soares de Oliveira, Ricardo. 2015. *Magnificent and Beggar Land: Angola since the Civil War*. London: Hurst.

SOS Habitat. 2012. *A justiça e os desalojamentos forçados em Luanda, Angola*. Luanda: SOS Habitat.

Stanek, L. 2020. *Architecture in Global Socialism: Eastern Europe, West Africa, and the Middle East in the Cold War.* Princeton, NJ: Princeton University Press.

Swanson, M. 1977. "The Sanitation Syndrome: Bubonic Plague and Urban Native Policy in the Cape Colony, 1900–1909." *Journal of African History* 18, no. 3: 387–410.

Tallie, T. J. 2019. *Queering Colonial Natal: Indigeneity and the Violence of Belonging in Southern Africa.* Minneapolis: University of Minnesota Press.

Tarbush, N. 2012. "Cairo 2050: Urban Dream or Modernist Delusion?" *Journal of International Affairs* 65, no. 2: 171–86.

Telo, F. C. A. 2021. "Mulheres e comércio (informal) em Luanda: Um olhar além da crise pandémica de Covid19." *Revista Espaço Acadêmico* 21: 13–24.

Thomas, D. A. 2019. *Political Life in the Wake of the Plantation: Sovereignty, Witnessing, Repair.* Durham, NC: Duke University Press.

Ticktin, Miriam I. 2011. *Casualties of Care: Immigration and the Politics of Humanitarianism in France.* Berkeley: University of California Press.

Tomás, A. 2012. "Refracted Governmentality: Space, Politics, and Social Structure in Contemporary Luanda." PhD diss., Columbia University.

———. 2014. "Mutuality from Above: Urban Crisis, the State, and the Work of the Comissões de Moradores in Luanda." *Anthropology Southern Africa* 37, no. 3–4: 175–86.

———. 2022. *In the Skin of the City: Spatial Transformation in Luanda.* Durham, NC: Duke University Press.

Trovalla, E., and Ulrike Trovalla. 2015. "Infrastructure as a Divination Tool: Whispers from the Grids in a Nigerian City." *City* 19, no. 2–3: 332–43.

Tsandzana, Dércio. 2018. "'You Just Killed Me': The Internet Meme Defying Angola's Government." Translated by Liam Anderson. *GlobalVoices Africa*, 8 March. https://globalvoices.org/2018/03/08/you-just-killed-me-the-internet-meme -defying-angolas-government/.

Tutton, M. 2011. "African City Named World's Most Expensive for Expats." *CNN*, 15 July. http://edition.cnn.com/2011/BUSINESS/07/14/luanda.expensive.city /index.html.

UNDP (UN Development Programme). 1999. *Relatório do desenvolvimento humano: Angola 1999.* Luanda: UNDP.

USAID (US Agency for International Development). 2010. *Review of Real Estate Financing in Angola, with Recommended Actions for the BNA to Meet New Challenges.* Luanda: USAID.

"Vamos salvar Luanda." 1993. *Jornal de Angola*, 28 April, 1.

van Noorloos, F., and M. Kloosterboer. 2017. "Africa's New Cities: The Contested Future of Urbanization." *Urban Studies* 55, no. 6: 1223–41.

Vines, A., et al. 2005. *Angola: Drivers of Change—An Overview.* London: Chatham House.

Vollgraaff, R. 2019. "Angola's Kwanza Plunges to Record Low on Black Market: Chart." *Bloomberg*, 12 July. https://www.bloomberg.com/news/articles/2019 -07-12/angola-s-kwanza-plunges-to-record-low-on-black-market-chart.

von Schnitzler, A. 2016. *Democracy's Infrastructure: Technopolitics and Protest after Apartheid*. Princeton, NJ: Princeton University Press.

Waldorff, P. 2016. "'The Law Is Not for the Poor': Land, Law and Eviction in Luanda." *Singapore Journal of Tropical Geography* 37, no. 3: 363–77.

Watson, V. 2014. "African Urban Fantasies: Dreams or Nightmares?" *Environment and Urbanization* 26, no. 1: 215–31.

———. 2020. "Digital Visualization as a New Driver of Urban Change in Africa." *Urban Planning* 5, no. 2: 35–43.

Watts, Michael. 1992. "The Shock of Modernity: Petroleum, Protest and Fast Capitalism in an Industrializing Society." In *Reworking Modernity: Capitalisms and Symbolic Discontents*, edited by Allan Pred and Michael Watts, 21–63. New Brunswick, NJ: Rutgers University Press.

———. 2012. "A Tale of Two Gulfs: Life, Death and Dispossession along Two Oil Frontiers." *American Quarterly* 64, no. 3: 437–67.

White, L. 1990. *The Comforts of Home: Prostitution in Colonial Nairobi*. Chicago: University of Chicago Press.

———. 2000. *Speaking with Vampires: Rumor and History in Colonial Africa*. Berkeley: University of California Press.

Wilson, Godfrey. 1941–42. *An Essay in the Economics of Detribalisation*. Manchester, UK: Rhodes-Livingstone Institute.

Wolfe, P. 2006. "Settler-Colonialism and the Elimination of the Native." *Journal of Genocide Research* 8, no. 4: 387–409.

World Bank. 2011. *The Case of Angola: Strengthening Citizenship through Upgrading Informal Settlements*. Luanda: Development Workshop and the World Bank.

Wright, G. 1991. *The Politics of Design in French Colonial Urbanism*. Chicago: University of Chicago Press.

Zenki Real Estate. 2013. *ZReport: Angola Property Market*. Luanda.

"Zona da Boavista regista tumultos." 2001. *Jornal de Angola*, 2 July, 11.

abolition, 70–71, 192n6

administrative divisions, 18, 19, 190n14, 192n15; unofficial, 91. *See also* GPL; local government; residents' committees

aesthetic, 9; politics as unstable, 8, 10, 125, 153

aesthetic dissent, 10, 153, 168–69, 174. *See also* Rancière, Jacques

aesthetics of belonging, 10, 125, 130, 140–41; as recognition, 182

aesthesis, 55, 127–30, 135–37

architecture, 13, 14, 34, 68, 165; as "foreign," 150–52, 164–65, 178; of musseques, 73–76

assimilados, 71, 161

Associação Kalu, 68, 156–57

autarquias. See local government

autochthony, 10, 69, 79, 106, 161–63, 164, 168; narratives of, 86–91. *See also* Indigeneity

autoconstruction (*autoconstrução*), 38, 39, 80–82, 87; directed (*autoconstrução dirigida*), 38, 44, 122, 190n7, 194n11; as urban autochthon, 88. *See also* musseques; self-building

AxiLuanda, 73–74

Bagdad (neighborhood), 1, 5, 98, 104

barracoons (*quintais*), 14, 69, 70

Black urbanism, 10, 68, 181

Boavista, 43–48, 55, 98, 109

Brazil, 7, 17, 42, 70–71, 98, 179

camponêses: definition of, 88, 192n9; as original inhabitants of the land but not city, 87, 88, 90–91, 166; purchasing land from, 84

CAP (party action committee), 94, 100, 103–5, 193n6

care: and infrastructure, 125–26, 128–30, 138, 140; national reconstruction as care, 19–20, 31; and the state, 32, 64–65; state's failure to provide, 33–34, 39; as violence, 31, 43–48, 57–58, 61, 64, 172

Cazenga: conducting research in, 23; histories of settlement, 87–89, 93–94; redevelopment of, 56–63, 166

China, 17, 23, 158–60, 163, 173, 189n3. *See also* oil; Sinophobia; xenophobia

cidades: and colonialism, 14–15; in need of redevelopment, 50, 135–37; relationship to musseques, 12–14, 68–69, 73, 141

citizenship: anxieties about, 153, 160, 161; and autochthony, 162, 168; and colonialism, 71; creation through urban planning, 56; defined by wealth, 129, 138–39, 141–43, 162; and infrastructure, 142–45; and oil, 8, 30–31, 64–65, 152; and state responsibility, 44. *See also* autochthony; class; Native Act; xenophobia

civil war, 6, 15, 21, 161, 189n2; and demolition, 107; effects of, on Luanda, 33–34; and urban land, 101–2

class: as aesthetic experience, 119, 128–29, 136, 137, 140, 142–43; and citizenship, 142–45; and consumerism, 7, 172; and housing policy, 137–42; and infrastructure, 130–37; and urbanism, 4, 8, 20, 50, 64–65, 118, 157–18, 165. *See also* citizenship; comfort; housing; new cities colonial urbanism, 4, 11–14, 36–37, 59, 134, 165, 178; in Angola, 70–73, 75, 106–7; and erasure of materiality, 76–78, 83–84

comfort: and the home, 125, 129–32, 140, 146; and infrastructure, 49, 53–55, 126, 136, 137; politics of, 20, 48–50, 152. *See also* discomfort

concrete, 73, 79, 150, 179; permanence of, 83, 84, 86. *See also* concrete-block houses; housing; musseques

concrete-block houses (*casas de bloco*), 27; cost of construction, 85; demolition of, 111–15; as evidence of urban belonging, 80, 82–83, 106; use as political strategy, 120–23. *See also* autoconstruction; musseques; self-building

Construction Materials Company, 39

corrugated-iron houses (*casas de chapa*): as not houses, 2; as proof of marginalization, 119; as provisional, 83

COVID-19, 176

CPBs (People's Neighborhood Commissions), 35, 92. *See also* residents' committees

Cuba, 15, 39, 86, 94, 107, 157, 161, 178–79, 192n14

Dar al-Handasah (Grupo Dar), 40, 47–48, 61, 191n14

demolition, 25, 59, 68, 74, 159; as care, 31, 44, 46–48, 57, 59; during the civil war, 42–43, 191n12; history of, 73, 106–7; and institutions, 109–11, 115; and Nova Vida, 118–19; personal accounts of, 108, 112, 113-114, 116–17; seeking compensation for, 120–24. *See also* Boavista; care; Cazenga; housing; musseques; Nova Vida

"detribalization," 74, 192n7

Development Workshop, 23, 26

discomfort, 38, 49, 119, 132, 146

displacement: by architecture and aesthetics, 164–67; after the civil war, 31, 109, 159; foreigners blamed for, 159–60; by urban planning, 14; during civil war, 15, 41, 83, 112. *See also* demolition; xenophobia

dos Santos, Isabel, 171

dos Santos, José Eduardo: as foreign, 161–62; as symbol of peace and reconstruction, 19–20; death of, 192n13; resignation of, 175–77. *See also* Presidency

dubaization (*dubaização*), 48, 50, 151, 155–58, 164, 191n15

EDURB (Urban Development Company), 42–43, 107

Eduardo dos Santos Foundation, 47

electricity, 49, 53, 130, 131–33, 140, 143

EMPROCI (Provincial Property Conservation Company), 37, 39

EMPROMAC (Construction Materials Company), 39

enslavement, 5, 13, 14, 69, 70–71, 128, 180, 192n6

FESA (Eduardo dos Santos Foundation), 47

FNLA (National Front for the Liberation of Angola), 15, 93

fugitivity, 14, 69, 79, 95, 181

GARM (Office for the Renewal and Rehabilitation of the Musseques), 38, 190n7

gender, 132–34

GOE (Office for Special Works), 17, 18, 43, 46, 109

GPL (Luanda Provincial Government), 42–45. *See also* administrative divisions

GRN (Office for National Reconstruction), 17, 18

GTRUCS (Technical Office for the Urban Reconversion of Cazenga, Sambizanga, and Rangel), 18, 61

heritage, 14, 54–55, 68, 71, 156–58
housing: colonial, 12, 60; as electoral strategy 20, 40; incremental (*casa evolutiva*), 141, 145, 195n11; musseque house as financial investment, 79; nationalization of, 35–37; privatization of, 40; social housing, 109, 138, 141; "with conditions" (*em condições*), 49, 125, 129, 137, 144, 146, 180. *See also* concrete-block houses; corrugated-iron houses; Kilamba; new centralities; Nova Vida; Panguila; rehousing; Zango

Imogestin, 95, 118, 140
Indigeneity, 10–14, 68–69; AxiLuanda as Indigenous 73; as critique of MPLA, 161; legitimating narratives of, 90, 91. *See also* AxiLuanda; autochthony; Indigenous urbanism; xenophobia
Indigenous urbanism: musseques as, 2, 10–15, 68–69, 78–79, 86–91, 96, 181; threatened by world-class city aesthetics, 167
informality, 2, 5, 61–63, 181; and infrastructure, 136; and materiality in African urban studies, 76–79, 83–84, 95; as mischaracterizing musseque construction, 11–14; as product of war, 33–34, 38–39, 41, 43. *See also* musseques; provisionality; residents' committees
infrastructure, 3–4, 16–18, 21, 130–32; breakdown of, during war, 37–38, as care, 59, 61, 63–64, 126; and inequality, 140–43; as peace dividend, 29–31, 34; people as infrastructure, 134–37; and political mobilization, 18–20, 49,

53, 140; as sensorial experience, 49, 53–55, 127–29, 133. *See also* aesthesis; care; comfort; national reconstruction; new cities
Iraque (neighborhood), 1, 5, 98, 104, 113

Kilamba: and aesthetic dissent, 174; cost of construction, 20; cost of rent-to-own, 64; and Hitler video, 99–100; and infrastructure, 138, 140–41; as propaganda, 49. *See also* new centralities

land tenure, 56, 101–4. *See also* law; legislation; property
law: appeal to, as strategy, 118; nationalization of housing, 35–36; limits of, for claiming ownership, 100, 101–6, 115, 123; as anti-poor, 101. *See also* land tenure; legislation; property
legislation: and colonial-era housing, 72; on land and property, 89, 100–104, 193n3; and post-independence housing, 35–36; and privatization, 40; and residents' committees, 92–93, 193n17; and urban planning, 43. *See also* land tenure; law
local government, 18, 92, 190n12, 193n16. *See also* administrative divisions; CPBs; residents' committee
Lourenço, João Manuel Gonçalves, 174–77. *See also* Presidency
Luanda Bay Project, 51–55, 156, 173. *See also* Marginal
Luanda Provincial Government, 42–45. *See also* administrative divisions
Luanda Sul Project, 42–43

Marginal (promenade), 40, 48, 50, 52, 54, 68, 151. *See also* Luanda Bay Project
Margoso, 145–47

materiality: and aesthetic dissent,
153, 163; critical potential of, 180; as
indicative of state incapacity, 37–39;
of neighborhood construction, 80; as
racialized, 72; used to elide importance of musseques, 77–78. *See also*
moral economy of materiality
May 1977 events, 92, 176, 192n14
Mingas, Ângela Branco Lima, 180,
191n4
moral economy of materiality, 27–28,
121–24; definition of, 98–99; determining compensation after demolition, 106, 109–11, 115
MPLA (Popular Movement for the
Liberation of Angola), 6–7, 15, 18–20,
161–64
musseques: aesthetic politics, 5, 6, 152,
165, 171, 179; during civil war, 38–39,
41, 42; as countergeography, 180–82;
demolition of, 107, 172; erasure of
material contribution to the city,
67–69, 76–78, 146, 180; governance,
91–95, 104; history of, 71–74; housing
and belonging in, 75, 83, 85, 86, 95,
164; as Indigenous, 2, 10–15, 75, 79,
86–96, 164; infrastructure of, 132–34,
143; process of construction, 80, 82–
87, 195n7; redevelopment, 56, 61–63.
See also Cazenga; concrete-block
houses; corrugated-iron houses;
demolition; land tenure; moral economy of materiality; provisionality;
residents' committees

national reconstruction, 3, 16–21, 60;
and comfort, 48–55, 64–65, 125–26;
and demolitions, 98, 109; as tool
of regime legitimation, 29–31; and
requalification, 57; and housing,
137–38; criticisms of, 29–30, 153–
59, 162–64, 167–68, 173. *See also*
care; comfort; Cazenga; housing;

musseques; new centralities; new
cities; requalification
National Program for Urbanism and
Housing. *See* PNUH
Native Act, 71
new centralities, 17, 20, 29, 138, 172. *See
also* housing; Kilamba; new cities
new cities, 3–6, 31, 168, 181; aesthetics
of, 5, 55, 125, 150–52, 171; criticisms of,
152–53; domestic origins of, 151–52,
177–79. *See also* aesthetic; Kilamba;
new centralities
Nova Vida, 20, 97, 138, 193n1; and demolitions, 115–18, 121–23; and infrastructure, 140; as object of desire, 143–45

Office for National Reconstruction, 17,
18
Office for Special Works, 17, 18, 43, 46,
109
Office for the Renovation and Rehabilitation of the Musseques, 38, 190n7
oil, 6, 7, 29, 171–75; loans, 16–17, 159, 173,
189n9
oil spectacle, 8–10, 30–31, 57–58, 64, 152,
181

Panguila, 98, 110, 138, 144, 193n2
party action committee, 94, 100, 103–5,
193n6
pedreiros, 13, 85, 181
People's Neighborhood Comissions, 35,
92. *See also* residents' committees
PHS (Program for Social Housing), 109
PNUH (National Program for Urbanism and Housing), 20, 138, 190n13;
1 million houses initiative, 20, 33,
137–38, 141
Presidency, 17–18, 46–47, 60–61, 101,
109, 118, 175
Program for Social Housing, 109
property: laws governing, 100–102,
193n3, 193n4; nationalization of,

35–37; private property, 190n6; unofficial recognition of, 89, 99, 103, 104, 115; tension between official and unofficial recognition, 102, 111, 123. *See also* land tenure; legislation; moral economy of materiality

protests: anti-MPLA, 22; for compensation, 120; against demolitions, 43, 44; during Lourenço's presidency, 175, 176; against rehousing, 145, 146

provisionality: defining musseques, 73, 82–83; criticism of use in African urbanism, 69, 76–78, 82–84, 86, 95, 180–81; as racialized discourse, 72. *See also* autoconstruction; musseques; self-building

PRP (Program for the Rehousing of the Population), 18, 109, 141, 145

Provincial Property Conservation Company, 37, 39

race, 13, 69, 70, 71, 161, 181; and construction materials, 72; and researcher positionality, 23–24; and urban planning, 72, 76. *See also* enslavement; musseques; provisionality

racial capitalism; 136, 179, 180

Rancière, Jacques, 9

rehousing, 20, 28, 46, 98, 107, 120, 143; as care, 43, 45, 129; institutional history, 43–48; process of, 109, 110; Rehousing Intervention Brigade, 7; reproduce class, 140, 141, 143, 144, 147; zones, 109, 138, 143. *See also* housing; Panguila; Presidency; PRP; Zango

requalification, 22, 56, 122; of Cazenga, 58–59, 60, 63, 166; versus "reconversion," 59; versus redevelopment, 57

residents' committees: and Boavista, 44; after demolition, 120, 123; governance of land and housing, 101, 103–5; legislation governing, 193n17; rejuvenation of in the 1990s, 42; and the requalification of Cazenga, 60, 63; and unofficial governance, 89, 91–94,192n15, 193n16. *See also* administrative divisions; CPBs; informality; legislation; local government; musseques

Savimbi, Jonas Malheiro, 15, 20, 161, 176

self-building, 3, 13, 22, 38, 56, 61, 75, 142; as inaccurate description, 82; as urban tradition, 86. *See also* autoconstruction; musseques

senzala, 70, 71, 73, 192n5

settler colonialism, 11–12, 14, 25, 69, 91; as legitimating myths, 90–91

Sinophobia, 155, 158

slave trade, 14, 70, 71, 181

sobrados, 14, 70, 156

SOS Habitat, 25, 118, 120, 123

Talatona, 29, 42, 131, 142, 146

Technical Office for the Urban Reconversion of Cazenga, Sambizanga, and Rangel, 18, 61

UNITA (Union for the Total Liberation of Angola), 15, 24, 30, 39, 40, 114, 161, 176

Urban Development Company, 42–43, 107

urbs nullius, 12, 14

water: access to, 131, 194n3; aesthetic experience of, 127–28; building infiltration, 37, 49; and class relations, 133–35; connection as proof of tenure, 115; cost of, 194n2; and gender, 132–34; informal connections to, 86, 130; and infrastructural politics, 49, 52, 59, 140, 145; in gated communities, 131; polluted, 52, 54. *See also* infrastructure

worlding, 4, 151–52, 167, 171, 178; domestic politics of, 154 world-class city aesthetic, 4, 27, 48, 49, 50, 157, 168, 178

xenophobia, 155, 159–63; and architecture, 168. *See also* Sinophobia

yard (*quintal*): and culture,165; as defining feature of Luanda's vernancular architecture, 75; as space of social

and economic reproduction, 85–86, 167

Zango: creation of, 44–48; and infrastructure, 140–46; as MPLA propaganda, 67; and rehousing, 98; and social housing, 138. *See also* Boavista; demolitions; housing; rehousing; social housing

www.ingramcontent.com/pod-product-compliance
Lightning Source LLC
Chambersburg PA
CBHW022354280326
41935CB00007B/184